A Nawab and a Begum

Sudipta Mitra is an author and a colonial researcher. He is also a freelance columnist and a regular contributor on historical anecdotes and nature. A doctor by profession, he is also associated with many NGOs. His commitment to acquiring first-hand and authentic knowledge on Awadh history down the ages has culminated in a remarkable experience. His bestselling book *Pearl by the River* was a fascinating depiction of Wajid Ali Shah's glamorous life in exile. He has more than 100 essays on colonial India, environmental sciences and wildlife history to his credit, both in English and Bengali. His other books, *Gir Forest and the Saga of the Asiatic Lion*, *History and Heritage of Indian Game Hunting* and *The Nitpicker's Chronicle: Flip Side Story of Indian National Movement,* are highly informative and useful references.

A Nawab and a Begum

Sudipta Mitra

Published by
Rupa Publications India Pvt. Ltd 2024
7/16, Ansari Road, Daryaganj
New Delhi 110002

Sales centres:
Bengaluru Chennai Hyderabad
Jaipur Kathmandu Kolkata
Mumbai Prayagraj

The views and opinions expressed in this book are the author's own and the facts are as reported by him which have been verified to the extent possible, and the publishers are not in any way liable for the same. Certain creative liberties have been taken to narrate the events presented by the author.

P-ISBN: 978-93-5702-652-9
E-ISBN: 978-93-5702-890-5

First impression 2024

10 9 8 7 6 5 4 3 2 1

Printed in India

This book is dedicated to my research guide and mentor, Late Prof (Dr) Meerza Kaukub Qadr, great grandson of Wajid Ali Shah and Begum Hazrat Mahal.

Contents

Foreword

by Rosie Llewellyn-Jones

Following the success of his book *Pearl by the River,* which recreated the life of Wajid Ali Shah in exile in Calcutta, Sudipta Mitra has explored the back story of the king and his consort Begum Hazrat Mahal. The Begum is known as a prominent freedom fighter in the Revolt of 1857 and is almost certainly more famous than her one-time husband.

Dr Mitra has skillfully woven together the story of the two ill-fated lovers who were never to meet again after the King left Lucknow when he was dispossessed of his throne by the English East India Company. Drawing extensively on both Indian and British sources, *A Nawab and a Begum* moves through the turbulent events that shook Victorian England and tells how it affected the royal couple.

It is a common assumption that after the British regained control of India, both Wajid Ali Shah and the Begum vanished from history. This is not the case, as Dr Mitra shows through careful research. After being defeated by the British, the Begum fled to Nepal where she received a grudging welcome from its ruler Jang Bahadur. The King, with wild extravagance, created a 'chhota Lucknow' on the banks of the Hooghly at Matiyaburj.

Theirs is a haunting love story set against a vivid background, told here in a very readable and straightforward manner. *A Nawab and a Begum* throws light on a forgotten episode of Indian history.

Rosie Llewellyn-Jones
London, May 2021

Foreword

by Irfan Ali Mirza

History is often flawed in two ways: the historian's version of events is generally imbued with the individual colour of the ink they use; and sometimes, history takes a long time to decide who the real victor was. It is the sincerity to get to the truth rather than the arrogance to defend what one perceives as the truth that distinguishes the better historian.

It is to Dr Sudipta Mitra's credit that he has tried to get to the bottom of this story and dissect facts from fiction with a kind of surgical precision that he has so diligently practised in his profession. His spirit of relentless inquiry to get to the truth lying under false assumptions and anecdotes is not only admirable in itself but also sets him apart as a very self-respecting historian. It is good that Dr Mitra has tried to register all this in this landmark book before history also forgets it.

A lot has been written about Wajid Ali Shah but not much about Begum Hazrat Mahal and her relationship with her husband. Dr Mitra has tried to explore precisely that and, as such, I am shedding some light of my own on why Begum Hazrat Mahal rebelled so furiously and preferred to die in Nepal instead of returning to an enslaved motherland.

During the First War of Independence in 1857, when Lucknow came under the siege of the British colonialists, out of the many wives and sons of Wajid Ali Shah, only Begum Hazrat Mahal and her young son Birjis Qadr had the courage to come out of the palace and openly defy the British. This daring rebellion, which pitted a lonely woman against the might of the British Empire, and helped vent people's anger and resentment against the colonialists, won the Poet-King's heart as it bled:

Usay angrezi faoj ghere hai,
Khanjar-e-gham jigar pa phere hai.

(She is surrounded by the English army,
Running the knife of sorrow on my heart.)

—Wajid Ali Shah Akhtar from *Behr-e-Mukhtalif*

Begum Hazrat Mahal had started in the spirit of Rabindranath Tagore's immortal one-liner, '*Ekla Chalo Re*', taking the courage of the first step in both hands. Hence, it was in the larger perspective: when the events of 1857 started unfolding on the timeline of Lucknow and the defining moment of reckoning came, it was Hazrat Mahal who stood firmly on the right side of history till her last breath. She was the one who sensed that her country was on the crossroads of history and she showed the green signal to her countrymen indicating the road to be taken.

In the longer timeline, we realize that Hazrat Mahal was not only a fierce freedom fighter but also one of the earliest forerunners in the dawn of Muslim feminism in the country. For a burqa-clad woman coming from an orthodox Muslim society, it takes enormous courage to defy not only Muslim conservatism but also the might of the British Empire at the same time.

The destruction of a historic city's blooming culture of poetry and civility by forcibly removing its highly cultured poet-king was the principal reason why Begum Hazrat Mahal had rebelled so furiously and fiercely, so much so that she refused to compromise with the British in spite of getting the most lucrative offers. The King had held the dream of a magnificent Lucknow in his heart till his last breath in Matiyaburj—a dream other kings could not have sustained, the dream of a Lucknow of refined aesthetic values, high in culture and poetry. The forcible dethronement of such an eminently talented and popular poet-king was a tragedy of epic proportions. It will remain one of the most regrettable colonial crimes committed under the grace and glory of the British Crown, and will go down in India's history as a monumental cultural blunder never to be forgiven or forgotten.

The decline of Lucknowi culture, slow but unstoppable, that started from the deposition of the King has continued unabated to this day. Today, Wajid Ali Shah's once glittering Lucknow, with majestic monuments dotting its landscape, has been reduced to a city of cacophonous crowds with its glorious Imambaras in ruins, sending even its famous Urdu dialect into exile.

Both Wajid Ali Shah and Begum Hazrat Mahal are relevant as role models in today's India: the King for his all-inclusive cultural and secular outlook, his genuine compassion for animals and his life-long emphasis on poetry, literature and culture; and the Begum for her inspiring courage in standing up to the ruling authority however mighty it might be, for defending her space and territory, and for her willingness and readiness for self-sacrifice when the moment comes.

Begum Hazrat Mahal displayed amazing courage in coronating Birjis Qadr right under the nose of the British highbrows—a coronation that became powerfully symbolic of a country's self-determination. Only Birjis Qadr can be recognized as the last king of Awadh in independent India, especially so when Wajid Ali Shah had designated Birjis Qadr, by name, as his heir apparent in the light of his many explicit poetical utterances.

Today, amid the ruins of 1857, Hazrat Mahal stands vindicated. She had provided a spark, and had led from the front, voicing loudly the simmering undercurrent of resentment against the colonial invaders. It was the prologue to India's nascent liberation movement. It was the courage of the lonely first step—Ekla Chalo Re! Begum Hazrat Mahal's determined effort at the very outset, like that of Rani Laxmi Bai and some other bravehearts—never mind that it did not succeed initially—was the incipient part of a national movement that grew in strength over the years to change the course of India's history.

Irfan Ali Mirza
Great-great grandson of Wajid Ali Shah
and Begum Hazrat Mahal,
Sr Trustee, King of Oudh's Mausoleum,
Sibtainabad Imambarah Trust,
Matiyaburj, Kolkata

Preface

The decisive war of Buxar and successive triumphs over Indian states goaded the British military generals of East India Company into the belief that the British were invincible on Indian soil, that they had perpetual authority over the omnipotent native kings. The confiscation of the Awadh kingdom was a bloodless exercise, as the monarch Wajid Ali Shah preferred to relinquish his turban than to take up arms. The offer of the landed gentries to build a consortium of armed forces and fight against the British was deemed immoral by the King; hence, it was turned aside with apathy.

Wajid Ali Shah was rather looked down upon by the *angrez* (English people) as a sensualist and a timid addict of dance and music than a macho-imaged supremo of a century-old war-mongering dynasty. Perhaps, the British had assessed him well but made a fatal mistake by underestimating his wife, Begum Hazrat Mahal, as they would soon come to realize.

Hazrat Mahal was one of the courtesans in the King's harem. She grew up as an abandoned child of her parents in the house of Lucknowi courtesans and charmed her way into the royal harem. She separated from her husband after she became the mother of her only child. She was accused of being inauspicious by her husband and ostracized in the *jenanas*.[1] Yet, destiny had ordained for her an audacious path. In 1857, the Begum came out of her

---

[1]The jenana is the inner apartment of the palace in which the womenfolk of the king's family live. It literally means 'of the women' or 'pertaining to women' in Persian language.

shell to teach a lesson to what then seemed like the invincible East India Company. Unprecedented in the history of India, not less than one lakh native sepoys and volunteers rallied behind Hazrat Mahal, ready to sacrifice their lives for their motherland.

When the Begum vowed not to end her struggle till the last angrez in the kingdom of Awadh was driven out, the King had no option but to strike a favourable deal with the Governor General. A twist of destiny had taken him away from the lap of luxury and driven him to a life of austerity. The 25-month-long rigorous incarceration had blotted his last hope of getting back his lost empire. He was thrown into stark misery, leaving behind several mouths to feed.

The King disavowed all his claims, repudiated the Oudh Mission in London, disowned his spirited wife and finally retreated into romance and art. He was preoccupied with his romantic sorrows, evoking memories of his sweet days with the begums. The struggle of Lucknow and the heroic role of Hazrat Mahal could not make a dent in his heart.

This is a humble attempt to explore the enigmatic relation between King Wajid Ali Shah and his unsung warrior queen, Begum Hazrat Mahal. The book will take the readers simultaneously through biographies of a nawab and a begum against the backdrop of sepoy mutiny and finally the pathways will fuse together. In the trail of my long research, I have come across scholars, collectors, respected members of the royal family of Awadh, including Prince Irfan Ali Mirza, Princess Manzilat Fatima, Prince Kamran Mirza and others, and the honourable trustees of Sibtainabad Imambara in Kolkata. I owe an enormous debt of gratitude to them; without them, this work would not have been possible. I am grateful to my commissioning editor, Saswati Bora, Rupa Publications, who first gave me the idea to write a comprehensive account elucidating the relation between

Wajid Ali Shah and Hazrat Begum. And finally my deepest gratitude to Late Prof (Dr) Meerza Kaukub Qadr, great grandson of King Wajid Ali Shah and Begum Hazrat Mahal, who was my research guide and mentor.

Sudipta Mitra
Kolkata, September 2023

Royal Family Tree of Awadh

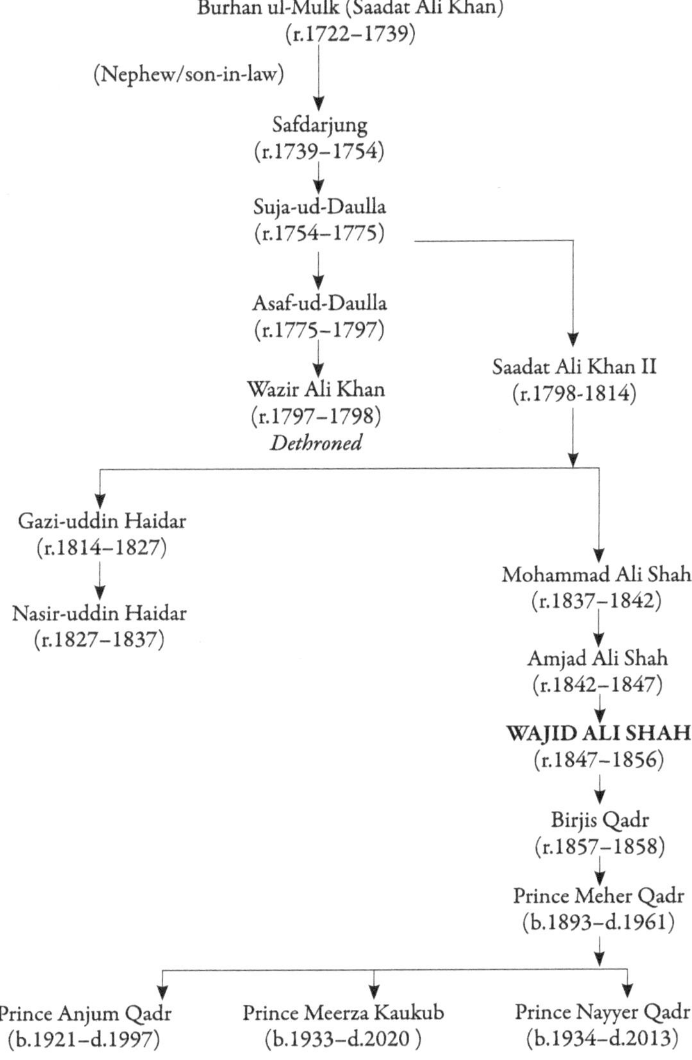

one

His Early Days

It was on 18 July 1853, the first Monday of Sawan—the most auspicious month in the Hindu calendar. Huzur Bagh, the King's most treasured garden facing his palace Rafat Manzil, was thrown open to the general public. It was richly adorned with flowers and lamps. An immense gathering stood amazed seeing a cluster of beautiful handmaidens—his *paree*s (angels), beautifully costumed for the much-awaited exhibition. Huzur Bagh had turned into a fairy ground. King Wajid Ali Shah came out from Rafat Manzil, dressed in saffron, his face and body smeared in ashes of pearls, with a yellow dupatta tied around his waist and a rosary in his hand. He masqueraded as a *jogi* (a Hindu ascetic).[1]

Slowly he came and sat on a high marble platform. Two of his most adored parees, Mashuqah-e-Khas and Sikandar Begum, were donned in costumes as 'joginis' by his side. The King was graced with melodious songs and exquisite dance, all skilfully choreographed by the King himself. The moon-lit night cast a spell over the minarets of Kaiserbag, the garden being bathed in its radiance. Only two days were left for Guru Purnima—the most auspicious full-moon night in the Hindu calendar dedicated to all

---

[1]Llewellyn-Jones, Rosie, *The Last King in India*, Random House India, 2014, p. 54. Also see Sinh, Ranbir, *Wajid Ali Shah: The Tragic King*, Publication Scheme, Jaipur, 2002, p. 102.

the spiritual gurus. The fete would continue till then. The King came out to the bank of a canal flowing near Rafat Manzil to see the fascinating fireworks illuminating the night sky. The mela went on splendidly.

The auspicious occasion developed into a *mela*, popularly known as Jogia Jashan, Jogi Mela, Qaisarbagh Mela, or, to his Hindu subjects, Sawan Mela. The King was extremely devoted to this mela. He mentioned this extravagant fete as his 'inspiration' in his autobiography, *Ishqnama*.[2]

The mela started to gain popularity as the biggest recurrent public event in Awadh. The celebration was open to all irrespective of caste and creed. But there was one caveat. The visitors must come dressed in saffron-coloured clothes, like jogis!

Wajid Ali Shah was born in Farhat Bakhsh Palace on 30 July 1822,[3] Tuesday, in the auspicious Hindu month of Sawan, in a Hindu-majority kingdom called Awadh. Sawan is sacred to the Hindus as it is the month of Lord Shiva. Lunar constellation in the year of his birth was such that Janmasthami, the birthday of Lord Krishna, was also observed in the same month. This was indeed an exceptional occurrence in the Hindu lunar calendar. Thus, the seed of his boundless devotion to Lord Krishna was conspicuously sown at the time of his birth.

After his birth, his mother, Aliya Begum, *khas* (chief) wife of

---

[2]Sinh, Ranbir, *Wajid Ali Shah: The Tragic King*, Publication Scheme, Jaipur, 2002, p. 102.

[3]Rosie Llewellyn-Jones, in her book *The Last King of India* (p. xi), and Mirza Ali Azhar, in his book *King Wajid Ali Shah of Awadh*, Volume 1 (p. 192), mention that Wajid Ali Shah was born on 30 July 1822. These sources are taken to be authentic. However, on the royal family website of Oudh, it is mentioned as 19 July 1823 or 10th Zeeqat 1238 Hijri, which is not correct.

Amjad Ali, called the royal astrologers to know about his fortune.[4] The royal astrologers predicted that due to the weak placement of stars in his birthchart, there was a chance that the prince would become a jogi, leaving all his treasure and duties behind. To nullify the adverse effects, the astrologers advised that the child be dressed like a jogi on his birthdays. His mother dressed the child in saffron-coloured clothes during the holy *chhathi* ceremony when he was only six days old. The prince never faltered in this practice, and even after ascending the throne at the age of 24, he would incarnate himself as a jogi on his birthdays. His mother restricted the ritual to the palace's prescience till 1853, after which the King took it to his faithful subjects, recasting the event as one of the greatest shows in Awadh. The Jogi Mela continued in public for the next two years till the King was self-exiled to Calcutta (now Kolkata).

Whatsoever the stellar constellation—favourable or unfavourable—Wajid Ali was never destined to be a monarch. He was born as the second son to Amjad Ali, who was not in the direct line of succession to the throne. When Wajid Ali was born, his grandfather's brother Ghazi-ud-din Haidar ruled Awadh. Only four years earlier, Ghazi-ud-din Haidar was awarded the title of Padshah-i-Awadh, or independent 'king' of Awadh, by British Governor General Marquess of Hastings. The Marquess had two furtive desires: to curb the power of failing Mughals and to make the king of Awadh more obliged to open their coffer.

When Ghazi-ud-din Haider inherited the throne from his father Nawab Sadaat Ali Khan, the royal reserve was brimming. Saadat Ali, who had a better command of the economy than his predecessors, recovered losses and raised the royal reserve to

[4]Azhar, Mirza Ali, *King Wajid Ali Shah of Awadh*, Volume 2, Royal Book Company, Karachi, 1982, p. 49.

₹14 crore.[5] Nevertheless, the real decline of Awadh started from Ghazi-ud-din Haidar's reign, who squandered the treasury and left behind a balance of ₹4 crore on his death.[6] Ghazi-ud-din had to bear ₹76 lakh per annum to the British to maintain the defence of Awadh as promised by his father. The Nawab also extended his help to the British to fight the Nepal war by giving a loan of ₹1.8 crore at 6 per cent interest per annum.[7] He was a weak-nerved and superstitious man and became an easy prey for his unscrupulous minister Agha Mir, who plundered an estimated amount of ₹56 lakh annually apart from unaccounted pieces of jewellery from the royal treasure.[8] On the flipside, Ghazi-ud-din Haidar was a patron of art and culture, and it was during his time that Lucknow was gifted with a series of fine monuments. He had much interest in literature and art, and promoted works of people who possessed natural talents for art and aesthetics.

Wajid Ali Shah was only five years old when Ghazi-ud-din Haidar died. However, the prince's upbringing was hardly influenced since his father was not in the line of succession. In his childhood, Wajid Ali was bashful and grew up most modestly, since his father Amjad Ali would only get a meagre allowance. Wajid Ali was brought up along with other princes and had his routine lessons in horse riding, shooting and reading Persian texts. Amjad Ali was a religious man and imparted sound religious education to his son. He had even appointed Imdad Hussain Khan, a scholar

---

[5]Cotton, James Sutherland, Richard Burn and William Stevenson Meyer, *Imperial Gazetteer of India*, Clarendon Press, 1908, p. 283.
[6]*The Pioneer Mail and Indian Weekly News*, Vol. 48, 1921, p. 36.
[7]Cotton, James Sutherland, Richard Burn and William Stevenson Meyer, *Imperial Gazetteer of India*, Clarendon Press, 1908, p. 283.
[8]Knighton, William, *Nawab Nasir-ud-din Shah of Oudh: His Life and Pastimes*, Northern Book Centre, New Delhi, 1990, p. xvii.

in Urdu, as *ataleeq*[9] to teach his son. Under the latter's guidance, Wajid Ali started to learn how to compose lyrics in Urdu. Imdad Hussain was an orthodox devout man who regarded music and dance as *haram* (forbidden under Islamic law). But Wajid Ali's penchant for music since his childhood days was such that often, involuntarily, he moved his feet in rhythm. Once Imdad Hussain slapped him on his face for doing so. Since then, he suffered the loss of hearing in one ear. Amjad Ali came to know about the incident but never spoke a word against his son's teacher.[10] Such was his ardour to impart moral training to his son.

Ghazi-ud-din Haidar's son Nasir-ud-din Haidar was the heir apparent, and had more European sensibilities than traditional Indian; he also had an English wife in his harem. His barber, George Harris Derusett, became one of the most influential persons behind the curtains of Awadh. His prolific expenditure could meet all his opulence in life; however, not much was spent on bringing about reforms as suggested by John Low, the then British Resident.

Nasir-ud-din moulded the ways and thoughts of young Wajid Ali, who witnessed his profligate uncle Nasir-ud-din maintaining a harem of accomplished dancers and singers called *jalsewaliyan* (stage performers). They would be expensively dressed and would perform fabulous dance-and-music concerts. Nearly 500 of them once participated in a spectacular dance concert called Raga Bhairavi, which was essentially a Hindustani-themed musical performance named after the Hindu goddess. The ladies were dressed in costumes with gold and silver jewellery as depicted in

---

[9]Ataleeq was a person who looked after right morals, general conduct and character of the princes apart from private tutor. See Azhar, Mirza Ali, *King Wajid Ali Shah of Awadh*, Volume 2, Royal Book Company, Karachi, 1982, p. 193.

[10]Adeep, Masud, *Lucknow ka Shahi Stage,* South Asian Languages and Civilizations, University of Chicago, 2019, p. 66; Azhar, Mirza Ali, *King Wajid Ali Shah of Awadh*, Volume 1, Royal Book Company, Karachi, 1982, p. 194.

the Ragamala paintings. It was a grand fete that lasted for 30 days.

Four years after Nasir-ud-din ascended the throne, Governor General Lord William Bentinck was about to assume the kingdom of Awadh, seeing that no attempt was made by Nasir-ud-din to undertake any reform. Lord Bentinck gave a strong warning to him as well. At one time, the Court of Directors authorized him to take over the management of Awadh without delay. However, the situation was saved by Nasir-ud-din's minister Hakim Mehndi Ali Khan, who had promised to make a change. Lord Bentinck, who had a high opinion of Hakim, gave up his idea of usurping Awadh and thus the kingdom was saved. Following the Treaty of 1801, Awadh was virtually a marionette in the hands of the British.

Wajid Ali's mother, Aliya Begum, came from Delhi's noble family and was an elegant lady with an assertive personality. She was educated and could read Persian fluently. Aliya Begum was appreciative of her son's literary talent but was apprehensive of his philandering nature. During adolescence, the prince looked charming with a fair complexion, with luscious and long springing hair bouncing around his neck. Wajid Ali had his first sexual encounter at the tender age of eight, when he was seduced by Rahiman, one of his female attendants. Soon after, he was sexually enticed by a 35-year-old lady Ameeran (his mother's help) and the romance continued till he was 11. When the prince was 11 years old, he was charmed by one Banno Saheb, but since she was married, there was no union between them. The prince fell in love with Banno's sister Haji Khanam, who was also married. Haji Khanam surrendered to the prince and their secret affair continued till he turned 14.[11]

[11]Azhar, Mirza Ali, *King Wajid Ali Shah of Awadh*, Volume 1, Royal Book Company, Karachi, 1982, p. 77.

Wajid Ali's fate took a new turn when his uncle Nasir-ud-din Haidar died a mysterious death on the intervening night of 7 and 8 July 1837. Since Nasir-ud-din Haidar did not have a legitimate child, the throne of Awadh was left without a successor. There was one Moonna Jan who claimed that he was the son of Nasir-ud-din Haidar and a contender for his father's crown. But the claims of Moonna were repudiated, raising doubts and questions on his paternity. Nasir-ud-din, in a declaration to John Low, declared that Moonna was not his son, rather the son of a slave girl who came to reside with him after the birth of Moonna Jan.[12]

Suddenly, the succession line changed and Wajid Ali's grandfather Mohammad Ali, at a worn-out age of 63, with trembling limbs and shaking head, ascended the throne. In the same year, Mohammad Ali's fifth son, Shahzada Amjad Ali, was sworn in as heir apparent. Amjad Ali's status was uplifted and so was his monthly allowance. As his royal rank elevated, Prince Amjad Ali then thought of arranging the wedding of his son Wajid Ali. Wajid Ali's parents started looking for a bride once he attained the age of 15.

After two unsuccessful attempts, his *nikah* was finally settled with Alam Ara Begum, the daughter of Nawab Ali Khan, who belonged to an illustrious family of Delhi. The bride was also a niece of Nawab Ali Naqi Khan. However, ceremonies were performed without any pomp on 14 November 1837 due to Nasir-ud-din Haidar's death as well as an aunt of the bride.

The company of his first wife could hardly give Wajid Ali the solace he aspired for. His passion, his romanticism and sensualities overwhelmed his relationship with his wife, Alam Ara Begum, who was a poet and a singer, too. Her talents were much cherished by her husband who admired his wife's intelligence and character.

[12]Ahmed, Muhammed Taqi (trans.), *Tarikh Badshah Begam: A Persian Manuscript on the History of Oudh*, Indian Press Limited, Allahabad, 1938, p. 51.

But she was incredulous about her husband's romantic encounters and kept a close watch on his movements. Wajid Ali's romantic flirtations with his attendants in the palace continued, while his relationship with his begum deteriorated.

Initially, the begum protested against her husband dallying with his womenfolk and even chased some of them out of his palace. But with time, she surrendered to her fate. The relationship turned worse when Wajid Ali appointed a girl named Moti Khanam as his personal attendant. He fell in love with Moti Khanam, who was a good dancer. The Prince even composed poetry in admiration of this woman, being aware of its impact on his deteriorating relationship with his wife. The begum made a great commotion and brought the matter to the notice of Amjad Ali. Eventually, the prince succumbed under pressure and left his mistress.

The Prince's failing character soon disseminated outside the covert realm of the palace, paving way for a fair proportion of crooks and opportunists inside the palace. The Prince got attracted to Saheb Khanam, a 32-year-old talented singer and his father's domestic worker. The begum taunted her husband for his sordid taste in dallying with a married woman. Wajid Ali retorted that the begum should cooperate with her husband in finding noblewomen instead of mocking his choices and added that doing so would earn her her husband's confidence!

The begum had no other choice but to compromise and fetch attendants from the higher class to charm her husband. Wajid Ali appreciated his begum's taste in collecting charming parees for his Pareekhana—a few among them were Suleiman Paree, Ajaibi Paree, Wajeer Paree, Shah Buksh Khawas Nur Afshan Paree and Bilkis Paree.[13]

---

[13]Akhtar, Wajid Ali Shah, *Mahal Khana-i-Shahi*, Mirza Fida Ali Khanjar Lakhnawi (ed.), Delhi, 1914, p. 13. See also Santha, K.S., *Begums of Awadh*, Bharati Prakashan, Varanasi, 1980, p. 211.

Thereafter, several women came into his life, such as Sarfaraz Begum, Nanni Begum, Umda Begum—the list goes on. They were married to him and became one of the first *Mutá* wives in his harem. The list is exhaustive, but they share some things in common. Wajid Ali was obsessed with the royal domestic workers—some of them were talented dancers and singers. Author and historian Abdul Halim Sharar was perhaps right in his assessment of Wajid Ali:

> He would fall in love with female palanquin-bearers, courtesans, domestic servants and women who came in and out of the palace, in short with hundreds of women and because he was the heir to the throne, he had great success with his love-affairs, the shameful accounts of which can be read in his poems, writings and books. His character appears to be one of the most dubious in all the records of history.[14]

As his relationship with the begum was getting more enigmatic, Wajid Ali's grandfather Mohammad Ali Shah passed away, leaving behind the legacy of a crumbling kingdom to his son Amjad Ali. Mohammad Ali had hardly been on his throne for two months when he signed an agreement that drove the last nail in the coffin of the kingdom of Awadh.

The treaty, which was executed in Lucknow on 11 September 1837, virtually gave the British government rights to assume any portion of the territory of Awadh if public tranquillity was found to be disrupted. The British authority reserved the right to take administrative control of such portions whenever the situation looked 'turbid' in their opinion. The expense of restoring peace in the region would be defrayed from the territory's revenue, which

---

[14]Sharar, Abdul Halim, *Lucknow: The Last Phase of an Oriental Culture*, Oxford University Press, 1994, p. 63.

the British administration would reserve exclusive right to collect. The balance, after meeting all expenses, would be deposited into the king's treasury. The fragile elderly man had no other option but to swallow the bitter pill, virtually giving away the control of his state.

The planetary positions once again favoured Wajid Ali when his father Amjad Ali coronated him at Farhat Bakhsh Palace on 7 May 1842. Wajid Ali was neither the first son of his father Amjad Ali nor the preferred heir for Oudh's people. The obvious choice of the people was Amjad Ali Shah's eldest son Mustafa Ali Haidar, who was also preferred by his grandfather.

However, Amjad Ali Shah chose his second son Wajid Ali as the heir apparent and ousted Wajid's over-ambitious elder brother Prince Mustafa, who was allegedly suspected of being a British informer. Wajid Ali, though the second child of his father, was the son of his principal wife. Mustafa was not only repudiated by his father, depriving him of his title, but he was also put under house arrest.

Of all his six brothers (the last one had died during infancy), the promise shown by Wajid Ali Shah in his intellectual pursuits was sadly lacking when it came to administration. The future king had no interest in state matters; rather, his romantic and literary pursuits started to reach unprecedented heights.

The Prince enjoyed being surrounded by beautiful women. Paintings of that era often depict him as a plump man with hair curling down to his shoulders, wearing a rich brocade *angrakha*, with his left nipple exposed. Wajid Ali gathered beautiful women, proficient in singing and dancing, irrespective of their caste and creed, and kept them under strict security. He named the abode as Pareekhana or the 'House of fairies'.

Wajid Ali spent a dear sum in maintaining his house of parees and trained them in music and dance behind the *purdah* (curtain). He appointed musical masters, whose job was to train the parees and make them adept in oriental music and dance. The house of fairies was closely guarded by a picked band of Abyssinian slave women.[15]

As time passed by, the Prince and his khas begum were enmeshed in a web of inscrutable relations. At times, he became unkind and dogmatic when it came to his fancies. Alam Ara Begum was his true wife—his only nikah marriage till then. But his romance with the many women was an insult to his begum's integrity.

The peril did not end there. The Prince put his khas begum in command of his Pareekhana or, literally speaking, his harem—overtly disguised as a college of music. It was the begum's responsibility to set the girls ready and to put them before her husband. The parees were his begums through *mutah* marriage but elevated to mahals if they gave birth to his sons. As soon as a mutah begum would get pregnant, she would be immediately shifted to a palace with special care and elevated position.[16] Naturally, the khas begum suffered from humiliation due to the goings-on in the Pareekhana. In his book, *Mahal Khana-i-Shahi*, the Prince accused his khas begum of being indifferent to his parees at times. Finally, she was relieved from her duty one day and released from her disgrace. He replaced her with one of his confidantes, Mohammad Hussain Ali Khan, who was later awarded the title of Dayanat-ud-Daulah.[17]

---

[15]Bhatnagar, G.D., *Awadh under Wajid Ali Shah*, Bharatiya Vidya Prakashan, 1968, p. 7.

[16]Nikah marriage is a permanent marital bonding and continues lifelong. The nikah wives were known as mahals. Meanwhile, mutah is a marriage custom followed by the Shia sect and indicates temporary marriage. The contract period could be few months to years. However, customarily, if, by chance, a Mutah wife gave birth to a child, she would be called 'mahal' and her status would be uplifted. She would be honoured with a lifelong marital bond and a separate room for the mother and child to grow up. She would also be entitled to a monthly allowance.

[17]Karbala of Dayanat-ud-Daulah in Lucknow was built by him during the reign of Wajid Ali Shah.

Amjad Ali Shah died prematurely at the age of 47 years, making room for his second son to become the eleventh nawab and fifth king of Awadh. Amjad Ali's cousin Nasir-ud-din Haider had squandered ₹6 crore during his reign and left in the treasury only a meagre amount of ₹70 lakh. Nasir-ud-din's uncle Mohammad Ali Shah had little to spend at the failing age of 63 and could save a little to leave behind a reserve of ₹80 lakh. King Amjad Ali was a devout person and a frugal ruler. After his death, Wajid Ali Shah came to sit on a throne worth ₹1.36 crore—a meagre sum, neither enough to carry out reforms nor to mollify the British.[18]

[18]Knighton, William, *The Private Life of an Eastern King: Together with Elihu Jan's Story; Or, the Private Life of an Eastern Queen*, Hardpress Publishing, 2013, p. 179.

two

Her Early Days

The city of Faizabad had lost its glory since Nawab Asaf-ud-daulah had shifted his capital to Lucknow. One hundred years before the birth of Wajid Ali Shah, his predecessor Burhan-ul-Mulk Saadat Ali Khan founded the kingdom of Awadh on the bank of river Saraju, revered as the birth place of the Hindu god, Shri Ram. Two years before the birth of Wajid Ali Shah in Lucknow, a girl child was born to a poor family of Sayyids in Faizabad, who claimed to be the descendants of Prophet Muhammad. Her name was Muhammadi Khanum, and perhaps no clairvoyant in the city could have ever predicted that the child was destined to rule the kingdom one day.

Misfortune fell on her since the moment she lost her mother during childbirth. She was the youngest child of her parents. Her father, a small artisan in Faizabad, migrated to Lucknow and passed away in poverty when she was only 12. Muhammadi became an orphan and was brought up in her uncle's house who earned his living by embroidering topis. Those woeful days were hard for the orphan girl. Living in a blighted area with poverty all around, it was becoming difficult for her aunt to make ends meet. Muhammadi could see her fate, her destiny, which was never to alter.

On one fateful day in her life, a palanquin stopped before the wretched house in the mohalla. Two ladies in burqa stepped inside the room and were received warmly by her aunt. Muhammadi's uncle was not at home. The ladies embraced each other, followed by a quick transaction of funds—an astounding amount that was beyond the poor family's wild imagination. Finally, Muhammadi was called to meet the strangers. She was immediately veiled and lifted to a palanquin. The women in burqas bid farewell to the lady of the house and the palanquin left the place.

Muhammadi could not guess how long the journey was, but she could feel the trepidation in her heart. A long journey had started in her life. The palanquin stopped near a house in a crowded place, and Muhammadi could hear the sweet resonance of euphony. It was chowk, the mohalla of tawaifs—the reputed performers of music in Lucknow.

The tradition of Lucknow Gharana was largely preserved and nurtured in Lucknow's dark alleyways since its heyday. If the exponents of dance and music in the court of Awadh went on to win laurels, the tawaifs living in *kothis* in obscurity embellished their creation, fostered the art and saved it from being lost in the sands of time.

Classical dance continued to live in its purest form amongst Lucknow's courtesans. The courtesans were not ordinary harlots in the streets; they were, in fact, the repositories of high art. Customarily, tawaifs skilled in singing were called Bais, while those who were accomplished dancers and singers were called Jaans. Yet, to the English, they all were *nautch* girls.

Muhammadi, amidst her life in misery, had a peaceful mind and a loving heart that harboured poetry. It was clear to Muhammadi that destiny had drifted her to a kothi belonging to the two burqa-clad ladies—Amman and Imamam. The ladies were former courtesans and had taken up the profession of grooming beautiful and talented girls for noble harems. Amman and Imamam were affluent and egregiously influential. They lived in a large mansion called kothi, which was virtually a centre for cultural learning.

Muhammadi was put to rigorous training in dance and music. There were other girls, too. Her day would start early and after prayer and a frugal meal, dancing and singing sessions continued till two o'clock in the afternoon. After a scrimpy lunch, the pupils were made to learn Persian—the court language—and codes of classical poetry. Evenings were free and Muhammadi, unlike her friends, would sit silently in a lonely corner, immersed in composing poetry. Dance was not her first choice; Muhammadi had her heart set on poems. It was not her dance but her poems that would bring her close to the prince one day. Was she forced to practise harlotry stealthily in the dark alleys of kothi? Modern authors, like Tasadduq Hussain, prefer to believe in the fact.[1] Even Wajid Ali indicated her as *zan-i-khangi* in *Ishqnama*, literally meaning a courtesan in her early life.

A twist of fate changed Muhammadi's path and took her away from the alleyways of kothis into a completely different destiny—the royal harem. She was in full bloom—23 years old, with a slightly dark complexion, sensuous and alluring, which had made scholars believe that she had African roots. Tracing the local land records, some would like to establish that both her father Umber and mother Mehr Fja were slaves in the court of Nawab Ghulam Hossain Khan of Farrukabad.[2] The king was attracted towards African women and married several, including Yasmeen Mahal. However, African lineage of Muhammadi Khanum is not tenable.

Wajid Ali was a flamboyant young man of 21, unpropitiously oozing with sensuality, when he was nominated as heir to his throne by Amjad Ali Shah. The prince was on a cherry-picking

---

[1]Hussain, Sheikh Tasadduq, *Begumaat Awadh,* Kitaab Nagar, p. 203.

[2]Naheed, Nusrat, *Jane Alam aur Mehak Pari*, Lucknow Library Helpage Society, 2005, p. 94.

spree, selecting fair-looking girls for his Pareekhana, and this is how he eventually came in contact with the city's two most influential procuresses, Amman and Imamam, who later offered Muhammadi to the Prince. Some scholars believe that Muhammadi came to the palace as *khawasin* (maid) who blossomed forth as a paree in the Pareekhana.

Nonetheless, Muhammadi Khanum metamorphosed to Mahak Paree soon. Wajid Ali confessed in his literary work *Pareekhana* that Mahak Paree wanted an honourable life and, thus, he gave her shelter in his harem as a dancing girl. Like the other parees, her grooming started as per the traditions of a sophisticated courtesan within the four walls of the Pareekhana.

Soon the Prince had his heart set on Mahak Paree and married her under a mutah wedding contract, and his courtship continued on legitimate terms. At the time of the wedding, the prince further honoured her with the title of Iftikhar-un-Nisa Begum (the pride of all women). He composed poems on Iftikhar-un-Nisa, glorifying her as a gift of miracles and one whose entire body exuded the fragrance of roses.

In early 1845, Wajid Ali came to know that Iftikhar-un-Nisa Begum was pregnant. The prince was overjoyed. Immediately, he gave her relief from all other activities and shifted her to Nageene-Wali-Baradari, a nearby palace. On 20 August 1845, Wajid Ali was blessed with a male child born to Iftikhar-un-Nisa Begum, announced by the sound of an 11-gun salute. King Amjad Ali was so delighted that he named the child Ramzan Ali with the title of Mirza Birjis Qadr Bahadur.[3] Little did he know then that this child of his son's mutah wife would one day step into his shoes.

---

[3]Shah, Wajid Ali, 'Chapter II', *Ishqnama, Lucknow, 1849–50*, p. 96; Hussain, Sheikh Tasadduq, *Begumaat Awadh,* Kitaab Nagar, p. 228.

After the birth of her child, Iftikhar-un-Nisa Begum asked her husband for a eunuch as her help. The Queen wanted a particular eunuch who had been serving a woman in the harem. The woman had died and the eunuch had lost their job. Mammu Khan was their name. He had earned a bad name of being an omen of doom by that time. Well-wishers cautioned the Queen not to take him, but the eunuch was gifted with the aptitude of being extraordinarily intelligent in resolving delicate matters and extremely conversant with the affairs of the Awadh court, and was hence awarded his place.

Wajid Ali readily agreed to the Queen's request and allotted Mammu Khan to serve her. Mammu was obliged to Begum Iftikhar-un-Nisa and pledged to serve the Queen to the best of his ability. After this, Mammu apparently went on to become the closest confidante of the Begum and remained so till his death.[4] Mammu stayed at Nageene-Wali-Baradari, which became the permanent residence of the Begum. Birjis Qadr spent his childhood in this mansion and grew up in luxury like the other princes. With the passing days, the Begum came closer to the eunuch, and was utterly dependent on him, for he served as her eyes and ears.

Birjis Qadr was the fourth son of Wajid Ali and had the unique honour of being the first son born to the prince after he became heir to the throne. Till the time of his birth, Wajid Ali had one nikah wife—Alam Ara Begum or later, Khas Mahal, who bore him his three sons before Birjis.[5] Her first son, Shahzada

---

[4]History reveals that Mammu Khan was a shrewd person with much political sensibilities. He was the main source of information for his mistress, particularly during the time when the king left Lucknow. There are several references to testify this statement. See Llewellyn-Jones, Rosie, *The Great Uprising in India, 1857–1858: Untold Stories, Indian and British*, Boydell Press, 2007, p. 123; Stuart, V.A, *The Cannons of Lucknow*, McBooks Press, 2003, p. 251.

[5]Santha, K.S., *Begums of Awadh*, Bharati Prakashan, Varanasi, 1980, p. 226.

Nausherwan Qadr, was deaf-mute and soon passed away. Her second child, Shahzada Falakh Qadr, who was heir to the throne, died prematurely of smallpox when Birjis was four years old. Her third son, Shahzada Kaiwan Qadr (Mirza Muhammad Hamid Ali), was nominated as the heir apparent after her second son's death. Birjis was the fourth son of the Wajid Ali and the only son of his mutah wife. Birjis was only two years old when his father ascended the throne.

Iftikhar-un-Nisa Begum had left her past long behind. She was no longer a nautch girl in the Prince's court, nor was she a dweller of the Pareekhana. She was next to Alam Ara Begum in stature. Indeed she was the second wife or mahal. Wajid Ali had fathered her child and given her due recognition, but that did not quench his fervent lust for his fairies or to raise the flock of his Pareekhana. The dance fete maintained its brilliance and so did his fervour in traditional performing art. Wajid Ali made full use of his Pareekhana to stage *rahas,* where he played the pivotal role of Krishna and wore the typical costume of a Hindu god. The divine sport of Raas Leela that had once been enacted by Krishna morphed into rahas in Lucknow. Wajid Ali's rahas was an opera with a perfect blend of dance from the Braj region, depicting Krishna's mystic life, with his added composition of kathak. The rahas dance and the Urdu opera was a week-long spectacular dance-drama festival held in Lucknow and was popularly known as *jalsa*.[6]

The first jalsa was performed in 1843. Hard to believe, this was also the last jalsa organized by Wajid Ali before he ascended the throne. What had prevented the heir apparent to restrict his passion for four long years remains a mystery.[7] The participation

[6]Misra, Susheela, *Musical Heritage of Lucknow*, Harman Publishing House, 1991, p. 103.

[7]Adeeb, Syed Masud Hasan Rizvi, *Urdu Drama Aur Stage*, Kitaab Nagar, 1957, p. 120–22.

of Mahak Paree in the dance fete is not known in history. It was an impressive congregation of renowned artists of North Indian gharanas and performers of drama and operas.

The heir apparent staged his first self-composed drama titled *Radha Kanhaiya ka Kissa*, based on the love story of Radha and Krishna. The Prince rediscovered the cult of traditional India that was firmly rooted in ancient understanding. Lord Krishna became his role model. Wajid Ali discovered within himself the archetypal romantic image of Krishna with his tenderness and mesmerizing beauty to inflame the desire of an individual soul for a union. Krishna's romance with his *gopis* (female devotees) under the luminance of a full-moon night on Jamuna's banks was a perennial theme of inspiration to Wajid Ali.

Begum Iftikhar-un-Nisa and Begum Alam Ara, the only wives of Wajid Ali who bore him sons, were prevented by social edits to participate in the spectacular fete. Begum Iftikhar-un-Nisa from the oriels of her *manzil* could apparently see the world through the eyes of Mammu. Her eunuch maintained an impervious intelligence system that could imbibe talks of the town from the air. Disturbing rumours were brewing in the labyrinth of manzil, prevailing over the triumph of rahas. Mammu's constant buzzing was likely to have flustered the Begum that something was looming large, which could change the fate of Awadh.

three

The Last King of Awadh

On 13 February 1847, at five in the evening, King Amjad Ali succumbed to cancer at Farhat Bakhsh Palace at the age of 46, leaving behind five sons and four daughters. His second son Wajid Ali was the designated heir to the throne, expunging the claim of his elder brother Prince Mustafa. If Elihu Jan[1] is to be believed, Amjad Ali also did not trust his second son and 'warned the queen not to allow Wajid Aly [*sic*] to ascend the throne in case he, Umjid Aly [*sic*] died.'[2]

Yet, Wajid Ali ascended the *musnaid* (throne) at nine in the evening after completing his prayer. He was ushered to the throne with the guard of honour at Qasr us-Sultan of Farhat Bakhsh Palace. The crown was placed on his head by none other than the British Resident Colonel Archibald Richmond himself. Nevertheless, when Wajid Ali was interring his father the next morning, inside the half-constructed Sibtainabad Imambara, the wheel of fortune turned in his favour.

Immediately after ascending the throne, Wajid Ali Shah bequeathed a series of honorific titles to his begums. Thus, Alam

---

[1]Elihu Jan was a maid who was brought up in the court of Lucknow from her seventeenth birthday.

[2]Knighton, William, *The Private Life of an Eastern King: Together with Elihu Jan's Story; Or, the Private Life of an Eastern Queen*, Hardpress Publishing, 2013, p. 31.

Ara Begum became Malika Mukaddera-uzm Nawab Badsha Mahal or simply, Khas Mahal, whereas Iftikhar-un-Nisa Begum became Hazrat Mahal. 'Mahal' was the highest appellation given to a mutah wife who bore the king's child. When he was a prince, Wajid Ali Shah elevated nine parees to begums by mutah marriage and Iftikhar-un-Nisa Begum was the only fortunate one to attain the highest rank of mahal, owing to the birth of her son Birjis Qadr. She was truly holding the privilege of his second wife.

The queens' allowances were equally raised. Khas Mahal was getting an allowance of ₹400 as pin-money and it was later increased to ₹5,000 a month. Hazrat Mahal's allowance was also raised but not as much as Khas Mahal's, and was limited to ₹3,000. Malika-i-Kishwar (Janab-i-Aliya), the widow of King Amjad Ali, became the dowager queen.

Desperate situations call for desperate remedies. Cutting through his fervent desire and romanticism, he turned over a new leaf after he accessed his title, focussing sharply on the questions of reformation of his administration. His Pareekhana went behind the purdah for the time being.

When Wajid Ali Shah ascended the throne, the territory of his kingdom was significantly reduced. His forefathers would often buy peace by giving away a slice of their territory to the British and favouring them to increase their treasury revenue. Wajid Ali's territory was extended to the north up to the boundaries of Nepal; river Ganga constituted the southern boundary; Gorakhpur in the east and Shahjahanpur in the west. The kingdom, which Lord Dalhousie cherished in his dreams as his bounty for Her Majesty the Queen of England, had a boundary to cover as much as 24,000 square miles and a population of 10 million people.[3]

---

[3]This figure was collected by Dr Rosie Llewellyn-Jones from a local historian, Roshan Taqui, using 1856 census figures published in local Urdu newspaper named *Tilism-i-Laknau.* See Llewellyn-Jones, Rosie, *The Last King in India,* Random House India, 2014, p. 287.

Just a month after Wajid Ali ascended the throne and when the ephemeral ecstasy of triumph was still wafting all around him, he faced the most stinging challenge that jolted him to realism. A strife between Hindus and Muslims in Awadh intensified around a temple. The story went like this: rumour had it that one Gulab Rai, a Hindu jeweller and a person closely known to chief minister Ameen-ud-Daulah, constructed a temple and sacrificed a Hindu Brahmin child on the day of installing an idol. The King was annoyed and sent his confidante Meer Mahdi to investigate the matter and give him a detailed report. Mahdi not only ordered dismantling the dome of the newly constructed shrine but also demolished two Shivalays and a temple at Haiderganj near his house.

Wajid Ali thoroughly investigated the matter and concluded that Meer Mahdi was at fault. He was immediately arrested and kept confined in his house for the excesses he had committed. Wajid Ali ordered the reconstruction of the desecrated temples and Shivalays at the state's expense.

Meanwhile, Wajid Ali Shah adopted various austerity measures, cracking down on extravagant court life. He curtailed excessive allowances of the nobles and princes, ignoring the Resident's warning that such curbing of personal leisure was 'injudicious' and might lead to rebellion within the palace. Before he constructed his dream palace Kaiserbag, the only construction he had gone through, or rather completed, was his father's mausoleum—Sibtainabad Imambara. The King gave a perpetual loan of ₹7 lakh to the East India Company against 5 per cent interest, from which the expenses to maintain his father's mausoleum were remitted.

The English Resident of Lucknow was keeping an eye on changes made by the new king without meandering much into his administrative matters. But Wajid Ali's endeavour to bring reforms in the army jarred the British from their slumber. Wajid Ali's priority for reforms was his army. He restructured his army and took a personal interest in attending morning parades and armdrills. Under him, not only did the army's strength enhance, the local landlords were also impelled to ensure the collection of revenue and the cavalry and infantry were reorganized. Fresh uniforms were distributed amongst the soldiers, and the King introduced new command in Persian language. He loved to call his troops of cavalry poetic names such as 'Banka' and 'Tircha', and named his infantry 'Ghangghore', 'Äkhtari' and 'Nadiri.'[4] Arms and accoutrements were purchased lavishly and the King spent £900 for his African regiment. He started to wake up early in the morning and attend the parade ground on his horse. He spent hours in scorching heat and dust every day to watch and ensure that his soldiers were obeying the commands.

The King's attempts to reinforce his martial strength and his tendency of turning a deaf ear to many of the Resident's intrusive requests produced a crescendo of discomfort to the foreign masters. The King argued that, on his accession, he had found the army in a bad state and it would not be possible to increase the collection of revenue without a powerful army to back him up. Wajid Ali Shah first tasted ignominy when Archibald Richmond advised him not to squander his treasure by increasing the strength of his army when the British Resident was duty-bound to take care of his kingdom in crisis.[5] Rather, the King should consider spending a little more on improving his police force.[6]

Wajid Ali Shah, like his predecessors, was scared of displeasing the British and, therefore, took the happy-go-lucky path to call off his plans of reforming, which he had once thought essential to rule over the refractory talukdars and zamindars. The matter could have

[4]Azhar, Mirza Ali, *King Wajid Ali Shah of Awadh*, Volume 1, Royal Book Company, Karachi, 1982, p. 196.

[5]As per Treaty of 1801

[6]Bhatnagar, G.D., *Awadh under Wajid Ali Shah*, Bharatiya Vidya Prakashan, 1968, p. 43.

ended here, but it did not. Richmond despatched an adverse report against the King to Viscount Hardinge, the Governor General who was about to retire. In those days, a farewell tour was customary for the Governor Generals before leaving the country for England. Hardinge added Kanpur and Lucknow to the itinerary. The Governor General was interested in meeting the incumbent of Awadh throne and intended a visit in November 1847 on his way back to Calcutta from Punjab. The Resident, too, was keen to meet the Governor General, who would allow him to quibble his ears against the King, since Richmond knew very well that he too was under scrutiny for his failure so far. He became busy in preparing his defence. Richmond would gloss over the truth that the King had corrected himself after his accession and had dropped the curtain of his favourite Pareekhana. His devotion to bringing reforms in the administration would never be spoken of before the Governor General.

Richmond was sure that the Governor General would neither subscribe the King's attempts to reorganize his army nor would he be happy to leave the stately affairs in the hands of the few musicians and dancers who were enjoying the King's blessings. Wajid Ali Shah strongly defended the appointment of Haji Ali Sharif—a 'common singer' who was put in charge of leading a cavalry regiment—or the appointments of other dancers and singers like Ghulam Raza Khan as commander of the Ghangoor Platoon or Anjum-ud-Daulah as the King's messenger to the Resident. The Resident was hell-bent against appointing an African eunuch, Dinanat-ud-Daulah, which finally did not get through. The King then agreed that his virtuosos would not be taken in the government but could serve him at a private level.[7]

Lord Hardinge's visit to Awadh was short and precise but significant enough to throw the King's life out of gear. The

[7]Llewellyn-Jones, Rosie, *The Last King in India*, Random House India, 2014, p. 76.

Governor General camped in Kanpur, on the bank of the Ganga on 3 November 1847, opposite to that of Wajid Ali Shah, who on the other side of the river within the territory of Awadh. The visits between the two sides were courteous and respectful. Wajid Ali Shah was first met by Henry Miers Elliot, the Governor General's secretary, along with two sons of Hardinge amidst incessant untimely rain. The next day, when the rain continued, the King attended a banquet hosted by the Governor General. He put a pearl necklace around the King's neck with his own hands, paying respect to him. A day later, when Hardinge crossed the river and reciprocated his visit to the opposite camp, he was honoured with a pearl necklace and 51 trays of costly articles and jewels.

On his way back to Calcutta via Kanpur, the Governor General paid a visit to Lucknow and met the King confidentially for two hours at his palace. Hardinge had a great time with the King who had organized for the former a sumptuous banquet and entertainment. However, while leaving Lucknow the next day, the Governor General surreptitiously dropped a strong and lengthy letter of a veiled threat written out of moral obligation.

The King was censured for his misgovernment in judicial and revenue administration of his country; the act of tyranny instigated by some ill-intentioned people in razing down Hindu temples; engaging musicians, singers and unworthy people in high stations; and his excess in organizing military activities when the Company was duty-bound to protect the territory of Awadh by all means. The King was advised to be more calculative to protect the interests of *ryots* (peasants); to rectify his defects in the police, revenue and judicial administrations; and always to act in conformity with the counsel of officers of the British government.

The Viscount gave the King two years to improve his administration or else the Company would take over full administration of Awadh in accordance with the Treaty of 1837 signed by the King's grandfather Mohammad Ali Shah. Hardinge's words reverberated the voice of Colonel Richmond in entirety.[8]

Hardinge had a preconceived idea about Wajid Ali Shah since it was reported by Captain H. Shakespeare in September 1845 that 'the heir apparent's character holds no prospect of good'.[9]

Before leaving the country, Hardinge wrote his last dispatch on Awadh containing 38 paragraphs to the Court of Directors in London, while cruising the Ganga on his way to Calcutta in *Soonamookee Yacht* off Monghyaron 2 December 1847. Hardinge's dispatch was more or less a reportage of his tour, intimating 'mismanagement' in the court of Awadh.[10]

However, his observations were influenced by the headsets of the Resident and the Company's officers. Hardinge was gradually building up the ground, speculating further that in the event of the King's sudden demise during the minority of his son, Awadh would be administered by the British Resident and a Native Council.

However, his conscience prevented him from a blatant act of falsehood. In paragraph 23, Hardinge confessed that as far as prosperity of the capital was concerned, Lucknow revealed no sign of bad governance in the state of its streets, bazaars and public building, which were kept in the most perfect order. Further, he revealed that the proportion of crime did not exceed that of cities under the Company's direct governance. It was Hardinge who first suggested that a trustworthy person should be engaged to traverse

---

[8]Bhatnagar, G.D., *Awadh under Wajid Ali Shah*, Bharatiya Vidya Prakashan, Varanasi, 1968, p. 215.

[9]Azhar, Mirza Ali, *King Wajid Ali Shah of Awadh*, Volume 2, Royal Book Company, Karachi, 1982, p. 377.

[10]Hardinge's letter to the Court of Directors in London dated 28 July 1847. See Azhar, Mirza Ali, *King Wajid Ali Shah of Awadh*, Volume 1, Royal Book Company, Karachi, 1982, p. 201.

the country thoroughly to understand the state of affairs of the peasants before jumping into any action.[11]

Wajid Ali Shah followed Hardinge's advice in entirety and dropped his plan to reform the army, at least on record. He diverted his attention in improving the revenue collection and decided to adopt the British system of revenue collection, at least experimentally, in those areas that were adjacent to British territories. Colonel Richmond supported the King's and Nawab Ali Naqi Khan's reforms. He engaged his assistant Resident, Major R.W. Bird, to get the reforms ratified by James Thomason, the Lieutenant Governor of the North-Western Provinces.

Finally, the plan was endorsed by Major Bird, Colonel Richmond and Thomason; the latter pruned the proposal to an acceptable form and placed it before the office of the Governor General in spring of 1848. Thomason was not true to his word. In order to goad 'misrule' and 'oppression' in the state, he deliberately rejected the King's proposal of disarming the local landlords on the plea that they needed to protect themselves against dacoits, so that he could have a pretext to justify British interference in the future.[12]

The Marquis of Dalhousie and his wife Susan reached the river port of Calcutta on 12 January 1848 to receive the baton of control from the retiring Lord Hardinge. The Viscount was growing old and became tired of waging a hundred battles. His health was failing fast and he sought to live a reclusive life in the quiet. In contrast, Dalhousie was in the prime of his life, at half the age of his departing predecessor, perhaps the youngest man to take over the supreme responsibility of the Indian Empire.

---

[11]Paragraph 26 of Hardinge's dispatch dated 2 December 1847. See Azhar, Mirza Ali, *King Wajid Ali Shah of Awadh*, Volume 1, Royal Book Company, Karachi, 1982, p. 515.

[12]See Azhar, Mirza Ali, *King Wajid Ali Shah of Awadh*, Volume 1, Royal Book Company, Karachi, 1982, p. 242.

Dalhousie's annexation mania had made him dream of Awadh as 'a cherry, which will drop into our mouths someday. It has long been ripening'.[13] However, he was not sure if 'the court would approve of my [Dalhousie's] shaking the tree to hold it down.'[14] Therefore, when the final draft of the King's pet project to adopt a British system of revenue collection was placed, it was immediately shelved.

Wajid Ali Shah did not give up; instead, he started to tighten his control over state administration. He issued a book of his regulation, which he named *Dastoor-e-Wajidi.* He concentrated all his efforts in the interest of ryots. He also focussed on the prisoners under detention and ordered enquiries afresh for the long detainees. The King assured safety on highways, stopped the excesses of his soldiers while executing his orders against the zamindars and reined in his men from bribery. Nonetheless, his tenets to build a society in all fairness had veered him to more difficulty.

Only eight months after his accession, Dalhousie started to stir things up with his policy of annexation. On 30 August 1848, Dalhousie came up with his idea of lapse and held that 'on all occasions, where heirs natural shall fail, the territory should be made to lapse and adoption should not be permitted'.[15]

Meanwhile, misfortunes continued to loom large over Wajid Ali. In 1849 January, he suffered a massive heart attack, which confined him to his palace for a whole year. When Wajid Ali was striving hard to make good on his promises to Hardinge by the end of the year, his very survival came to be at stake. The King,

---

[13]Baird, J.G.A., *Private Letters of the Marquess of Dalhousie,* William Blackwood and Sons, 1910, p. 169.
[14]Chhabra, G.S, *Advanced Study in the History of Modern India,* Lotus Press, 2007, p. 215.
[15]Kaye, John William, *A History of the Sepoy War in India, 1857–58,* Longmans, Green, and Co., 1896, p. 73–4.

even during crisis, would count on his hakims[16] instead of English doctors whom traditionally he found untrustworthy, conniving to murder him. It was said that when the King was in crisis, the ladies of the *harem* even indulged in witchcraft to cure him.

When the cloud of uncertainty was lurking high over Awadh, a man in his sixties whose reputation was to suppress the thuggees' (thugs') secret societies, stepped into the British Residency of Lucknow on 6 January 1849. Colonel William Henry Sleeman was the most versatile character in the history of British India—the thuggee-hunter, the discoverer of dinosaur fossil in Asia as well as the 'wolf child' that later inspired Rudyard Kipling.[17] He was assigned by the Government of India for 'the reconstruction of its internal administration'.[18] of Awadh and 'his appointment sealed the doom of Oude and its dynasty.'[19] By then, Colonel Sleeman had earned the nickname 'Thuggee Sleeman' (having slayed 1,400 thugs). He was quick to grab the coveted post of the Lucknow Residency.

Colonel Sleeman was appointed to prepare an inquiry report in the way Hardinge had advised—a reliable British person to traverse the country and gather accurate information of the present state of affairs, but the intent of the report was made clear to him even before he entered Awadh.

---

[16]A traditional physician to practise indigenous medicines

[17]Kipling, Rudyard, *Jungle Book*, Penguin Classics, 1989, p. 18; Sleeman, Sir William, *A Journey through the Kingdom of Oude in 1849–1850*, Volume 1, Richard Bentley, 1858, p. 206. Sleeman, during his stay in Lucknow, narrated an eyewitness account of wolves nurturing a human child in her den. His article, 'An Account of Wolves Nurturing Children in Their Dens', inspired Rudyard Kipling to portray the account of Mowgli in his famous, *Jungle Book*.

[18]Lord Dalhousie's letter to Colonel Sleeman dated 16 September 1948. See Sleeman, Sir William, *A Journey through the Kingdom of Oude in 1849–1850*, Volume 1, Richard Bentley, 1858, p. xvii.

[19]Lucas, Samuel, *Dacoitee in Excelsis; or, The Spoliation of Oude by the East India Company, Faithfully Recounted*, J.R. Taylor, London, 1857, p. 109.

As Major Bird succinctly put it: 'He [Sleeman] professed to examine, but he was under orders to sentence; he pretended to try, but he was instructed simply to condemn.'[20] The enormous reserves of ₹92 lakh and the 124,000 gold *mohurs* (coins) in the King's treasury and government security worth ₹24 lakh[21] were coveted by the Governor General. Dalhousie's order 'with special reference to the great changes which, in all probability, will take place'[22] gave Colonel Sleeman to understand that the Governor General had assigned a thief to catch a thief, to carry out a historic dacoity!

Wajid Ali Shah's heart attack had put Sleeman in a terrible dilemma. The thuggee hunter was not sure about the future of the dynasty and once wrote to H.M. Elliot that 'the King continues very ill, but no danger seems to be apprehended.' Sleeman was sceptical and after a few days, he again wrote to Elliot: 'The King continues much the same as when I last wrote.'[23]

Sleeman was almost certain that the King would not survive anymore, and promptly signalled danger to Elliot, proposing to form a Regency Council without delay, suggesting to place the heir apparent on the throne immediately after the King's death. William Sleeman's new strategy in line with the new changes in Awadh was about to come to an abrupt halt.

---

[20]Ibid.

[21]Sleeman, Sir William, *A Journey through the Kingdom of Oude in 1849–1850*, Volume 1, Richard Bentley, 1858, p. 310.

[22]Dalhousie's letter to Colonel Sleeman from Government House Calcutta dated 16 September 1848. See Sleeman, Sir William, *A Journey through the Kingdom of Oude in 1849–1850*, Volume 1, Richard Bentley, 1858, p. xvii.

[23]Sleeman's letter to H.M. Elliot on 20 March 1849. See Sleeman, Sir William, *A Journey through the Kingdom of Oude in 1849–1850*, Volume 1, Richard Bentley, 1858, p. l.

four

A Wind of Change

Iftikhar-un-Nisa Hazrat Mahal Saheba's world had been limited to the bounds of Nageene-Wali-Baradari. Disturbing news was floating into her ears. The angrez were not happy with her husband and were plotting to sieze the kingdom. Whenever Mammu Khan went to the chowk, he was likely to have brought daunting stories for his mistress. The King was full of beans before Hardinge's visit, but the air changed abruptly after he received a letter from the Governor General on his departure. The Begum was unaware of the content, which the King would be reluctant to share, but it was not difficult to apprehend that the letter was veiled intimidation. But Jan-e-alam was not a timorous man and, often, it was difficult for Hazrat Mahal to decipher the real man from all that had been said about him.

With rising vehemence against the British, Wajid Ali Shah went on with his reforms. Taking the help of his *wazir* (prime minister) Ali Naqi Khan, the King concentrated in preparing a proposal of introducing a British system of revenue collection. Time was short for him and he would not be granted a period of more than two years by the English masters. But his well-thought-out proposal never saw the light of the day after being shelved by the new Governor General Lord Dalhousie.

Mammu Khan was likely to have brought the news first. Colonel Richmond was leaving Lucknow shortly and would be replaced by a new Resident who was about to come from Gwalior. But what was apparently not known to Mammu Khan was that the new Governor General's ruthless assertion of power had already marked the beginning of a rapacious English dominance in the country.

On assuming his office, Dalhousie worked hard for eight months to lay down his policy of assuming the native states, either by the ploy of misrule or doctrine of lapse, Satara being his first thriving experiment. On 18 September 1848, less than a month after putting forward his policy of annexation, Dalhousie wrote, 'Meantime I have got two other Kingdoms on hand to dispose of—Oude and Hyderabad. Both are on the high road to be taken under our management—not into our possession; and before two years are over, I have no doubt they will be managed by us.'[1]

Awadh's fate was decided much before Sleeman joined; the 'thuggee hunter' was merely there to facilitate the process. The King's illness was seen by some authorities as calculated British propaganda with a vested intention to prepare the ground for a rumour that the King was not physically well to continue with his stately functions. Sleeman exerted his influence over the King's trusted minister Ameer Ali Khan, author of *Wazeer Namah*, to reiterate that the King was suffering from melancholy, and overindulgence in sex had led him to a mental disorder bordering on insanity. Furthermore, the court physicians had sent him to rest and advised him to stay free from all courtly matters. Rather, the King was advised to keep himself busy with music and other ways of recreations to prevent straining his heart and brain. He purposely avoided European physicians, as he feared being poisoned by unknown doctors. This fact was not unknown to Sleeman.[2] He

---

[1]Baird, J.G.A., *Private Letters of the Marquess of Dalhousie*, William Blackwood and Sons, London, 1910, p. 33.

[2]Azhar, Mirza Ali, *King Wajid Ali Shah of Awadh*, Volume 1, Royal Book Company, Karachi, 1982, p. 264.

sent British Resident physicians Dr Bell and Dr Leekie to meet the King as required by tradition. Sleeman was baffled when the English physicians, who had a long conversation with the King in the presence of Major Bird, announced that the King was in a sound state of health and mind and showed no signs of confusion!

Wajid Ali recovered from his illness, but luck was still not in his favour. Prince Falak Qadr, the second son of Khas Mahal and the heir apparent to his throne, died of smallpox on 26 May 1849, when he was only 11 years old. It was a severe shock to Khas Mahal, and the King who had recently recovered from his illness. Mammu Khan informed Hazrat Mahal that the third son of Khas Mahal, Prince Mirza Muhammad Hamid Ali, would be sworn in as the heir apparent to the Awadh throne. Hamid Ali was only seven years elder to Birjis Qadr and both princes had the same upbringing in the royal court. This led Mammu Khan to ponder that destiny had pushed Hazrat Mahal a little forward in the power race. In case of any adversity to Hamid Ali, Birjis Qadr's fate would smile on him!

On the other hand, Wajid Ali Shah's fate was pierced by a triple-edged sword—the enduring impediment created by the British Resident to bring reforms within the stipulated period laid down by Lord Hardinge, the death of his beloved son and his failing health. Unlike his predecessors, Wajid Ali had no political ambition; rather, he preferred to be a backroom monarch in his court precincts. The Sultan-e-Alam, as his people called him, started to decentralize his responsibilities to his trusted ministers. He had handed over the Dastoor-e-Wajidi, his code of conduct of running the kingdom, to his ministers and gradually pulled out from stately matters.

It wasn't hard to ruminate that Wajid Ali Shah had sunk deep in depression. He was expeditiously losing confidence in himself. His mind was muddled when he remembered one of the aphorisms of his mother. If William Sleeman is to be believed, the dowager queen Aliya Begum had woven a story for Wajid Ali to diffuse his son's mind from being enamoured by one of his women. The begum narrated that it is a bad omen for her son to be captivated by a girl who bore an evil sign of a *sampun* (a coiled figurine of a snake) on the back of her neck, underneath her hair. She further added that if a man cohabited with a woman having such a mark, he and his children would perish. Even Sultan-e-Alam would not be spared if any of his begums bore this evil mark, the dowager queen explained.

When adversities devastated Sultan-e-Alam's life, when misfortune had led to losing his dearest son, the heir to his throne, when his health was failing rapidly, his mother's apophthegm had taken a deep root in the innermost recesses of his weak mind. His plight made him believe that a bad omen in his palace must be prevailing upon his wheel of fortune.

'No doubt,' said the old queen dowager, 'we have long thought so; but Your Majesty gets into such a towering passion when we venture to speak of your wives, that we have been afraid to give expression to our thoughts and fears.'[3] Sultan-e-Alam immediately called Bashir, his eunuch, and forthwith ordered him to inspect the back of the necks of all his queens. Khas Mahal, the fated queen who had lost her favourite son and the heir apparent, was spared from frisking.

The fated motion of weeding doomed Hazrat Mahal's destiny. She was one of the eight begums in the King's palace whom Bashir found to bear the evil mark of sampun. The King called an assembly of *moulvis* (Muslim religious scholar) and later, Hindu brahmins in the court for their opinion. While the moulvis inferred separation

[3]Sleeman, Sir William, *A Journey through the Kingdom of Oude in 1849–1850*, Volume 1, Richard Bentley, 1858, p. 107.

as the safest option, the brahmin pundits who were supposed to have mastered the art of prophecy took a liberal view. The pundits ordained that though the mark partly resembled sampun, there was hardly any merit in the omen. They resolved that the omen, if any, could be averted by singeing the head of the snake with a hot iron. The situation was humiliating for Hazrat Mahal. The mother of the King's fourth son was determined, out of conviction, not to give in to the barbaric custom, nor was she ready to leave her palace.

No one in history has ever mentioned that the King had divorced Hazrat Mahal; nor did the King ever deny his relationship with her in any of his writings.[4] Yet her love turned futile as a twist of fate changed her path and took her away from Jan-e-Alam and onto an altogether different destiny. The fated queen lived the rest of her life in seclusion, cut off from all conjugal relations with her husband.

Destiny had ordained for Wajid Ali Shah a merry existence within the precinct of his Pareekhana. When Wajid Ali Shah was over engrossed with his reforms, the Pareekhana was deprived of all his tender care. The 'fairies' and his 'begums', who partook in his indulgence, were now forced to stay behind the curtains. This period

---

[4]The enigmatic relation between the King and the Queen has led to a century-old controversy. The royal family, based on documentary evidences, strongly believe that although the King and the Queen were separated, the King never divorced the Queen. Wajid Ali Shah, being a prolific writer, composed a small *masnavi* (a long poetic collection of anecdotes and stories written in rhythmic verses) named *Bahr-e-Mukhtalif* about his wives during his incarceration at Fort William. The masnavi, which is in custody of the royal family, does not mention that the author had divorced Begum Hazrat Mahal or repudiated the marriage by pronouncing 'talaq'; rather the King eulogized his wife for the bravery she had shown in recovering his ancestral kingdom. The dynasty is proud to believe that the *suryabanshi* and *chandrabanshi* kshatriya rajputs would not have had rallied behind the Queen if she was a divorced lady. However, English sources still hold the opinion that the King had divorced Begum Hazrat Mahal.

did not last for long as soon, the King, baffled by British political intrigues, took recourse to love and decided to spend more time with his 'fairies'. The King, who had been ill since January 1849, recovered from his illness in October 1850, with a reinvigorated love for music and dance. The lights of his Pareekhana started to gleam once again. After ascending his throne, the King had put all his efforts to construct a palace complex, which amalgamated all the intricacies of a paradise garden. He named it Kaiserbag. The palace complex had taken four years to build from 1848 to 1852 and had incurred an expense of ₹8 lakh.[5] Kaiserbag became the platform for his artistic efflorescence. His literary eloquence continued in the meantime.

The masnavis, which he composed during his teens, were re-edited. Thus, *Darya-e-Ta'shuk, Afsana-e-Ishaq* and *Behr-e-Ulfat* were spruced up in new forms.[6] Wajid Ali's jalsas came to a halt after he ascended the throne. Perhaps, the King found it beyond his dignity of merit. But his annual custom to become a jogi continued with royal splendour for the first two years of his rule. It was turned into Shahi Jasan in the years to come. His famed musical fete, rahas, where the King impersonated a jogi and Qaiser Begum and Gilzar Begum assumed the characters of jogins had come to an abrupt halt for almost the whole of 1849 and early 1850 due to his unprecedented sickness.

Contrary to British propaganda about the King's indulgence in music and other frivolous pursuits, it is a fact that no jalsa was held for as long as nine years after the first one. The King could not devote much time to music after ascending the throne. Besides, his illness had kept him away from the stage till 1850. Wajid Ali's penchant for performing arts once again breathed new life when

---

[5]Llewellyn-Jones, Rosie, *The Last King in India*, Random House India, 2014, p. 57.
[6]Qureshi, M.A, *Wajid Ali Shah's Theatrical Genius*, Lahore Vanguard Books Ltd, 1987, p. 5.

he was brushing up the masnavi *Darya-e-Ta'shuk*—the romance of Ghazalah and Mahru, which he wrote in his younger days. He had a brilliant idea to dramatize his long poem and gathered more than 250 womenfolk from different strata and an almost equal number of musicians and male actors for the stage. The fete was finally put on stage after a year-long preparation in February–March 1851. Wajid Ali himself mentioned the extravagance in *Ishqnama* as *Tayyari Rahs Mubarak*. He used the term 'rahas', although the drama did not depict Krishna's life.

Mammu Khan was excited and rushed to his mistress to be the first to give a commentary of the series of events unfolding. Hazrat Mahal was not surprised, as the whiff of King's extravagant fad was already hanging in the air of Nageene-Wali-Baradari. The Queen, although relieved to find Jan-e-Alam recovering from his infirmity, was disturbed by his mulish obstinacy to stay away from courtly duties, which were handed down to him by his forefathers. His dependence on Ali Naqi Khan was looked down upon by Hazrat Mahal. Mammu warned her many a times that Ali Naqi Khan, being a British stooge in garb, could plot against Jan-e-Alam.

But Mammu was bubbling over with enthusiasm as the King retreated into romance and his arts—the lamps over the fringes of the newly built Kaiserbag palace complex would glitter for the first time since its construction. Mammu recalled the splendour and participation of around 250 stunning beauties, dressed in gorgeous costumes heavily embroidered with gold strings, accompanied by hundreds of musicians. There were about a hundred sarangi *nawaz* or fiddlers and the same number of *tal-dar*s (chime players). The fete started with European music played by the King's regimental band trained to play English music including 'God Save the King'.

The story continued to recreate a king's durbar studded with gold and silver, his court, his queen, princes, princesses, ministers, courtiers, astrologers, pundits, macebearers, demons, fairies, *dervishes* and *khwaja sera*s or attendants of the harem. Spectators were flabbergasted to see a live, theatrical kingdom recreated within a real kingdom, showing mock fights, jousting and archery, tableaux and processions with real elephants and many such wonderful set crafts. Mammu reported to the Begum that the show continued for a day and dusk in palatial Farhat Manzil, Shah Manzil, Qaiser Manzil and Ma'shud Manzil. The old Daulat Khana was decorated as Paristhan or fairyland.

The show continued for a month, staging 14 episodes with intervals of a day or more. Wajid Ali resumed his magnificient regal style, his power, his unquestioned authority and resources to spend £12,000 to stage ephemeral merriment!

The grand success of Tayyari Rahs Mubarak emboldened Wajid Ali Shah to stage more rahas in the subsequent period. Perhaps what was most worrisome to Hazrat Mahal was Jan-e-Alam's new obsessions, which would eventually run the kingdom into the ground. Pareekhana became the epicentre of his artistic efflorescence and parees, his incentives to live.

Hazrat Mahal was most likely apprehensive that the King's renunciation of courtly matters might herald dark times for the kingdom. Jan-e-Alam's trusted men were not worth their salt and had never been subservient to their master. Mammu Khan rightly pointed out that the King's trusted ministers would take undue advantage of his repudiation from stately affairs and his overindulgence in romantic escapades.

Nevertheless, Mammu must have not expected that his premonition would come true so soon. Wajid Ali Shah himself was wary of his prime minister Nawab Ali Naqi Khan's treacherous mind with the threat of insurgency looming at large.[7] Eventually,

[7]Azhar, Mirza Ali, *King Wajid Ali Shah of Awadh*, Volume 1, Royal Book Company, Karachi, 1982, p. 39.

the King's decision to marry Ali Naqi's third daughter, Raunaq Ara Begum, to avoid being assassinated by his own father-in-law, incited Sleeman to deride, 'Ali Naqi would keep the King alive'.[8] Thus, 11-year-old Raunaq Ara Begum, with her stunning beauty, became Malikah-e-Oudh Nawab Akhtar Mahal on 4 June 1851. The King's second nikah wedding was celebrated with much grandeur and a magnificent *jashan* (celebration) was held on the banks of river Gomti.

After his wedding with Akhtar Mahal, Wajid Ali Shah staged the second jalsa from his masnavi *Afsana-i-Ishq*, the love story of Sim-tan and Mah-paikar in 1852, with unprecedented splendour. Wajid Ali Shah organized his third jalsa based on his masnavi *Behr-e-Ulfat*, or the story of Mah Pervin and Mehr Parwar, probably in 1853. In his own words, the King trained 40 to 50 charming women with a dulcet voice from the house of Lucknowi courtesans for the stage. This was his last jalsa in Lucknow before leaving for Matiyaburj. In 1852, Wajid Ali Shah wrote a book titled *Saut-ul-Mubarak* devoted to the rahas he had composed, wherein 32 kinds of rahas dances had been described. But before he could put more jalsas on show, political hostility forced him to leave Lucknow.

[8]Letter from Colonel Sleeman to the Marquis of Dalhousie dated 11 November 1853, in Sleeman, Sir William, *A Journey through the Kingdom of Oude in 1849–1850*, Volume 2, Richard Bentley, 1858, p. 468.

five

Annexation of Awadh

Sir William Henry Sleeman was the most distinguished yet controversial servant of British India. His service was recognized for more than 40 years by three Governors General of India—the Earl of Ellenborough, Viscount Hardinge and the Marquis of Dalhousie. However, he virtually failed to deliver his task, which was vested upon him by Lord Dalhousie.

Sleeman planned on using an opportune moment to enforce a new treaty by taking the King's discontented elder brother Prince Mustafa and the dowager queen into confidence and bringing them over to his side—a plan that never saw the light of day.[1] His attempt to engage a regent to guide the heir apparent did not work either. His aspiration to play the role of a virtual ruler analogous to the model prescribed in Gwalior or Lahore never came to fruition.

At the end of his career and when his health was failing, Sleeman had no reason to flatter his masters. The annexation of Awadh took place eventually, but not as a consequence of his report. Post-annexation results proved beyond doubt that Sleeman had judged the mind of the people of Awadh better than Dalhousie. This versatile character in the history of British rule

[1]Sleeman's letter to Mr H.M. Elliot from Lucknow dated 20 March 1849. See Sleeman, Sir William, *A Journey through the Kingdom of Oude in 1849–1850*, Volume 1, Richard Bentley, 1858, p. l.

in India left Lucknow with his wife on 5 October 1854, never to return.

Dalhousie's successful annexation of 12 princely states—from Satara (1848) to Tanjore (1855)—had made him obsessed with power. The East India Company, which was no longer an autonomous corporation but principally under the control of the British Crown, rapidly spread its roots and became the predominant power in India. Dalhousie's annexation of Awadh, his thirteenth 'cherry', entailed grave political danger.

It was neither Sleeman nor Dalhousie, but the King himself who paved his path to ruin. Colonel Sleeman wrote that the King inherited a coffer of ₹92 lakh and 124,000 gold mohurs, which his father had saved from his income. Wajid Ali Shah squandered the wealth on his lofty dreams and was left with little more than ₹6 lakh and a few gold mohurs since he ascended the throne. His expenditure superseded his annual income by ₹22.5 lakh while keeping the salary of his troops and stipends of his dependents as arrear for one-and-a-half years. The King was trapped in a debt of ₹50 lakh—a depiction of the decline of the kingdom.[2]

On 5 December 1854, a dark-looking, short-figured Englishman with a Jewish beard came from Calcutta to set foot on Lucknow's soil. He was Colonel James Outram, the successor of Colonel Sleeman. Outram was received by the heir apparent on an elephant and had left his howdah for that of one of the sons of Wajid Ali. The Residency officers attended him with a large procession of elephants, camel, cavalry and infantry.

Before moving to Lucknow, Outram came to Calcutta for a briefing from Lord Dalhousie. But the Governor General had already started on a voyage along the coast of Orissa (now Odisha)

---

[2]Colonel Sleeman's report dated 20 October 1851. See Bhatnagar, G.D., *Awadh under Wajid Ali Shah*, Bharatiya Vidya Prakashan, 1968, p. 107.

to recoup his health. Dalhousie left his instructions with Sir John Low. The instruction was short and *ad rem*. Precisely, Outram would continue working on annexing Awadh, the resolution decided by the government and 'wait no longer for ridiculous improvements from within, but at once, to shape their measures for the assertion'[3]. Outram did not have to be hasty in winding up the net; rather, the measures were to be carried out deliberately after certain preliminary formalities of inquiry and reference.

Unlike Sleeman, Outram confined himself within the four walls of the Residency except taking a short stroll at the break of dawn on the terrace of his quarter. He was to take a hurried breakfast before setting to work at his office till evening. Meanwhile, Dalhousie was losing his patience. His failing health and impending retirement made him restless. Excessive smoking and a wasting disease took a toll on him and when he returned to Calcutta from the Nilgiris in October 1855; he was almost crippled.

However, his physical incapacitation could not prevent him from his last task of annexing Awadh. The report prepared by Outram, even though it had no sum or substance, bolstered Dalhousie to prove Wajid Ali's reckless spending and his worthless reforms before the Court of Directors.[4] Dalhousie prepared his minutes for the board of governors of East India Company, mainly based on the observations and reports of Colonel Sleeman and James Outram.

Dalhousie offered three options to assimilate Awadh: first, the King should surrender the province of Awadh to the British

---

[3]Kaye, John William, *A History of the Sepoy War in India, 1857–1858*, Longmans, Green, and Co., 1896, p. 143; Azhar, Mirza Ali, *King Wajid Ali Shah of Awadh*, Volume 1, Royal Book Company, Karachi, 1982, p. 102.

[4]Baird, J.G.A., *Private Letters of the Marquess of Dalhousie*, William Blackwood and Sons, 1910, p. 344.

Government for a limited period of time; second, he should be allowed to retain his title and his throne while the administration would be vested in the hands of the British forever; or the third, that Awadh should be fully and permanently annexed to the British domain. Dalhousie was in favour of the second option.[5]

It was a long wait for the Marquis, and the delay was becoming unbearable. The incessant strain took a heavy toll on Dalhousie's health, which was slowly giving up. The Marquis was almost at a point where he had to cling onto crutches, when the despatched duly signed by the Court of Governors on 21 November 1855 reached his hands in Calcutta at midnight on 2 January 1856, as 'a specimen of the art of writing important instructions to avoid responsibility'.[6] Dalhousie's 75-paragraph minutes, covering 144 pages, appeared to be overstated, but after meticulously weighing the merits, the Court of Directors and Her Majesty's Ministry gave him the go-ahead. Dalhousie was given a free hand by the Court to choose the best option out of the three as he deemed suitable.

Dalhousie was confident of his ability to overcome Wajid Ali in handing over the baton of the administration in lieu of preserving his title. He thus remarked: 'The King won't offend or quarrel with us and will take any amount of kicking without being rebellious.'[7] However, he also prepared an alternative proclamation, lest his confidence was misplaced. 'We shall offer him a treaty and

---

[5]Kaye, John William, *A History of the Sepoy War in India, 1857–1858*, Longmans, Green, and Co., 1896, p. 143; Azhar, Mirza Ali, *King Wajid Ali Shah of Awadh*, Volume 1, Royal Book Company, Karachi, 1982, p. 390.

[6]The statement was made by Sir Charles Jackson in Bell, Evans, *Retrospects and Prospects of Indian Policy*, Trübner, 1868, p. 51. The argument behind this was that the Court of Directors bestowed full liberty and confidence on Dalhousie to choose his own course of action to assume Oudh.

[7]Letter dated 2 May 1855. See Baird, J.G.A., *Private Letters of the Marquess of Dalhousie*, William Blackwood and Sons, 1910, p. 344.

if he refuses it, swallow him,'[8] Dalhousie was adamant. '[Either] the King must give up administration, or we shall take it. I think he will give; if not, we certainly shall take.'[9]

Outram reached Lucknow from Calcutta on 30 January 1856, with the Governor General's decree and his alternative proclamations in hands. Regardless of his master's explicit approbation, Outram was doubtful—rather apprehensive—whether the British would succeed in annexing Awadh without taking recourse to arms. Outram had known the King closely for one entire year and had reason to believe that the King would not enter into any such arrangement to give up his government in place of the Crown.

The news was disclosed as the British troops in Kanpur were in a state of readiness to act.[10] Rumours reached the King's palace and conjecture was all around. It was unbelievable for Wajid Ali Shah that the honourable East India Company could stoop so low as to instigate a breach of reliance and violate the Treaty of 1801. The King rebuffed the rumours and reprimanded the tattlers. Nevertheless, the rumours did not die down and forced the King to send his emissary to the Resident to enquire about the truth of the matter. Outram had no other way but to take refuge in a flagrant lie. He fibbed that the concentration of troops in Kanpur were part of pre-emptive steps to quell a rebellion on the Nepal frontier. The King felt relieved.

---

[8]Letter dated 6 January 1856. See Baird, J.G.A., *Private Letters of the Marquess of Dalhousie*, William Blackwood and Sons, 1910, p. 367.

[9]Letter dated 20 January 1856. See Baird, J.G.A., *Private Letters of the Marquess of Dalhousie*, William Blackwood and Sons, 1910, p. 365.

[10]Ludlow, John Malcolm, *British India, Its Races and Its History Considered with Reference to the Mutinies of 1857: A Series of Lectures Addressed to the Students of the Working Men's College*, Volume 2, Macmillan, 1858, p. 210.

However, the relief was short-lived because the rumours rang true. Outram, on his arrival on 30 January 1856, met the prime minister, Ali Naqi Khan, and explained what the British government had in mind and talked about the new treaty, which his Lordship would like to enforce. The task, which Outram was given to perform, was difficult as well as delicate. Outram's apprehension was correct and, as anticipated, Ali Naqi Khan refuted the charges concocted against the King and remonstrated the concentration of British troops at Kanpur. The prime minister made all possible efforts to impress the Resident, citing the reforms the King had brought about following Hardinge's visit, the amelioration of law and order of the state, the Treaty of 1801 and, last but not the least, the century-old faith that the dynasty had affirmed to the British Crown but all in vain.

The Resident's hands were tied and he was bound by his duties. He had nothing further to add, nor did he deny the arguments adduced by Ali Naqi Khan. Even so, Outram could not defy the great task entrusted to him.

A second meeting was arranged on the following day at the Lucknow Residency, where Ali Naqi Khan was shown a copy of the new treaty. The prime minister also read Lord Dalhousie's letter addressed to the King, explaining the government's resolution and the terms of the treaty, which His Majesty would be requested to sign. The discussion was brief and Ali Naqi Khan questioned if the King could be allowed to seek an appointment with the Governor General and, if required, with Her Majesty, the Queen of England, for a more favourable resolution.

Outram was focussed on signing the treaty for which he gave the King only three days to decide, following the official handing over of the document. Thereafter, the Company would have no other option but to assume the governance of Awadh, and the King would be responsible for the consequences. On the other hand, if His Majesty acceded to sign the document, the Company would agree to a pension of ₹1 lakh per month for the King and would allow him to retain his title.

Tattlers fanned out the gossip that the King's obsession with dancing and singing had frustrated the British lords and sooner or later, Awadh would be annexed. The air was heavy at Nageene-Wali-Baradari. Mammu Khan first brought the news of the battalion stationed at Kanpur, waiting in the wings to take over the Lucknow territory. It was a congregation of 1,600 soldiers at the beck and call of General Wheeler, the army commandant of Kanpur cantonment. The angrez would take over the kingdom disposing off Sultan-e-Alam. The heydays of Lucknow would become history, Mammu expressed his trepidation.

People of Lucknow would prefer to be ruled by their own king, whatever his faults may be, rather than by the angrez. They would prefer to take the side of a revered dynasty, discounting all miseries in life. The gentries and talukdars, who were afraid to lose their lustre and authority as well, were ready to reluctantly take to their guns, as they were not warriors as such. They belonged to the sophisticated elite class and despite the impending threat, some of them were just not ready to give up on their indolent life.

Hazrat Mahal was inclined to lay the blame on Sultan-e-Alam for this unforeseen misfortune. The King should have ruminated much earlier that tending to his hedonistic, aesthetic tastes and flamboyant private life would not have been a noble choice for a king. Hazrat Mahal got wind of the fact that the Resident was adamant about making a treaty signed by Sultan-e-Alam, or else he would have no other option but to assume the power of the kingdom and the King would lose his title and privileges.

Ali Naqi Khan's second meeting with the Resident on 31 January miserably failed as expected. When the chief minister was about to leave the Residency, he was handed over a letter from

Dalhousie and a draft treaty for the King to examine.

On his return to the palace, Ali Naqi Khan, after much hesitation and rolling of tears, handed over the missive to the King. The letter jolted the King to hard reality. Dalhousie had built a castle on blatant lies. How could people live in poverty in the 'garden, granary and the queen province of India', Sultan-e-Alam wondered. He never faltered to undertake the reforms prescribed by Hardinge. Soon after the Governor General left Lucknow, the King proactively reviewed his reforms and prepared a fresh set based on the English model advocated by Hardinge. It was precisely the wealth of Awadh that had lured the British to abrogate his government. Wajid Ali Shah immediately called a *durbar* (court) to vent to his cabinet men whom he held culpable for his impending misery. It was a wake-up call for the ministers and advisors. Fountain of harsh words spouted the durbar to describe the treachery of the British whose arrogance was unwarranted in the context of the dynasty's loyalty for nearly a century.

Advisors remained mostly unequivocal, with the only exception being Raja Jai Lal Singh. Raja Jai Lal, who was the talukdar of Azamgarh district and a prominent courtier with a military background, advised the King to wage war against the British. He was a trusted name in the King's cabinet since his father's time. His father was a companion and faithful confidante of Sultan-e-Alam's uncle Nasir-ud-din Haidar who had once saved the king while on a hunt.

Raja Jai Lal was determined to congregate the talukdars, each one with a small army, under one umbrella. The talukdars became scared of the impending changes and feared losing authority and privileges under British rule. Together with Sultan-e-Alam's troops, there would be a combined force of 70,000 men to fight against the British and to lay down their lives for their masters. Ali Naqi Khan was not confident about the ideas of Raja Jai Lal and pleaded that the talukdars' troops were barely fit to repel the bandits and would not be capable of standing against the British canons. The chief minister inclined to argue in favour of a peaceful settlement—signing the new treaty as per which the King would retain his title as well as would get a monthly sum of ₹1 lakh for his expenses.

Meanwhile, Hazrat Mahal argued that Nawab Ali Naqi Khan was a wolf in the garb of a sheep. Rumours were then already rife that Outram had won over the King's chief-minister-turned-father-in-law by offering him his old *jagir*[11] of Machhrehta in Sitapur, yielding an annual income of ₹1 lakh, if he could prevail upon the King to affix his signature out of his free will.

The King listened to his men and took a balanced path. Neither did he consent to sign the treaty nor did he allow Raja Jai Lal to take the sword. He was not prepared to burn his fingers like his great-great grandfather, Nawab Shuja-ud-daula. The King, being confident of getting justice from the Governor General in Calcutta, decided to write to Outram and refute the charges framed against him. An optimistic Wajid Ali misjudged the danger and deception of the colonial rulers just like his predecessors.

The next day, on 1 February, the British Resident received a letter from the King, which bore an acquiescent tone. The King refuted charges framed against him by the Governor General but submitted to adopt any other reforms that the British government felt would be in the interest of his people. The King enumerated manifold reforms undertaken during his regime since the visit of Lord Hardinge and once again expressed his fidelity to the British Crown, but declined to endorse the contents of the treaty.

The Resident acknowledged the receipt of the letter on the

---

[11]Landed property. The jagir was given to Ali Naqi Khan's grandfather in 1767, and was held by the family for 42 years.

same day, but his reply was sharp. It said that the resolution passed by the British government was irrevocable and the Governor General would not accept any more communication in this regard; the Resident regretted that he could not extend the period for more than three days and no further delay would be contemplated.

Wajid Ali Shah was taken up entirely in the pursuit of his gratifications. He had no desire of taking any interest in public affairs and in running the government. No one could judge him better than Hazrat Mahal, who had understood the King since her days in Pareekhana. He lived exclusively in a shell of fiddlers, eunuchs and women since his childhood and was likely to do so till his last breath. The reforms, which he initiated after ascending his throne, were short-lived and ended soon after the King became a victim of British political intrigues. He took recourse in love and decided to spend more time with his 'fairies'.

At the start of the day on 1 February, the Queen Mother received a sealed envelope from the prime minister. She was getting dressed after a bath. Leaving everything aside, she tore open the letter and was baffled by its contents. Without caring to cover her head or her feet, she rushed into her son's quarters with the letter in her hands. 'The kingdom is destroyed,' she wailed.[12] The King was sitting alone in a corner, his face covered by his hands. He sobbed at the sight of his mother but could not utter a word.

Hazrat Mahal knew that the King's future was dark, and if he was deposed, she would have no other option left but to live on her resources, which she had been stockpiling since her heydays. The pension, which the King might agree to receive, would not

[12]Knighton, William, *The Private Life of an Eastern King: Together with Elihu Jan's Story; Or, the Private Life of an Eastern Queen*, Hardpress Publishing, 2013, p. 61.

be sufficient to make ends meet freely. What would be the fate of his queens, his children, his begums, his fairies, his courtiers, his musicians, his animals and his spectacular show of rahas?

With the danger of losing the kingdom looming large, Hazrat Mahal was worried sick about her only son Birjis Qadr, who was not even 11 years old and was growing up with all the resources and grandeur in the royal place. No matter how enigmatic the relationship between Hazrat Mahal and Sultan-e-Alam, the King loved Birjis and did everything he could to ensure his happiness and well-being. Hazrat Mahal felt that her world was about to change and tried to clutch at straws. The only person on whom she could rely to save the kingdom was Aliya Begum. Perhaps the Queen Mother could make the clock roll backwards. Even the British narrators spoke in respectful terms of her personal qualities. Hazrat Mahal sent her humble request to the Queen Mother to call the Resident to her palace and convince him to change his mind.

On the first day of February, around four o'clock in the afternoon, General Outram stepped inside Zurd Kothi Palace at the invitation of the Queen Mother. A futile attempt at reversing the British dictate began. Aliya Begum's efforts to defend her son and to prove his fidelity to the British Crown did not cut ice with the Resident. Outram accused the King of being responsible for misgovernance and said that the decision to assume the state to restore peace was irrevocable. Aliya Begum had upbraided her son for his obsession with dance, music and women, saying that his profligacy would one day ring in his ruin.

Outram hoped that the Queen Mother would be able to convince her son, so that the British command could avoid the unpleasant task of dethroning the King. He trusted that being a sensible woman, she would influence her son to accede to the terms. However, the Resident had no answers to several questions fielded by the begum regarding governance. If Wajid Ali was the reason for British wrath, she was ready to replace him in the throne with his younger son Sikandar Hasmat or for that matter, the heir apparent Prince Mirza Muhammad Hamid Ali.

The King's grandmother and the widow of Mohammad Ali Shah, Mukhaddara-e-Uzma, who was listening to the conversation behind the purdah, preferred to back Mustafa Ali Khan, the stepbrother of Wajid Ali Shah, to replace him if the latter was found unfit.[13] The Resident could not refute the irrefragable argument put up by the graceful royal ladies. The meeting concluded without a resolution as all attempts failed.

Dalhousie was desperate to get the treaty signed. He would not hesitate to increase the King's stipend to ₹18 lakh per annum to please him. Outram, in his meeting with the Queen Mother, assured to compensate the King with a sum of ₹1 lakh rupees per *mensem* (month), which would be guaranteed to his heirs forever. In addition, a sum of ₹3 lakh per annum would be spent on His Majesty's guards and men.[14] Lord Dalhousie's extravagant offer could not impress the Queen Mother.

Outram was frantic and tried to lure her with a social promise that he would recommend his government to allow her to get an annual stipend of ₹1 lakh, provided the King would accept the treaty readily. The merchants' offer soared up to ₹16 lakh per annum to take control of the 'queen province of India'! When Outram found both threats and allurements ineffective, the British government chose the option of hostile operation. General Wheeler marched his troops and halted at Nawalgunj, 20 miles from Lucknow.

---

[13]Azhar, Mirza Ali, *King Wajid Ali Shah of Awadh*, Volume 1, Royal Book Company, Karachi, 1982, p. 460.

[14]Notes of a conference with the Queen Mother. See *Accounts and Papers of the House of Commons,* Volume 45, Great Britain Parliament, London, 1856, p. 284.

Behind-the-scene diplomatic manoeuvres continued and Outram was putting all his efforts to persuade the King for his signature through agents and cronies. The next day, on 2 February 1856, Ali Naqi Khan stealthily entered the Residency after the talks with Queen Mother had broken off. Although the purpose of his visit remained unknown, Mammu Khan reported that the chief minister, allured by the fortune he was promised, finalized the deal. Rumours began to pour forth that Ali Naqi Khan affixed the royal seal on the new treaty in front of the Resident.

Traditionally, in those days, affixing the royal seal on a paper would imply subscribing signature of the king. Ali Naqi Khan, being the safe custodian of the royal seal, took advantage of the King's faith in persuading him to affix his signature to the treaty. Yet, Lord Dalhousie was finical and categorically instructed Outram to obtain the King's physical signature as well. Outram had spoken of his desire to meet the King formally on 4 February. Wajid Ali Shah was courteous enough to formally invite the British Resident for a meeting that morning at his palace.[15] Meanwhile, General Wheeler further advanced his troops on the Kanpur Road now, only eight miles away from Lucknow.

In the history of Awadh, 4 February 1856 became a watershed moment. When Outram stepped into the Zurd Kothi Palace in the morning at eight o'clock along with Captain Fletcher Hayes, the assistant to the Resident and Weston, the superintendent of the Awadh Frontier Police, much to their surprise, the Englishmen found the court deserted and the guns dismounted. The guards of honour at the gate were disarmed and saluted with bare hands. The Englishmen were received by the King and his brother Sikandar Hasmat in the most befitting and courtly

---

[15]Enclosure 11 in No.4, Major General Outram to the Secretary to the Government of India. *See Accounts and Papers of the House of Commons,* Volume 45, Great Britain Parliament, London, 1856, p. 286.

manner to welcome them inside the palace. The conversation started with the King, his brother, Ali Naqi Khan, the Residency *vakeel* (lawyer), Musheeh-ud-daulla, his deputy Shahab-ud-daulla and the finance minster Raja Balkishen on the one side, and the Resident and his team on the other. Queen Mother Aliya Begum and grandmother Mukhaddara-e-Uzma were present behind the purdah.

It can be easily assumed that a cloud of uncertainty enveloped the Zurd Kothi. The air of Nageene-Wali-Baradari must have been thick and misty too. The palace complex of Kaiserbag, which heretofore reverberated like the jingle of sitar and was captivated by the spectacular public fetes, must have been shrouded in dreadful silence, with the sentries dismounting their guns and dawdling like marionettes. An assembly of nervous faces were likely to have gathered around the horse-drawn phaetons that had brought the Englishmen to the palace. Curious faces must have kept watch on the door of Zurd Kothi from a distance. Mammu Khan was apparently one of them. A meeting was going on inside, which would potentially decide on the fate of people of Awadh. Rumours had blossomed forth that the angrez were annoyed with the Sultan-e-Alam and the Resident had come to take away the country from him.

The Council Hall of Zurd Kothi was likely to have engulfed in the air of uncertainty and doubt. Outram declared an end to the Treaty of 1801, before formally handing over the draft prepared by East India Company to the King. The new treaty was made ready and irrevocable with the royal seal affixed to it and the King was only to put his signature. Presumably overwhelmed and beleaguered, Wajid Ali Shah received the treaty and showed his dismay with utmost dignity that was in keeping with his refined culture. In a brief note, the last King of Awadh acquiesced:

> Treaties are necessary between equals only: who am I, now, that the British Government should enter into Treaties with? The kingdom is a creation of the British, who are able to make and to unmake, to promote and to degrade. It has merely to issue its commands to ensure their fulfilment; not the slightest attempt will be made to oppose the views and wishes of the British Government; myself and subjects are its servants.[16]

Saying thus, Wajid Ali Shah walked over to Outram, removed his crown and handed it over to him.

[16]*Accounts and Papers of the House of Commons*, Volume 45, Great Britain Parliament, London, 1856, p. 287.

six

Beginning of a New Life

Hazrat Mahal must have known that the *fait accompli* could neither be prevented nor averted. The rumours had come true in her life. Mammu's speculations were perhaps right. The Queen should waste no more time to start a long battle. The news had spread like wildfire as soon as James Outram's phaeton left the gate of Zurd Kothi palace. The meeting had led to a futile end. Wajid Ali Shah had shown his solidarity with the British government and handed over his *taj* or crown to James Outram, once bestowed on the head of his grandfather Ghazi-ud-din Haidar in 1818 by the East India Company.

His uncovered head signalled the end of a title, rank, honour and the last ethos of Awadhi culture. Lucknow witnessed the fading pride of a tragic king whose limitless extravagance and indolence had led the British to usurp his crown. He was not a man of politics, much less a warrior. He lived in a world of dreams and tried his best to head off a confrontation in his life.

Outram had given time to respond within three days, failing which he would ask Dalhousie to sign a proclamation and abrogate the kingdom directly. The Company would then enjoy the power to dispose of the state's revenue at its free will; rather, the offer of his pension would also be revoked. The King would be held responsible for ushering misfortune in his life and that of his people. Yet, the King was determined not to endorse the treaty, nor would he allow his adherents to take up arms. Outram's proposal was about to end in the morning at nine o'clock on 7 February. Sharp at eight o'clock, the Resident received a letter from the King. Under no circumstances whatsoever was the King prepared to sign the new treaty.

From her apartment, Hazrat Mahal is likely to have kept a close watch on the changes that were occurring rapidly, thanks to Mammu Khan's impervious network. Mammu Khan had a consequential upstart and was playing a decisive role in the queen's palace. He had allegedly already beguiled his mistress, protecting her from all worldly intimidation and adversities. Hazrat Mahal could likely perceive the great changes through Mammu's eyes and commentaries—the eunuch had been her confidant in slump days, her informer and her only navigator to tide over the crisis.

Jan-e-Alam was more concerned with his poetry than politics, but his bare head displayed his determination to confront the ordeal. He had not followed the advice of his talukdars and avoided the armed conflict. Rather, when he came to know that his subjects were preparing for an armed revolt, he dissuaded them to stand down. Nonetheless, in the land of his blue god, peace was his priority. Mammu was likely to have ensured that Sultan-e-Alam was loved by all his subjects, and after the news of his ill-fated discourse with the Resident broke out, thousands of people came out on the streets to attest their support for Sultan-e-Alam. A signature campaign was launched to drum up the reign of Sultan-e-Alam as the most peaceful era in Awadh history. Awadh was annexed as it was misgoverned—if the argument was accepted, then no kingdom on earth would be safe from the aggression of a powerful neighbour.

Wajid Ali Shah accepted his fate with dignity. Soon he removed his troops, police and *kotwalees* (executioners) to make room for the British government. The King promulgated two proclamations—one for the talukdars, amirs and landlords, and the other for his army, urging them to uphold peace and to refrain from insurgency. The people were instructed to pay revenue to the British government. The King disarmed the talukdars and stopped them from joining the Royal Army to set the mutiny in motion. Outram had no difficulty in taking possession of Awadh, nor did he mobilize British troops to confiscate the throne. Through a public proclamation, Outram declared the State of Awadh annexed to British territory on and from 7 February 1856. There was no need to have a royal court and hence no need to have a British Resident. Colonel James Outram was declared the first commissioner of Oudh, virtually the king of Awadh.

Wajid Ali Shah decided not to deploy any opposition against the measures adopted by the British government, but in what Outram called 'a fit of petulance', he ordered all his troops in Lucknow to be paid up and discharged. What had mutated Sultan-e-Alam from an avant garde devotee of art to an astute politician, defeating British egotism without shedding a drop of blood?

Wajid Ali had in his court 48 trusted European associates till 1849. John Rose Brandon was one of them. Presumably, Brandon advised him not to sign the new treaty but to seek justice in Calcutta and also to call on Queen Victoria in case justice was denied. He offered to facilitate the King's mission to England for his reinstatement if the situation so demanded. Brandon was an English merchant who had come to Lucknow to make a fortune.

Speculations and rumours filled the air of Residency. Outram was also receiving upsetting news. Tattlers were whispering salacious gossips that the talukdars were plotting a holy battle against the British while the former King and his retinue were preparing to cross the oceans to plead justice before Her Majesty

Queen Victoria in London. The new commissioner Colonel Outram was presumably not comfortable with the news since in all likelihood, the company would be in trouble if Wajid Ali was determined to continue with his plan to visit London. Outram issued two proclamations. In one, he promulgated that after assuming the Government of Oude, the army would take heed to obey the orders of the British government. Under no circumstances should the army resort to mutiny since the British government would thenceforth reserve the power to punish the soldiers. The proclamation also directed that if the Majesty decided to proceed to Calcutta and/or London for further justice, no one should follow him or accompany him in his journey. In the second proclamation, Outram declared that all officers of the King's army, by default, had come under their control and assured the troops in regards to the payment of their arrears. The *sipahis* (soldiers) should remain on duties in the same posts and no one should resort to violence and unlawfulness. Lord Dalhousie continued his effort to persuade Wajid Ali for his signature through his agents and cronies even when Awadh was officially confiscated.

Three days after the annexation of Awadh, Wajid Ali wrote a letter to Colonel Outram on 10 February, informing the commissioner about his intention to leave Lucknow for Calcutta. He requested for Commissioner's assistance in arranging accommodations and proper reception at the respective stations, where the retinue would intend to halt. Wajid Ali's letter was a cautious attempt to test his freedom of movement, which was advised to him by his British aide Brandon. When his letter remained unanswered, Waid Ali issued a reminder on 13 February. Colonel Outram reluctantly replied, asking him to furnish a 'complete list of attendants and cattle' to accompany him to Calcutta, based on which the government would take a call. Outram placed a note before the Secretary of Government of India to place it before Lord Dalhousie.[1]

The Commissioner of Oudh had no intention to either take risk of detaining Wajid Ali at Lucknow or prevent him from visiting the Governor General in Calcutta or sailing to London and throw himself at the feet of Her Majesty, the Queen of England. But to make his journey a living hell, the new commissioner detained 22 members of the former king's inner circle and ordered them not to leave Lucknow as they would soon be required to appear before the commission of inquiry and investigations. Both Ali Naqi Khan and Raja Balkrishen, the King's finance minister, were detained despite Wajid Ali's personal request to release the former.

Mammu Khan, however, was allegedly convinced that the detention of Huzur Aalam Ali Naqi Khan, Outram's most trusted man in the King's cabinet, was a ruse to hide him from the public gaze. Babu Puran Chand, the custodian of government records, was also detained. Outram did not want to take any risk and even went to the extent of confiscating all the King's carriages and horses.

Wajid Ali was determined to go to Calcutta and eventually cross the black water for London—an impending journey of great uncertainty and despair. It was at the mercy of the whims of the chief commissioner to decide who would go with Wajid Ali. As days went by, the government began putting more constraints to bewilder Wajid Ali and to stop him from leaving Lucknow.

Regarding the British arrangement for the supply of provisions during his journey, the chief commissioner issued a communiqué and limited the number of heads in his retinue. A state of impasse was already prevailing, and Sultan-e-Alam found it most difficult to draw a line. The begums and mahals were restlessly waiting

[1]*Accounts and Papers of the House of Commons,* Volume 45, Great Britain Parliament, London, 1856, p. 296.

for their turns and, nonetheless, a queen would take with her her attendants, hookah bearer, fan bearer, children, their attendants and trainers and a host of maids.

On the other hand, Wajid Ali preferred to have with him some of his musicians, parees, singers and dancers to keep him alive. Nevertheless, his mother Janab-i-Aliya Begum, his brother General Sahib Sikandar Hasmat, his heir apparent and son of Khas Mahal Prince Muhammad Hamid Ali, and last but not the least Khas Mahal Alam Ara Begum were to join him in his journey. His courtiers Nawab Munawwar-ud-daulah, Raja Yusuf Ali Khan, Munshi Mir Baqar Ali; and his physician Hakim Mir Muhammad Ali also had the blessings of Sultan-e-Alam.

Quite a few of Jan-e-Alam's wives presumably lost his favour. The numbers were limited and Wajid Ali had to cut corners with a heavy heart. Only three of his wives could make their way in his long march. Apart from Nawab Alam Ara Begum, fortune smiled upon Akhtar Mahal and Mashuq Mahal, who were invited to join Wajid Ali. Akhtar Mahal was his second nikah wife and daughter of Nawab Ali Naqi Khan, while Mashuq Mahal was his first mutah wife. She was elevated to mahal after she was blessed with a son—Farid-ud-din Qadr.[2]

Elihu Jan, the personal hookah bearer of the Queen Mother, recounted an interesting account of palace life with the help of William Knighton, under whom she worked as a helping hand of his wife after the mutiny. Elihu Jan's entry runs a fascinating story on the Queen Mother's preparedness before the journey. The hookah bearer narrated that her mistress constructed a secret vault underneath a water reservoir and concealed all her jewels, gold and silver furniture worth several lakh of rupees, which she felt scared

[2]Llewellyn-Jones, Rosie, *The Last King in India*, Random House India, 2014, pp. 224–5. No authentic record is available to confirm the name of any other wife who accompanied the King to Calcutta.

to take with her. But, unfortunately, that was dug out and looted during the mutiny.[3]

The begums outside Wajid Ali's charmed circle most likely accepted their humble fate as an immutable happenstance. But it must have been a jolt to Hazrat Mahal. The mutah queen-turned-mahal first came to know from the Queen Mother that her destiny was doomed—she was not amongst the travellers.

The dowager queen shared an enigmatic relationship with her son's khas wife, and it can be assumed that she did not have faith in her. She was always apprehensive of being stabbed in the back by Khas Mahal. If Elihu Jan is to be believed, there were attempts on her life on at least two occasions and the prime suspect was Khas Mahal. Somehow, by the grace of god, the attempts failed. Neither could she rely upon Akhtar Mahal. The Queen Mother was a bit unsure of Akhtar's father, Nawab Ali Naqi Khan, who was allegedly hobnobbing with the English masters. Rather, the dowager queen found Hazrat Mahal more amenable than Khas Mahal and she also admired her intelligence. But it was the Queen Mother, who without any ulterior motive, brought misery to Hazrat Mahal's life by infusing a belief into her son's ears that a woman carrying sampun on the back of her neck is inauspicious and one must avoid her at all costs. Alas, it was Hazrat Mahal who bore the mark of sampun on the back of her neck. Thereupon, she became a victim of Wajid Ali's superstitious belief. Most likely since then, he tried to repudiate Hazrat Mahal and shunned her from his life.

Hazrat Mahal's rival was the King's first wife—Khas Mahal. It was she who disliked Hazrat Mahal and infused poison into her husband's ears against his favourite begum. Khas Mahal adamantly refused the companionship of Hazrat Mahal. She impressed on

---

[3]Knighton, William, *The Private Life of an Eastern King: Together with Elihu Jan's Story; Or, the Private Life of an Eastern Queen*, Hardpress Publishing, 2013, p. 65.

her husband that Jan-e-Alam should exercise the sovereignty of his choice between Hazrat Mahal and Khas Mahal. Fearing losing his first wife and crown prince simultaneously, Wajid Ali was left with no option but to draw a line between his two wives.

But Jan-e-Alam was counting on Hazrat in crisis. He did not want to be a rebel with a cause but had firm faith in Hazrat Mahal that she would try her best to regain his lost glory. She was an ace up his sleeve. The King revered her valour and his grief of parting had distilled into an exquisite poem.

Gharon par tabahi padi saher men,
khude mere bazaar Hazrat Mahal
Tu bi bayse aesho aaram hai garibon ki,
gambkhwar Hazrat Mahal

[Calamity visits houses and families in the city
My markets were uprooted, Hazrat Mahal
You are the only means for comfort
You who shares the pain of the poor, Hazrat Mahal][4]

Even then, the unfortunate Hazrat Mahal had to stay back in Lucknow. Little did she know that the destiny had ordained for her an indelible identity—of that of a revolutionary, who would fight the battle to regain the freedom of the country that her husband had miserably lost at the hands of foreign usurpers.

The approval for Wajid Ali's shift to Calcutta came more than a month after his appeal, but Colonel Outram had limited the number of his companions to 500.[5] The chief commissioner was scared of Wajid Ali's popularity and his long march, which could put to the test the 'atrocious' image of Wajid Ali Shah, which had

[4]Misra, Amaresh, *Lucknow: Fire of Grace,* Rupa Publications, 2004, p. 111.
[5]Azhar, Mirza Ali, *King Wajid Ali Shah of Awadh*, Volume 1, Royal Book Company, Karachi, 1982, p. 491.

been portrayed to the British people. Though Outram made an appeal saying, 'The King was in a hurry for his journey to London for lodging his complaint, but we have, *somehow*, put it off. Now orders are awaited,' it was vetoed by a reply from the new Governor General Lord Canning from Calcutta who said, 'The King has not shown any disobedience to the Government orders, he should not be stopped.'[6]

On 13 March 1856, Wajid Ali stepped out of his favourite Zurd Kothi Palace for the last time. The caravan left at eight o'clock in the evening, taking the route of Hazaratgunj road for Kanpur from where the former king would then go to Calcutta. The caravan left Lucknow with Wajid Ali seated in a bedecked carriage drawn by a pair of his favourite horses. A thousand of his followers, displaced from the city, trailed behind the royal carriage.[7] The farewell was heartbreaking and Lucknow was plunged in grief. People wailed over their beloved King.

Wajid Ali Shah was finally accompanied by the Queen Mother; his wives Khas Mahal, Akhtar Mahal and Mashuq Mahal; Prince Mirza Sikandar Hasmat, his brother; Mirza Hamid Ali, his son and the crown king; Raja Yusuf Ali Khan; Munshi Mir Baqar Ali; Hakim Mir Muhammad Ali; Mr John Rose Brandon, the English merchant of Kanpur and Major R.W. Bird, amongst many other followers. Ali Naqi Khan's wife wanted to join the group but was given the cold shoulder by Wajid Ali. He could not accept his father-in-law's tilt towards the British. Only Mr Brandon sat with Wajid Ali Shah in the coach box. It was a long and mournful

---

[6]Qureshi, H.A. (trans.), *Qaiser-ut-Tawarikh of Kamal-ud-din Haidar*, Volume II, New Royal Book Co., 2008, p. 159; Azhar, Mirza Ali, *King Wajid Ali Shah of Awadh*, Volume 1, Royal Book Company, Karachi, 1982, p. 48.

[7]Singh, Nagendra Kumar, *Encyclopaedia of Muslim Biography: S–Z—Volume 5 of Encyclopaedia of Muslim Biography: India, Pakistan, Bangladesh*, A.P.H. Pub. Corp., 2001, p. 415.

march for the King—a journey that would take him to his new home in Calcutta. The King, in his optimism, had misjudged the danger and deception of the colonial rulers like his predecessors. Nothing had caused him more anguish than being forced to leave his beloved Lucknow forever.

The retinue tailed off as the bewailing citizens on foot slowly gave up. When Wajid Ali reached the riverbank of Ganga at Unnao, it was dawn. He sat for namaz. His men formed a bridge by joining the boats across the Ganga, and finally at five o'clock in the morning of 14 March 1856, Wajid Ali Shah walked into Kanpur. He preferred Brandon's house to rest in.[8] Wajid Ali spent the whole month of Rajab (Islamic Hijri Calendar) in Kanpur.

On 7 April 1856, the first day of Shaban and after sighting the 'Moon of Shaban', Wajid Ali Shah left Kanpur and started his journey for Benaras (now Varanasi). He cruised down the Ganga in a private steamer to Allahabad (now Prayagraj), where he rested in a mansion called 'panchghar' for eight days. From Allahabad, the King reached Benaras by a horse-driven carriage on 16 April 1856.[9] Ishwari Prasad Narayan Singh, the Maharaja of Benaras, was courteous enough to offer his best palace in Ramgarh to Wajid Ali and his begums.

Ali Naqi Khan, after great effort, managed to free himself and joined the party at Benaras.[10] However, a conflicting literary

---

[8]Mohan, Surendra, *Awadh under the Nawabs: Politics, Culture and Communal Relations 1722–1856*, Manohar Publishers & Distributors, 1997, p. 170.

[9]Azhar, Mirza Ali, *King Wajid Ali Shah of Awadh*, Volume 1, Royal Book Company, Karachi, 1982, p. 492; Hyder, Qurratulain, *River of Fire*, Oxford University Press, 1999, p. 152.

[10]Kaye, John William, *A History of the Sepoy War in India, 1857–1858*, Longmans, Green, and Co., 1896, p. 401. Another source says Ali Naqi Khan was released from Lucknow in the month of July and started his journey towards Calcutta on 15 July 1856. His caravan reached Allahabad from where he boarded a steamer and reached Calcutta on 29 July 1856.

source reveals that Ali Naqi Khan was released from Lucknow in the month of July and started his journey towards Calcutta on 15 July 1856.

From Benaras, the royal retinue divided itself into two groups. Wajid Ali, accompanied by his begums, mother, son, Ali Naqi Khan and other confidants, embarked on a ship named *General Mcleod* on 25 April 1856.[11] His followers boarded large *bazras*[12] to sail down the Ganga, while some of them travelled by road. Wajid Ali cruised continuously for 18 days in the incessant summer heat and reached Calcutta on 13 May 1856.

[11]Azhar, Mirza Ali, *King Wajid Ali Shah of Awadh*, Volume 1, Royal Book Company, Karachi, 1982, p. 97.

[12]Country vessels with rows.

seven

Her Lonely Battle

When Wajid Ali Shah was preparing for his journey to Calcutta, Lord Dalhousie was growing increasingly impatient to get back home. Eventualities over time had taken a toll on both. The King had lost his kingdom, his dynasty, his wealth and his future. On the other side, the Governor General had lost his health, his peace of mind and his family as well.

Dalhousie's health was failing fast. The wasting disease had reduced him to a decrepit man who could hardly walk. Lady Dalhousie, too, had not been able to stand the enervating climate of India and had breathed her last on her voyage back to England three years before, even as the ship was within sight of the English shore. Dalhousie was only 41 years old at that time and fated to face the supreme trial of his life. Moreover, his doctors strongly advised him to cut short his tenure in India and return to England. But when asked to extend his stay in office, he could not bring himself to refuse. He did not allow his misfortunes to come in the way of his professional duties.

A week before Wajid Ali's retinue had left Lucknow, Dalhousie bid farewell to a throng of his friends and admirers waiting in the lawn of the Government House in Calcutta. It was a pleasant evening when his horse-driven phaeton took him and his elder daughter, Susan, off to Princep Ghat from where he boarded the ship named *S.S. Firoze*. After seven years of strenuous labour, Dalhousie set sail for England on 6 March 1856.

Viscount Canning assumed the office of the Governor General of India on 29 February. He shared his office with Lord Dalhousie for six days before the Marquess set sail for England. The Viscount was only eight months younger than his immediate predecessor and possessed sound health. His characteristic endurance and self-restraint nature made him best suited to rule a country of 250 million people.[1]

Meanwhile, Begum Hazrat Mahal had confined herself within the four walls of her palace, spending most of her time in writing poetry. Her renunciation, however, gave her no liberation from her impending responsibility. Birjis Qadr was not even 11 years old and had been entirely entrusted to his tutors. Birjis was the apple of her eye—the only immortal chain that bound her to her husband. She could never confide in the women of the palace who passed time by whispering salacious gossip; instead, she would prefer to remain discrete. Her only link to the outside world was her confidant—Mammu Khan.

Mammu apparently preferred to spend much of his time in mosques and chowks to get his information. He would spend hours with the people and enter into luscious gossip to know what was on their minds. Thus, it was he who first brought the startling news that Mustafa Ali Khan, the King's elder brother, had suddenly woken up from a deep slumber and was trying to fish in troubled waters. Mammu had gathered furtively that the prince was plotting a fiery uprising against the British to capture the vacant throne of Awadh. The news reached the Residency too. Colonel Outram was sceptical of the gossip and went for a first-hand enquiry himself. He was accompanied by Residency surgeons Dr Fayrer and Dr Nasmyth. However, his suspicion was proven wrong. The King's discontented elder brother was found in a wretched state, confined

---

[1]Malleson, G.B., *The Indian Mutiny of 1857*, Rupa Publications, 2016, p. 15.

to his house on his father's orders on the basis of the allegations of reaching for the throne and involvement with the British. He had been confined within the walls of his kothi for 14 years, having no access to even a piece of paper or ink. Outram rescued him from the dungeon and shifted him to the Residency. The prince recuperated well under the supervision of Dr Fayrer. Keeping him under close observation for some period, he was released by the order of the Governor General and a pension was sanctioned for his living expenses.[2]

The malady of 'misrule' was not tenable anymore in Awadh. The hedonist tyrant had gone away. Hence, shaping the destiny of Awadh was vested in the hands of foreign masters whose priority presumptively would be to serve people's interests. All the excess and extravagance left behind by the former King of Awadh needed to be undone. The British showed their true colours soon after the proclamation was issued. The remnants of Wajid Ali Shah and his rule were to be erased from the face of Awadh.

The first attempt, in the name of reforms, was to wipe away the former King's entire collection of animals while he was still in Lucknow.[3] His collection of magnificent tigers, lions, elephants, horses, exotic animals and finest birds was soon disposed of and the profits from sales were added to the treasury of the Company.

British authorities alleged that the former King did not pension off his troops and police. When the British took over, they found that the troops and police had not been paid for 18 months. The East India Company had to arrange their back payments and pensions. The Company sold off the former King's possessions, and there were a number of sales from the Royal

---

[2]Bhatnagar, G.D., *Awadh under Wajid Ali Shah*, Bharatiya Vidya Prakashan, 1968, p. 92.

[3]Rizvi, S.A.A. and M.L. Bhargava, *Freedom Struggle in Uttar Pradesh*, Volume 1, Uttar Pradesh Publications Bureau, 1957, p. 109.

Armoury too, trying to raise enough money to cover the cost of the pensions.

Evil tidings ride fast. Mammu Khan allegedly came running with the story that the angrez would next invade the *jenanas*.[4] He had his own cronies in the Residency and the news took no time to reach his ears. Mammu's anxiety most likely soared when he learnt that Chatter Manzil would not be spared.

On 8 May, James Outram handed over his office to Colville Coverley Jackson—only to further inflame the already fiery plight. Coverley Jackson was known for his implacable animosity towards the natives, which he never tried to hide. If annexation policy of Dalhousie is blamed for the Mutiny, it was Coverley Jackson who tolled the death knell. His wrath on the native King fell on the bricks and stones of ancestral monuments. On the pretext of widening roads for public interest, the new chief commissioner of Lucknow started to pull down old edifices, right before hundreds of tearful eyes. A campaign of demolition was commenced by the newly appointed deputy commissioner Colonel Simpson and the City Magistrate of Lucknow Major Carnegie, ignoring the former King's innumerable appeals made before the new Governor General in Calcutta to stop wrecking his ancestors' memorials. Icons of the great dynasty would either be confiscated or demolished. Jilan Khana near Baillie Guard was pulled down; the gates of Hazratganj were demolished to widen roads; and Farhat Bakhsh palace, which served as the residential palace for the kings of Awadh, was converted into kennels and stables.

Hostility was taken to new heights when Kadam Rasool, the shrine where the footprint impression of Prophet Muhammad was kept, was converted to a storehouse of gunpowder. Coverley Jackson shamelessly used the city magistrate's office in the state-

---

[4]The part of the palace reserved for the king's wives

sponsored loot and confiscated the King's library of more than 15,000 rare books and manuscripts.[5]

The chief commissioner sequestered the collection of rare books and manuscripts from the prestigious imperial library located at old Daulat Khana of Nawab Asaf-ud-daulah, which was converted into a storehouse of artillery and magazines. The library contained more than 10,000 books, most of which were collected since the reign of Shuja-ud-daula and further enriched by Ghazi-ud-din Haider. Apart from imperial library, Wajid Ali Shah had his personal collection of rare books at libraries in Moti Mahal and Farhat Bakhsh Palace.[6] The books were confiscated on the pretext that the chief commissioner was fond of reading and therefore shifted those to Claude Martin's kothi. The books became the private property of City Magistrate Carnegie and access was denied to the denizens of Lucknow. The disappointed King kept crying out from Calcutta that the books were being manhandled.

The people of Awadh did not accept annexation as *fait accompli*. The growing apprehension among the talukdars of Awadh of losing power and prestige once they took over indeed rang true. On 18 August 1856, Coverley Jackson passed a decree, directing complete disarming and demolition of the talukdars' forts scattered all over the countryside of Awadh, the estimated number of which was around 574.[7] A notice was also served on 3 September to surrender the military stores to the chief commissioner within a month.

The talukdars were once all-powerful in the state of Awadh

---

[5]See Lucas, Samuel, *Dacoitee in Excelsis; or, The Spoliation of Oude by the East India Company, Faithfully Recounted*, J.R. Taylor, London, 1857, pp. 145–6.

[6]Taher, Mohamed and Donald Gordon Davis Jr, *Librarianship and Library Science in India: An Outline of Historical Perspectives*, Concept Publishing Company, 1994, p. 61.

[7]Archaeological Survey of India, *The Residency, Lucknow—An account of the Residency*, 2003, p. 37; Rizvi, S.A.A. and M.L. Bhargava, *Freedom Struggle in Uttar Pradesh*, Volume 1, Uttar Pradesh Publications Bureau, 1957, p. 115.

and possessed more than two-thirds of the land in the countryside. Some of them even owned paid foot soldiers and cavalry, varying in strength from 200 to 300 or even 1,200! They had the power of collectors and magistrates as well, and held durbar and issued orders so long as they accepted the lordship of the Nawab.[8]

The talukdari system was virtually put to an end by the British with the implementation of Summary Settlement Act, 1856. This was done to alleviate the peasants from the web of extortion and to settle the land amidst its actual owners.

However, there was something deeply flawed within the revenue assessment system and eventually, the peasants were laden with obnoxious taxes levied on stamps, petitions, food, houses, eatables, ferries and opium.[9] Annexation had a severe economic impact on Awadh, which had led to serious unemployment and soaring prices of food grains and essential commodities—the worst sufferers being the weavers. With the abrogation of talukdari system, soldiers and courtiers of the talukdars turned jobless and soon became political rivals of the British Empire.[10] The peasants sided with their old masters to revolt against the colonial sovereign. The oppressed foot soldiers of the feudal heads were now ready for a clinching revolt against the tyrannies of colonial power.

Mammu Khan's apprehension was likely to have compounded into reality when the British turned their eyes towards the hapless womenfolk of the jenana. The former king left behind a reserve from where the livelihood of his women was to be

---

[8]Singh, Surya Narain, *The Kingdom of Awadh*, Mittal Publications, 2003, pp. 62–6.

[9]Majumdar, R.C., *The History and Culture of the Indian People, British Paramountcy and Indian Renaissance,* Volume IX, Bharatiya Vidya Bhavan, 1965, p. 536.

[10]Mukherjee, Rudrangshu, *Awadh in Revolt 1857–1858: A Study of Popular Resistance*, Orient Blackswan, 2002, pp. 36–7.

defrayed. Carnegie issued an order to stop all payments to the King's descendants from the royal reserve. The City Magistrate summoned the King's supervisor to stop paying the dependents. Strict order was issued by Carnegie that 'not a single *cowree* shall be paid at all to anyone from this day without orders of the authority, or there shall be severe consequences.'[11] It was indeed a vengeful attempt to throw the King's dependents permanently at the mercy of the chief commissioner. Hazrat Mahal's monthly allowance of ₹3,000 was thus discontinued and history has no record as to whether it was resumed in the future. Nevertheless, the Queen's accrual of gold, jewellery and cash was enough to support her all through her life.

The greed kept mounting. The British attitude towards the begums was becoming more and more unbearable, and plundering continued on one pretext or the other. In August, the city magistrate went to Machhi Bhawan for a raid to delve into the King's secret vault of artillery, weapons and tents. Carnegie ordered to vacate the possession of Machhi Bhawan without delay. The British pressure to vacate the palaces intensified even though the edifices were occupied by the King's dependents. The chief commissioner fixed 14 August as the last date for vacating the palaces.

But the most immoral act, which forced the former King to send a written complaint to the Governor General in Calcutta on 14 September 1856, was the vandalism faced by his womenfolk residing at Chatter Manzil.[12] It was at the crack of dawn on 23 August when the women in Chatter Manzil woke up to a clamour and clattering of weapons of the British guards. It was Major Carnegie, the city magistrate, who was seen outside the

[11]Azhar, Mirza Ali, *King Wajid Ali Shah of Awadh*, Volume 2, Royal Book Company, Karachi, 1982, p. 4.

[12]Ibid. 150.

portico with his armed men, trying to break through the sentinels of the mansion. Major Carnegie evicted the women from Chatter Manzil and threw out their belongings into the street. The women ran pell-mell without knowing what to do, where to protest and, more so, where to go.[13] The ancestral jewels and ornaments of the Queen Mother were excavated from the hidden tank and looted. The resentments and arguments of the begums fell on deaf ears. The month of Muharram was approaching. They begged and implored for relief, but their streams of tears could not move Carnegie from his stubbornness. While most of the begums rushed desperately to take shelter in Kaiserbag, some stayed back to face their destiny.

Chatter Manzil served as the central durbar of the Awadh kings till Wajid Ali Shah had shifted his palace from Farhat Bakhsh to Kaiserbag. Chatter Manzil was the house of royal ladies during the reign of Wajid Ali Shah. It was one of the buildings preserved by English authorities for the King's family, and a *sunud* (agreement of grant) was also granted by the King to the royal ladies.

Lord Canning could no longer turn a deaf ear to the series of appeals made by the King in Calcutta and asked for an explanation from Coverley Jackson of his alleged 'misdeeds'. The chief commissioner denied the charges and mentioned in his reply before the Governor General that 'the building [Chatter Manzil] has again been placed at the disposal of the king who will deal with it at his pleasure'.[14] Coverley Jackson claimed innocence and elucidated that the King's English library was found in a decrepit state and, therefore, to preserve the rare books, he had shifted

[13]Lucas, Samuel, *Dacoitee in Excelsis; or, The Spoliation of Oude by the East India Company, Faithfully Recounted*, J.R. Taylor, London, 1857, pp. 145–6.
[14]Rizvi, S.A.A., and M.L. Bhargava, *Freedom Struggle in Uttar Pradesh*, Volume 1, 1957, p. 109; Azhar, Mirza Ali, *King Wajid Ali Shah of Awadh*, Volume 2, Royal Book Company, Karachi, 1982, p. 14.

those to Martinere College with due consent of the King's vakeel Sehut-ud-Dowlah.

The tyranny continued and uncertainty grabbed the jenanas of the deposed King. Not a single kothi was found safe for the women and the royal family's descendants. As Coverley Jackson could not get rid of his colonial ego, the fear of dispossession remained an ubiquitous phenomenon for the begums. Hazrat Mahal found herself unsafe in the kothi of Nageene-Wali-Baradari. She had learnt her lessons from what had happened in Chatter Manzil. Hazrat and Mammu, with a cartful of household articles, books, ornamented costumes and vaults of jewellery, shifted to Kaiserbag—a much safer destination for the King's ill-fated descendants.

After a long time, the Begum was on the road. Peeping through her palanquin, she could hardly recognize her city. Lucknow had undergone sea changes within a short period of time. Many of the ancestral houses of her in-laws had been raised to make ways for broad avenues. Finally, she reached Kaiserbag, the dream abode of her husband. The Begum had chosen a dozen spacious and beautiful rooms. She wrote a series of letters to Jan-e-Alam, but either the letters did not reach him or they fell on to deaf ears. Rumours were flying thick and fast—Sultan-e-Alam was busy recreating a sprawling empire in Calcutta, or he had set out on his journey to England, or shockingly, he had been put in jail by the Governor General in Calcutta!

eight

The King Cries for Justice

Since landing at the Bichali Ghat in the suburb of Calcutta on 13 May 1856, Wajid Ali Shah had been striving to establish his living in Calcutta. He was given a cold shoulder by the British government. Although he had been promised safety by the government en route and assured of 'proper arrangements for the supply of provisions',[1] there was no sign of any British agent to receive the royal retinue at any place on his way to Calcutta. The reception was utterly unceremonious in the British capital as well, with the government merely sending an officer to receive the former King as he disembarked on the banks of Hoogly. The commissioner of Awadh in his letter clearly advised that '[O]n his (Wajid Ali Shah's) arrival at Calcutta he should make his own arrangement for his accommodation, for he will be looked upon as an uninvited guest. In fact, he is going to undertake this journey against the wishes of government.'[2]

---

[1]Letter from the Chief Secretary addressed to Wajid Ali Shah. See Azhar, Mirza Ali, *King Wajid Ali Shah of Awadh*, Volume 2, Royal Book Company, Karachi, 1982, p. 491.

[2]Azhar, Mirza Ali, *King Wajid Ali Shah of Awadh,* Volume 2, Royal Book Company, Karachi, 1982, p. 491; Rizvi, S.A.A., and M.L. Bhargava, *Freedom Struggle in Uttar Pradesh: 1857–59*, Volume 1, Uttar Pradesh Publications Bureau, 1957, p. 110.

Historians believe that the Wajid Ali sent Moulvi Masih-ud-deen to arrange accommodation in Calcutta, which he did by renting the riverside abode of the Maharaja of Burdwan. Rumour has it that the former King had to wait in the steamer for a couple of days while his people hunted a house for him. Local records revealed that he rented a palatial riverside resort from the Maharaja of Burdwan in Garden Reach paying ₹500 per month. Wajid Ali Shah's book *Sheo-e-Faiz* testifies: '*Raja Bardhawan ki kothi panch saye ki kiraet per raisa* (Burdwan's Maharaja's kothi was rented at five hundred rupees per month).'

By all records, Wajid Ali was optimistic about receiving justice from the Governor General in Calcutta and was eager to send his representative to the Council. Asan Hussain Khan, Mir Aulad Ali and one Mr Patteson—a British advocate of the Supreme Court—came forward to plead for him. The outcome was as expected. The Governor House in Calcutta paid no heed to the former King's appeal and refused to admit his case for hearing. Wajid Ali had lost his faith as well as his face. He realized that he was left with no other choice but to appeal directly to Her Majesty, the Queen of England. Surely Her Majesty would not be unscrupulous like her people in India and would gracefully give him a patient hearing.

Wajid Ali started preparing for his journey to England. But this was not to be. The hapless former King was dissuaded by his doctors, as the exhausting sea voyage would negatively affect his ill-health. He was suffering from dysentery and scabies in his passage to Calcutta during the incessant, scorching summer.[3] Moreover, he would lose face if he had to return from England empty-handed.

[3]Shah, Wajid Ali, *Masnavi Husn-e-Akhtari*, Munshi Nawal Kishor, Lucknow, 1922, p. 41.

The King himself was not certain of getting due justice in British Parliament. He was in a helpless state. Who would be his envoy to cross the 'black water'?

The Queen Mother, 'with some substance of masculine vigour still left as God had given it'[4] stepped forward to lead the mission. At the age of 60, she was truly the one who took the revolutionary decision to cross the 'black water'. The assertion was indeed astounding for a noble lady from a traditional Indian ancestry who would otherwise flinch at the idea of crossing a river!

It was then decided that the 'Oudh Commission' would be led by Moulvi Masih-ud-deen Khan, a confidant of Wajid Ali Shah since his heyday in Awadh, as his *mukhtar* (lawyer) and envoy plenipotentiary. He was also accompanied by the King's brother, General Saheb Sikandar Hashmat, and his heir apparent, Mirza Hamid Ali Bahadur, who was then a lad of 18. Brandon and his wife Mary Ann joined them too at the time of departure. However, Major Bird was not in sight. He had come to Calcutta from Lucknow with the former king in his caravan but left Calcutta soon after assuring the latter that he would join the retinue in proper time.

One-and-a-half months after Coverley Jackson assumed his office in Lucknow and started to reveal his true colours, a steamer was weighing anchor early morning at seven o'clock at the ghat of river Hoogly in the suburbs of Calcutta. The former King had chartered the steamer named *S.S. Bengal* to take a voyage from Calcutta to Suez, sailing with 140 passengers. It was 19 June 1856; the banks of the Hoogly suddenly came alive and were bustling with hundreds of coolies going up and down the gangway, busy loading the goods. A large crowd had gathered at the dock to bid

---

[4]Malleson, George Bruce, and John Kaye, *Kaye's and Malleson's History of the Indian Mutiny of 1857–8*, Volume 1, W.H. Allen & Co., 1888, p. 295.

farewell to an entourage of the royal family of Awadh as it set off to an uncertain destiny.

All eyes were in search of the one adored by the multitudes—Aliya Begum, the King's mother. She was accompanied by her son Prince Sikandar Hasmat and the King's son, the heir apparent, Prince Hamid Ali Mirza. The dowager queen of Awadh would meet Her Majesty Queen Victoria to plead for her son. She carried with her valuable gifts of gem-studded rings, diamond necklaces and costly apparel for the English Queen. Bahran Nissa accompanied her mistress along with her husband Piyari Saheb. One can imagine Aliya Begum's eyes becoming moist to see her people wailing as they bid her farewell. Her son, the former King, stood in the portico of his palace to accept the farewell salaam of his brother and son. Lord Canning, who had known of the impending voyage, crossed his fingers and simply said, 'Let them go.'[5]

The steamer cruised down the Hoogly into the Bay of Bengal and turned south towards Ceylon. It touched the shores of Ceylon and cruised northward to enter the Red Sea through the Gulf of Aden. The *S.S. Bengal* ended its journey at the Port of Suez[6] and the royal entourage travelled on land in carriages to Cairo. They stayed in Cairo for 10 days and boarded the steamer of the Peninsular and Oriental Steam Navigation Company of England called *S.S. Indus* from the port of Alexandria and sailed off the Mediterranean.[7]

S.S. Indus finally dropped its anchor in the coast of Southampton at five o'clock in the evening on 20 August 1856, after touching Malta and Gibraltar. The commission was received by a huge crowd that

[5]Malleson, George Bruce, and John Kaye, *Kaye's and Malleson's History of the Indian Mutiny of 1857–8*, Volume I, Longmans, Green and Co., 1914, p. 296.
[6]The Suez Canal was excavated in 1869, and the wayfarers had to follow the land tract in Egypt to reach the Mediterranean.
[7]Azhar, Mirza Ali, *King Wajid Ali Shah of Awadh*, Volume 2, Royal Book Company, Karachi, 1982, p. 102.

applauded its arrival. Major Bird had kept his word and appeared as soon as the royal members disembarked at the port of Southampton. Brandon rented the Royal York Hotel at Southampton for the royal entourage for 10 days at the cost of £100.

On 30 August 1856, as early as six o'clock, the royal retinue left Southampton and boarded a special train for London.[8] The train reached London on Sunday, 31 August 1856. Only a few people could be seen on New Road, in front of Harley House, where Brandon had made all arrangement for the Queen Mother to stay. Harley House, the former residence of Duke of Brunswick on New Road was rented for one year at the cost of £550. Some of the adjacent houses were also rented to accommodate the rest of her retinue.[9] Intimation was sent to the directors of the East India Company to announce their arrival.[10]

Wajid Ali Shah, in a letter addressed to Queen Victoria, entrusted Moulvi Masih-ud-deen as his mukhtar and envoy plenipotentiary to express his complaints, while other members of the commission had no definite role in the presentation. Masih-ud-deen had been a British servant for 12 years until he was accused of being an informer of the King of Awadh and expelled, even though the charges against him could not be proved. Masih-ud-deen extensively studied British laws, which had helped him to spearhead the Awadhi movement.[11]

The British were reputed as being honest and trailblazers in the dispensation of natural justice. The honourable members of the House of Lords could not deny the accusations of debauchery

---

[8]*Times*, Monday, 1 September 1856.

[9]*Times*, Tuesday, 2 September 1856.

[10]Azhar, Mirza Ali, *King Wajid Ali Shah of Awadh*, Volume 2, Royal Book Company, Karachi, 1982, p. 108.

[11]Fisher, Michael H., *Counterflows to Colonialism: Indian Travellers and Settlers in Britain 1600–1857*, Permanent Black, 2008, p. 412.

brought against their Indian counterparts, which had vilified their great nation. British Parliament directed the counterpart in India to prepare their argument in support of their deed. The *Oude Blue Book*,[12] officially called *The Parliamentary Papers: Papers Relating to Oude Presented to Both Houses of Parliament by Command of Her Majesty, 1856*, was the most controversial paper ever published on British policy during the Company's days in India. It was presented to both Houses of Parliament by command of Her Majesty after the House debate on 10 April 1856. In it were framed a series of charges against the King for his dereliction of duties. The report was nothing but a collective 'fiction of official penmanship'[12] by a few prejudiced contributors, such as Richmond, Sleeman, Dalhousie, Outram and others.

After reaching London, the Oudh Commission engaged Gregory Skirrow and Company—a British law firm—to solicit its support in getting copies of relevant papers from the Company that spoke of the charges framed against them. The solicitors had to persuade Parliament to release those papers after the Company had denied their appeal. The papers truly helped the Commission to refute charges framed against the former King to justify annexation.[13] Possibly, the *Oude Blue Book* came into the hands of the King at Metiyaburj during that time. The preface of Wajid Ali Shah's *Reply to the Oude Blue Book* testifies that he had to ship his defence

[12]This description of the *Oudh Blue Book* was given by one British official who had been involved in the operation described in the parliamentary Blue Book (or paper) on Oudh; Dalrymple, William, *The Last Mughal: The Fall of a Dynasty: Delhi, 1857*, Alfred A. Knopf, 2007, p. 534.

[13]Letters of Mussehood-Deen. See Fisher, Michael H., *Counterflows to Colonialism: Indian Travellers and Settlers in Britain 1600–1857*, Permanent Black, 2008, p. 417.

arguments from Metiyaburj well after sending off his commission. Wajid Ali's reply was initially in Persian and later translated to English. This version had seven chapters covering 58 pages. The former King spent lakhs of rupees to print 300 copies of his 'reply' in English and to send them off to England for widespread distribution amongst interested readers and also the British prime minister, Prince Albert and Her Majesty Queen Victoria.

The public sentiment took a 180-degree turn in favour of the former king as soon as the *Reply to the Oude Blue Book* reached London, probably on 12 December 1856. The publishing of Major Bird's pamphlet *Spoliation of Oudh* in 1857, and *Dacoitee in Excelsis*[14] in the same year spurred a series of propaganda. The commission was triumphant in creating a public clamour in its favour.

On 19 January 1857, an envoy of royal princes, Moulvi Masih-ud-deen and Major Bird met the directors of East India Company at India House, the headquarters of East India Company, for reconciliation. They were received cordially by the chairman and directors of the Company as they reached the portico of India House. The atmosphere was warm and Moulvi gave an eloquent speech in favour of liberation while challenging the annexation.

On 21 January 1857, the directors paid a counter visit to Harley House and offered a pension of ₹5 lakh per annum and an annual jagir of 10 miles of land, surrounding Lucknow to the King of Oudh.

On the other hand, the proposal came like a weapon in the hands of Oudh Commission. The generosity shown by the directors was taken as their admission of mistakes in India. Oudh

---

[14]The book *Dacoitee in Excelsis; or the Spoliation of Oude by the East India Company* was co-authored by Robert Wilberforce Bird. Although the book is attributed to Samuel Lucas, barrister-at-law, it is clear that Bird's input was considerable.

Commission, after long discourse, rejected the offer and Moulvi Masih-ud-deen placed it before the ministers and Members of Parliament as evidence to prove the weakness of the freewheeling mercantile body of men. The wind drifted in favour of the Oudh royalty. Yet, the Queen Mother of Awadh had to have her endurance tested for 10 long months before she could pass through the doors of Buckingham Palace on 4 July 1857.

nine

A Bullet from the Musket

In mid-November, 1856, people of Lucknow noticed a strange man in town in the disguise of a fakir but having all accoutrements to tell tales of a secretive royalty. He was staying in the *sarai* (resting place) of Motamad-ud-Daulah and later shifted to a house at Ghasiari Mandi—little more than a mile away from Kaiserbag where Hazrat Mahal had recently opted to live. People called him by the name Moulvi Ahmadullah Shah. The fakir was a tall and lean but brawny man in his mid-30s with large, deep-set eyes, beetle brows, a high aquiline nose and lantern jaws. He remained surrounded by a throng of *murids*[1] and disciples from all walks of life. His language was overwhelmingly charming, which had led the people to believe that neither fire could burn his disciples nor sword could do them any harm. People of Lucknow visited him in large numbers, regularly on Mondays and Thursdays, to take part in mystic gatherings called *majlis-i-hal-o-qal* and joined him in enchanting religious feats.[2]

Moulvi Ahmadullah Shah's mere presence in Lucknow had filled up many columns in contemporary newspapers and spurred

---

[1]Student disciples who are committed to receive spiritual enlightenment under a spiritual guide

[2]*Tilism-i-Laknau*, 21 November 1856.

endless myths amongst the readers.[3] Every rustle of his movement was followed by newsmen and one such reportage in *Tilism* on 30 January 1857 reports a public address where Moulvi Ahmadullah Shah affirmed before a huge assemblage that whatever he wished to say, a large crowd stood enthralled to hear him speak. In his speech, he often pleaded for jihad,[4] which was his clarion call—jihad or holy war against the enemy of the motherland. The message, which Moulvi attempted to put across the people of Lucknow, was clear and without any conjecture. The British had confiscated the country and resorted to tyrannical rule; it was the sacred duty of all Hindus and Muslims to join him in the holy war to expel the interlopers that had come from European shores.

Hazrat Mahal was eager to know more about the strange man who had arrived in the city; she seemingly had a weird feeling. Mammu Khan was likely to have told her that the Moulvi believed in Sufism and that he had come from the south. He was in England for a while and got acquainted with *angrezi* (English language). Mammu explained further that the Moulvi possessed supernatural

---

[3]Most of the scholars studying annexation of Awadh rely exclusively on European sources. One reason is certainly the dearth of indigenous source. But there are some reliable and popular Indian sources, one of them being the Urdu newspaper, *Tilism-i-Laknau*. The main authors of the article related to the changing political situation of Awadh were Anjum Taban Faruqui and Iqbal Hussain. *Tilism* was edited and published from Firangi Mahal in Lucknow by one Muhammad Yaqub. It was published between 25 July 1856 and 8 May 1857, and covered the period from Awadh's annexation to the 1857 Sepoy Mutiny. All 41 issues of this newspaper, except issue number 37, are preserved at Aligarh Muslim University. The description of Moulvi Ahmadullah Shah, the fakir, as published in *Tilism-i-Laknau* is also mentioned vividly in Khan, Nadir Ali, *A History of Urdu Journalism, 1822–1857*, Idarah-i Adabiyat-i Delli, 1991. See also, Ahmad, S.K. Ehteshamuddin, 'The Impact of the Annexation of Awadh on Local Merchants: Based on the Evidence in Urdu Newspapers', *Indian History Congress*, Vol. 66, 2005–6, pp. 852–58.

[4]Holy war against the enemies of Islam

powers like a prophet, which helped him captivate his disciples. The British were scared of his popularity and feared that his arrest would perhaps stir up too much controversy.

As days went by, Moulvi Ahmadullah Shah became more desperate. Mammu Khan often visited his *majlis* (closed gathering) in the disguise of a disciple and pried into his secret affairs. Mammu apparently came to know that Moulvi was plotting a fiery uprising against the British. He had planned to pitch a surprise attack on Christians when they would assemble in a church on Sunday. Unfortunately, the plot was leaked and the plan consequently failed. The British sent a kotwal and the Moulvi was driven out of town. Ahmadullah Shah left Lucknow with 10 to 12 of his men, mostly armed, but his endeavour did not perish.

Ahmadullah Shah halted in Faizabad and once again called for jihad in a mass gathering. The authorities did not take any risk. The Moulvi was arrested and placed behind bars in the cantonment as 'he seemed too dangerous a character to be kept in the city jail'.[5] After a brief trial, he was removed to a jail in Faizabad. But soon, Moulvi proved that no jail was strong enough to hold him. Hazrat Mahal had never found a man who had the audacity to challenge the British authority out in the open and to speak the language of rebellion in public. The Begum started to revere the man as his gallantry began to unfold to her.

Hazrat Mahal started her new life of a recluse at Kaiserbag, speaking only to her son and Mammu Khan, spending her time in devotion and poetic ecstasy or writing letters to Jan-e-Alam without expecting any reply. The British stopped hounding her. Birjis was in his teens and was receiving his education at home. Hazrat felt reassured when she first came to know that a

---

[5]Taib, Fateh Muhammad, *Tawarikh-i Ahmadi*, Tegh Bahadur Press, Lucknow, 1925; Jafri, Saiyid Zaheer Husain, 'The Profile of a Saintly Rebel: Maulavi Ahmadullah Shah', *Social Scientist*, Vol. 26, No. 1/4, 1998, pp. 39–52.

commission had set forth for London to appeal before the Queen of England. She was hopeful that her husband's petition would be heard with compassion by the British sovereign and his authority over his kingdom would be restored.

A rumour was flying thick and fast in the city of Lucknow. The tattle was buzzing around the walls of Kaiserbag. The rumour said that in the cantonment area of Dumdum, some nine miles away from the Governor General's house in Calcutta, a lower-caste lascar, working at Dumdum ordinance factory, was thirsty and begged for water from the lota of a brahmin sepoy, which the latter refused to share. The lascar was hurt by the casteism of the brahmin and ridiculed him that soon all the Hindus and the Muslims would lose their religion as the new cartridges smeared with beef-fat and hog-lard were being made in Dumdum depot for all the sepoys in the country.

In early 1857, the British decided to replace the old musket, known as Brown Bess, with a newer, improvized version of Enfield P-53 rifle in India. Loading the new rifle called for the sepoy to bite off a paper cartridge, allegedly greased by the proscribed animal fat. The brahmin sepoy, terribly upset by the lascar's derision, carried the news to his comrades. The sepoys were convinced that it was a ploy by the British to desecrate both Hinduism and Islam in order to spread Christianity.

The agitation was immense and, soon, the story was thrown up to the sepoys stationed at Barrackpore cantonment, some eight miles away from its place of origin. A section of sepoys from Barrackpore, who had come to Bahrampore, poured their suspicion into the willing ears of their comrades. The following morning, sepoys of 19th Native Infantry, located in Bahrampore, disobeyed the command and refused to pick up cartridges that they had been using for many years. An order was passed to Colonel Mitchell to instruct his regiment, 19th Native Infantry, to march down from Bahrampore to Barrackpore cantonment.

The news of grease cartridge spread like wildfire and reached Lucknow with incredible rapidity and murmurs. Mammu Khan noted clusters of people in every chowk holding meetings furtively to keep themselves abreast of every new change. A mutiny was brewing in Lucknow. The open defiance of authority by the sepoys of 19th Native Infantry invited a Court of Enquiry and eventually, the 19th Native Infantry was disbanded on 31 March 1857.

The disbanded sepoys were sent back to their native states. Most of them were from Bengal, along with many from Awadh. The sepoys were aggrieved and united with the refractory talukdars and zamindars to wage war against the Raj. But Mammu Khan had more interesting news to give to his mistress, a news that had jolted the country into a shocking reality. Sepoys from the countryside of Awadh comprised an overwhelming number in the Bengal Army and their ire was threatening to create a colossal furore against the British masters in a cantonment that was not more than 20 miles from Wajid Ali's riverside abode in Calcutta. Mangal Pandey, a sepoy of the 34th Bengal Native Infantry of Barrackpore, raised his musket against his white-skinned masters and started an open mutiny on 29 March 1857, almost single-handedly. Pandey's rebellion was devoid of any personal agenda but aimed to protect Hinduism and Islam against the alleged British motive of converting people to Christianity. Pandey's ardent appeal to his comrades to join him in the war against the British, the soldiers' aversion to disarm Pandey or even the *jamadar*'s[6] apathy to rein in Pandey were all looked upon by the British as gross treason.

---

[6]Jamadar is the term used for native commanding officer under whom the native soldiers were kept posted.

Eventually, Pandey tried to take his life by firing from his musket when he found himself cornered at gunpoint. He was mortally injured and taken into custody but recovered from his wounds. The court martial sentenced him to death, which was executed on 8 April 1857 without any delay. The jamadar Iswari Prasad was also hanged on 22 April at Barrackpore cantonment. The 34th Native Infantry was disbanded as a collective punishment on 6 May 1857.

The disbandment of two native infantries had sent back to Awadh nearly a thousand men, flaring the fires of disgruntlement and treason against foreign masters. Awadh was the best recruiting ground for the native infantries. There was hardly a family in Awadh that was not represented in the native army. Yet the Englishmen had confiscated land and jagirs and besmirched holy places in Awadh. Price of commodities had increased and the threat of famine was looming large. The seeds of distrust had already been sown after the dismissed sepoys reached their country house, and Awadh became the chief centre of the rebellion. There was ammunition and only the spark was awaited. Mammu would have known very well that in waging war against the English, there ought to be some space in the frontline for a monarch. And this could only be possible if Hazrat Mahal agreed to take the lead.[7]

The day when the 19th Native Infantry was asked to vacate the Bengal cantonment of Bahrampore, the people of Lucknow witnessed a tall and lanky angrez, with a long beard around his conical chin, get down from a horse-drawn phaeton and step into the residency. He was greeted and ushered inside by the outgoing chief commissioner of Lucknow, Coverley Jackson. The incoming person was an Irish gentleman who was born in Ceylon to his

---

[7]Edwardes, Michael, *The Orchid House: Splendours and Miseries of the Kingdom of Oudh, 1827–1857*, Cassel, 1960, p. 199.

military father and knew the country like the palm of his hand. He was called by his official name—Major General Sir Henry Lawrence.

Fluent in Hindi, Sir Lawrence, as he liked to be called, was sent to Lucknow by Lord Canning, anticipating a brewing discontent amongst the people of Awadh. The unhappiness of the citizens stemmed from unrestricted haughtiness shown by the last incumbent. Lawrence observed the people of Awadh closely and his first step towards reformation was to stop the carnage initiated by his predecessor and ordered not to spade a single brick in the city without his permission. Sir Lawrence wrote to the Governor General that he had solemnly made it his mission to rectify the mistakes committed for years by his countrymen. He had to face disdain in the streets and deep discontent among people all around.

Nearly a month after Sir Henry Lawrence set foot in Lucknow, he was warned by his officers to keep a close watch on a controversial native prince who had been seen recently meandering around the alleyways of the city. Nana Sahib, the last Maratha Peshwa,[8] whose animosity towards the British Empire was well known, came to Lucknow on 20 April for a surprise visit with his handsome and glamorous Muslim *dewan* (prime minister) Azimullah Khan and his brother. Suddenly, the discontented people of Lucknow started to idolize the Maratha Peshwa in their city as a pacesetter of a neoliberation movement. Nana was the adopted son and heir of Maratha Peshwa Baji Rao II, who had been exiled by the British to a place called Bithoor near Kanpur, just outside the realm of Wajid Ali Shah's kingdom. Baji Rao II used to be paid a generous pension of ₹8 lakh per annum by the British, which was discontinued after his death under Dalhousie's Doctrine of Lapse.

---

[8]Peshwa means prime minister. He was the virtual ruler of the Maratha confederacy.

After Baji Rao II's death, Nana had inherited the title and possessions of Peshwa but not his pension. Since then Nana had been fighting to recommence the pension in his favour. He had sent Azimullah Khan as his envoy to plead his case before the Board of Control and the British government in London. Azimullah was a young Pathan from a northwestern territory and a part of Afghanistan, the land that remained ever invincible to the British. The sparkling youth was Nana's favourite advisor, his aide-de-camp. Azimullah's mission to England had failed, but he did not return to his country empty-handed.

While he had been in England, the Crimean War had broken out. Initially, the British army had taken a backseat, which flickered a flash of new ideas in his mind. On his way back home, Azimullah had stopped in Constantinople, which was then part of the Ottoman Empire. There he had met *The Times*-famed Irish reporter William Howard Russell, who was covering Britain's war against Russia. Russell had painted heart-rending stories from the seat of war to underline miseries of the British army. Azimullah had also developed contacts with Russian agents in Constantinople, who assured him to extend all possible help to fight the British. Azimullah, who was in his mid-20s, with soaring fervour, started to believe that the British were not invincible and could be ousted from India if the leaders fought unitedly. On his return to Bithoor, he influenced Nana Sahib to wage war against the British and win back his lost kingdom and glory instead of wasting time and crying for justice. It was Azimullah who planted the idea of retaliation in Nana's mind.

The Peshwa was reportedly spending his vacation in Lucknow with his brother and his dewan. But his visit was a mystery and everybody knew that it was a ploy. Yet, the gentlemen took advantage of their visit and held secret meetings with discontented nobles and disbanded sepoys of Lucknow. Sir Lawrence met Nana at his residency. He was sceptical of the Peshwa's motives and wrote to Sir Hugh Wheeler, his commanding officer stationed at Kanpur, to not trust the loyalty of the prince. But Wheeler, who had seen the country for more than half a century, complimented Nana as 'friend of the English'.

Meanwhile, Hazrat Mahal was a great admirer of Nana and his dewan since the day she first saw them from behind the purdah when he had arrived as her husband's honoured guests. After a long time, Nana also met his childhood companion Maharani Laxmibai in Jhansi—another victim of Dalhousie's infamous 'doctrine'. Nana Sahib was travelling around, cementing ties with his allies and inviting the native chieftains to large-scale open warfare. All that was needed was a consortium of native power.

From Kaiserbag, Hazrat Mahal was keeping a close watch on the situation, which was changing fast. She had already engaged her intelligent eunuch to mingle intimately with people and to keep close vigil on any stranger found roaming in the streets. Mammu Khan was shrewd and a master reporter. Mammu's snooping mind would have known that new cartridges had arrived in the city and were supplied to the 7th Oudh Irregular Infantry stationed at Marion cantonment.[9]

Nana Sahib's visit to Lucknow had an instant effect. In the morning parade of 7th Oudh Irregular Infantry, native soldiers marched to a different tune. Mammu gathered that the incident that happened on 2 May in the parade ground of 7th Oudh Irregular Infantry was the first indication that a mutiny in the army was brewing and it was only a matter of time. The native sepoys refused to pick up the new cartridge supplied to them for the Enfield rifles. Major Carnegie, who was inspecting the

---

[9]Malleson, George Bruce, *History of the Indian Mutiny, 1857-1858, Commencing from the Close of the Second Volume of Sir John Kaye's A History of the Sepoy War*, Volume 2, William H. Allen and Co., 1878, p. 362.

parade, failed to convince the sepoys that cartridges were the same as supplied before and not smeared with the forbidden fat. The sepoys disobeyed Carnegie's order. They had probably lost their faith in the angrez after their country was annexed, treaties were flouted and their beloved King was dethroned. They could not trust Major Carnegie anymore. Chaos ensued and the cantonment and parade was abandoned.

The following day was a Sunday and poised to be a watershed moment in the history of Awadh. The D-day, 3 May, marked the onset of sepoy mutiny in India. It was not a sporadic incident or an expression of fury of any individual against an angrez, but an unprecedented organized revolt of a battalion against the commander. Brigadier Grey had already warned Lawrence about the growing mutinous state of 7th Oudh Irregular Infantry. Sir Lawrence rushed to the cantonment and immediately disarmed the discontented sepoys with the help of native commanders who were still loyal to them. As Sir Lawrence returned to the Residency, a startling rumour spread that 14 Indians at Marion cantonment were hanged to death. The flame of vengeance soared. Native soldiers of 8th Calvary revolted, and after a brief exchange of fire, the commanding officer Captain Parkinson was killed. Twenty native soldiers were arrested and hanged after 10 days of trial.

Another incident happened on 3 May. Agha Mirza Kambalposh, along with a subedar named Chotte Khan, revolted and made a failed attempt to kill Major Carnegie. On his failure, Agha Mirza ran away unhurt but organized a march with rebellious soldiers and thousands of people to retaliate. Both rebels were defeated in an encounter with the British force near the Rumi Gate. Agha Mirza sustained serious injuries. Next day, Aga Mirza was hanged in a moribund condition at Jelo-Khana of Machhi Bhawan. His companion, Chote Khan, who was also caught in the strife, eventually shared the gallows.

Hazrat Mahal was probably sad to hear that Agha Mirza Kambalposh had been executed. She had known the man for a long time, since he had come to Sultan-e-Alam to serve his army. Agha Mirza was closely known to Huzoor Alam Nawab Ali Naqi Khan, who recommended him to the former King. He came from a respectable family living at Mansoor Nagar and his father's name, as Hazrat could still recall, was Mahmood Mirza. A week after the incident, Mammu Khan informed the Begum that the angrez had brought down a large portion of a Dargah located on the northern side of Darshan Vilas palace in Kaiserbag. The Dargah was the residence of famous Awadhi poet Amanat Lucknowi, who was the author of *Inder Sabha,* a play once enlivened by Sultan-e-Alam in Kaiserbag. The poet was thrown into the street and eventually, he left for a safer place to Hussainabad.

The bullet that had popped out from the musket of Mangal Panday and whizzed past the ear of the English duty officer finally struck the minds of discontented natives in the entire northern realm. Rumours rocked the city of Meerut that flour sold in the market was adulterated with powdered beef bones, outraging religious sentiments. The story had added fuel to the raging controversy regarding cartridges. As a result, 85 sepoys of the 3rd Native Light Cavalry in Meerut refused to accept cartridges for their morning parade. The sepoys were rounded up, court-martialled and finally sentenced to imprisonment varying from six years to a decade.

On the morning of 9 May, the condemned sepoys were brought to the parade ground, shackled in iron chains, and forced to march for 2 miles to the jail in front of hundreds of staring and sobbing native eyes. The following day, sepoys of the 11th and 20th Native Infantry stormed the jail in Meerut and released the 'convicted' sepoys and other prisoners. Colonel Finnis of the 11th Bengal Native Infantry was shot to death on the parade ground.

The bungalows of the European officers were torched and many of their families murdered. The carnage went on for the whole night and at the crack of dawn, the mutineers left Meerut and marched towards Delhi, covering a distance of nearly 60 miles.

The ember of Meerut soon blasted into an inferno, burning through the British smugness across Delhi, Mathura, Faizabad and Lucknow. Two days after the fateful incident in Meerut, Sir Henry Lawrence called a grand durbar at Lucknow Residency and invited the talukdars and zamindars along with his European officers to renew social correlation and solidarity. He addressed the masses in Hindi. Sir Henry Lawrence regained some amount of confidence from the native leaders and his Governor General as well. But it was too late. The evil seeds sown by his predecessor had begun to bear fruit. The supporters of the native ruler were united and began to conspire. Hazrat Mahal was keeping a close watch over the situation. Mammu too kept his eyes and ears open and reported on every new event that he would come to know about.

The news of the mutiny had rekindled the flame of vengeance in the Begum's heart. Her grief turned to rage and called for revenge against the ushers of her family's misfortune, but revenge was not enough. Birjis was still a lad of 12. What Sultan-e-Alam's blue blood had restrained him from doing was done by the native sepoys. All they needed in that hour was a leader.

The sepoys reached Delhi on 11 May at daybreak and marched straight to the Red Fort. They urged the last Mughal emperor Bahadur Shah Zafar to lead their movement. On 13 May, after much hesitation, at the age of 82, he agreed to their proposal and was proclaimed the Emperor of India. He was a titular king under the auspices of British hegemony, whose authority was limited only to the walled city of Shahjahanbad (Old Delhi). The city witnessed massive carnage against the Europeans after the new band of mutineers marched down the street from Meerut.

Eventually, after a week or so, Delhi was devoid of Europeans, whether civilian or military personnel. The success of the mutineers was evident and they became unchallenged masters of Delhi under the authority of Emperor Bahadur Shah. Soon, the wildfire of the mutiny spread across northern India. Reports of insurgencies were coming in from Etawah, Mainpuri, Rurki, Etah, Mathura and, last but not the least, Lucknow, just within the period of half a month.

ten

A Cloud on the Horizon

The colossal furore against the Raj was no longer limited to a bid to uphold religious solidarity but a crusade to remove the foreign shackles that had enslaved the nation for a century. Barely a century back were the seeds of British hegemony in India planted at Battle of Plassey, not so much by armed forces directly but by mercenaries. The outcome had provided the East India Company with a firm foothold on Indian soil and allowed them the breathing space to plan their strategy of bringing the rest of the country under their rule. The British did not come on their own; rather, they were brought by the natives to rein in a tyrannical native king. After a century had passed, the same natives once again united to drive the British out. The chieftains and the sepoys somehow banded themselves together to form a decrepit consortium, led by a happy-go-lucky man of 82 years of age, living in a palace under the tutelage of the East India Company, writing poems and strolling under the sky, protected by the shadow of 500 pigeons flying over his head!

Bahadur Shah's reaccession as Emperor of India was more allegorical than physical. Hazrat Mahal was excited about the possibilities of good things happening in Delhi, but she was uncertain about how long the flame would remain alive. Mammu Khan reiterated that Awadh had all the preparedness for a holy war but lacked a seminal character on the frontline. Fervent gatherings among notables in Lucknow continued before the news of Meerut and Delhi broke out. One Munawar-ud-daulah Ahmad Ali Khan held a secret meeting with prominent religious leaders and *mahajans* (money lenders) at his house. He was a close confidant of Wajid Ali Shah and went to Calcutta with him but came back to Lucknow after six months. Munawar-ud-daulah Ahmad Ali Khan, who was a guest in the durbar of Sir Lawrence the night before, wanted to form a junta against the angrez but not at the cost of maintaining peace in Lucknow. The last bit sounded contradictory to the leaders present in the assembly.

The protracted discussion went on for a long time without the convergence of thoughts. People loyal to the royal family of Awadh preferred Nawab Rukn-ud-daulah, youngest son of Saadat Ali Khan, to be the vanguard. The 52-year-old Rukn-ud-daulah came to light in the city when he was thrown out from Farhat Bakhsh palace by Carnegie's cops. While Rukn-ud-daulah was under strong consideration, a line-up of names, such as Sah Behari Lal and Raghubir Dayal, was also thought of. However, no conclusion could be arrived upon. Rukn-ud-daulah called a meeting on the following day at Daulat Khana, inviting resaldars (army commanders) and sepoys of the native army to gauge his strength. The meeting ended inconclusively.

Disturbing news of sporadic attacks on the whites started pouring in from across the city. People were displaying their hatred for the Europeans though symbolic violence. Effigies of Europeans were erected and beheaded in public places, much to the appreciation of the crowd that was gathered. The chief commissioner was not in a mood to take any chance. He ordered to dig a moat surrounding Residency and Baillie Guard gate. Hundreds of coolies were made to come from all corners to dig a wide and deep trench. The news of siege at Delhi reached Lucknow on 17 May.

Mammu Khan's intelligent reportage of the incidents unfolding in Meerut and Delhi presumably inspired the women staying in

Kaiserbag. With Bahadur Shah Zafar in power, the old glory of the Mughal Empire had been rejuvenated and the prestige of Muslims and Hindus was revived. It seemed like the time had come for Muslims and Hindus to unite and enter a holy war for freedom. Jihad would drive the foreign oppressors out of the country and Sultan-e-Alam would get his crown back.

Mammu was greeted by the cheering women. Hazrat Mahal was also listening to him with great interest. The arrow had already been fired and could not be taken back. The rebels sparked a massive violence and killed many angrez, not even sparing the women and children. The sepoys had no other choice but to continue with the siege or die on the gallows. Hazrat Mahal was not sure if the people of Lucknow would take up arms against the angrez, and more so, who would lead the battle.

Yet, legitimate rights needed to be restored without any delay, so that Jan-e-Alam could be brought back home. The Begum had an astute sense of political foresight unlike other members of the King's jenanas, which she nurtured since her husband succeeded to the throne. The Queen would often come out from her kothi in a burqa, moving stealthily in her phaeton around the city to catch the whispers wafting in the air. Sunken in the deepest morass of despair, the hapless citizens had nothing to lose. The Begum was happy to see the spirit of her people waiting for a change. But as days passed, a lull settled in. The city had returned to its usual calm.

For the first time, Hazrat Mahal could see a frown on the face of the angrez, a nuanced depiction of losing confidence. None of them dared to move unarmed in the streets. Mammu believed that the 'prophecy of Plassey' would soon come true and angrez would be wiped out from India a century after the momentous battle.[1]

---

[1]Harlow, Barbara and Mia Carter (eds), *Archives of Empire Volume I: From the East India Company to the Suez Canal*, Duke University Press Books, 2003, p. 548.

John Kaye also recorded the prophecy that circulated by word of mouth and acquired the character of a rumour.[2]

Hazrat Mahal was sitting in her room and leafing through the pages of the Lucknow daily *Payame Azadi*, which was known for its seditious editorials from Mirza Bahadur Bakht. She was allegedly intrigued by the editorial column, which called upon the Muslims of Awadh to rise and fight a holy war against the British. Graffitis appeared on the walls in the city, appealing the Hindus and Muslims to unite for a holy war against the angrez. Mammu Khan was apparently always the harbinger of surreptitious news. On 22 May, the eunuch allegedly came to inform that Nawab Rukn-ud-daulah had been detained by angrez cops the night before. The youngest son of Saddat Ali Khan, who was known for his animosity towards the British, was running a secret military training camp, which got exposed. Rukn-ud-daulah was arrested and put behind bars at Machhi Bhawan.

In the wee hours on 18 May, Mahmood Mirza was going for his namaz and saw a long convoy of carts filled with grains, sugar, water, tea, coal, animal fodder and weapons, snaking through the streets leading to Residency. Mirza was an ex-soldier of the King and father of Agha Mirza, the first martyr in Lucknow. Only a day had passed after the news of the fall of Delhi had broken out, when Sir Lawrence started his preparations. Churches were converted to the godowns of food. A swimming pool inside the Residency was dried up to store grain. Lawrence called his chief engineer and ordered to erect a fortified wall surrounding the Residency. The chief commissioner evacuated more than 20 houses close to the Residency and prepared those to shift the Europeans in the city and also to prevent the mushrooming of rebellious haunts near

---

[2]Malleson, George Bruce, and John Kaye, *Kaye's and Malleson's History of the Indian Mutiny of 1857–8*, Volume 1, Cambridge University Press, 2010, p. 356.

the British headquarters. Machhi Bhawan became a storehouse of munitions. Only one European battalion having 600 soldiers was stationed at Awadh as against 20,000 sepoys standing on the opposite side. But still, Lawrence was confident of getting support from the elderly sepoys in his regiment who were loyal to their old masters. All he needed was the confidence of local sepoys to win the war.

Disarming the sepoys in Lucknow would not be a good idea as it would speak of British weakness. Two days after the news of Delhi broke out in Lucknow, Lawrence received a favourable 'order' from the Governor General. To empower him even more, the Governor General had vested him with absolute military power in Awadh and the rank of 'brigadier general of Oude' with supreme command over the Awadh army.

Roads near the Residency were cleared and all houses closer to it were vacated by Major Carnegie and some were even demolished. The evicted families were thrown out on the streets, giving them no time to pack their belongings. The house of the former King's brother, Prince Sikandar Hasmat, who was in London to plead for the King, did not escape Carnegie's rage. The prince's kothi was near Farhat Bakhsh Palace. The women and children were thrown out of his kothi and all valuables were looted. The family of Prince Sikandar took refuge at Kaiserbag, the ultimate abode of the royal family. Prince Sikandar's kothi was razed down after five days. The nobles and members of royal families were passing through a nightmarish phase and several houses that belonged to them around the Residency were plundered and grounded.

Eid-ul-Fitr was observed by the people with red eyes and sullen faces on 24 May. The Muslims assembled in masses in the city mosque and Christians in the church for Sunday prayer. Eid was peaceful but lustreless and the Eid mela near Rumi Gate was called off. Sir Lawrence cleverly removed all the police and army men from the roads to avoid conflict. On the following day, Sir Lawrence directed all British women and children to leave their bungalows and shift to the Residency. The ladies living luxurious life in decorated bungalows were forced against their will to shift. Although the distribution of rooms was made according to rank and file, living in the Residency could not have been a pleasant experience.

The first bugle of war was blown after sunset on 30 May 1857. Sir Lawrence was dining with his officers in his headquarter, when he was alarmed by the sound of cannons, followed by volleys from muskets. He was informed by a messenger that 71st Infantry had rebelled in Marion cantonment and gunned down Brigadier Handscomb.[3] They were joined by the native sepoys of 13th and 48th infantries. The loyal sepoys of 7th Cavalry Regiment tried to defend but were summoned to their side by the native sepoys. The mutinous sepoys attacked the English bungalows, plundered their wealth and set the bungalows on fire to take revenge for century-old British misdeeds. The flame of burning bungalows soared high into the air and could be seen from the Residency roof where Martin Gubbins stood dumbfounded. Gubbins was there to control the intelligence department in Awadh. The rebels made a long procession with effigies of angrez in their hands. The march started from the chowk and finally reached the palace gate of Kaiserbag. They rallied below the windows of Hazrat Mahal's kothi, displaying their ecstasy by chopping off the heads of effigies with swords and raising slogans against their foreign foes. Hazrat Mahal, looking down from her windows, must have wondered why the sepoys had chosen the gateway of Kaiserbag. Was it that they would like to convey a message to the deposed King or simply an

---

[3]Gubbins, Martin Richard, *An Account of the Mutinies in Oudh, and of the Seige of the Lucknow Residency*, Richard Bentley, New Burlington, 1858, p. 104.

attempt to inflame the queen's heart with the flame of rebellion? The native sepoys could have hoped to receive blessings from their queen. Begum Hazrat Mahal was the glamorous queen of Wajid Ali Shah and in the absence of the King, only the Begum could lead them to win the war!

The morning was appalling to Sir Henry Lawrence. He rode to Marion cantonment, only to come across the smouldering embers. The place was deserted as the rebels had left the scene. The bungalows were gutted and charred. Dead bodies remained scattered all around. Sir Henry's fury fell on the native sepoys who were there in the cantonment the night before. In a fit of rage, he ordered them to stand before the firing squad. His order was immediately executed and the sepoys were gunned down. But one of them was wounded. He feigned death till he was thrown into a dunghill. The wounded soldier managed to escape to Husainabad and allegedly relayed the story to his comrades.[4]

A riot broke out in the Husainabad quarter, which was quelled by civil police and irregular cavalry with much effort. There was devastation all around in Moosabagh. British soldiers brutally offered grapeshots[5] to slay the rebels en masse. Sir Lawrence was terrified by his misdeeds and did not take any chance to shift his headquarters from the cantonment to the Residency. He promised a reward of ₹100 for every mutineer captured or slain.[6] Sporadic killings continued in Lucknow resulting in casualties on both sides. The sepoys were gaining ground and swelling in number as well.

---

[4]Taqui, Roshan, *Lucknow 1857: The Two Wars at Lucknow—The Dusk of an Era*, New Royal Book Co., 2001, p. 73–4.

[5]Grapeshot is a type of ammunition that consists of a collection of smaller-calibre round shots packed tightly in a canvas bag and separated from the gunpowder charge by a metal wadding.

[6]Gubbins, Martin Richard, *An Account of the Mutinies in Oudh, and of the Seige of the Lucknow Residency*, Richard Bentley, New Burlington, 1858, p. 107.

Arms and ammunition were allegedly smuggled into the hands of the sepoys. The insurgency was spreading like wildfire, not only in Awadh but throughout North India. Decades of cold-blooded suppression and barbarity meted out to the people of Awadh had left them no recourse but to resort to violence.

In the early morning on 4 June, 36 mutineers who were found guilty in the eyes of the British were hanged publicly in front of Machhi Bhawan.[7] On the same day, a rebellion was recorded in Sitapur, followed by another at Faizabad, and then in succession at Daryabad, Sultanpore and Salon—all within the territory of Awadh and not far away from the capital city of Lucknow.

When the mutiny spread from Meerut to Lucknow, Kanpur appeared to remain in peace. British officers dutifully slept amongst their sepoys to show confidence in their men, thanks to Nana Sahib's loyalty to the British. Even the half-Indianized General Hugh Wheeler, who had seen the country for half a century, misjudged Nana as a 'friend of the English' when Sir Lawrence sounded a note of caution after meeting the mighty Maratha.

When the flame of mutiny was blazing high in Delhi, Sir Wheeler looked towards Nana for their safety, who assured him of his support. He had already declared his allegiance to the British and sent his volunteers at Wheeler's disposal to defend Kanpur! The General gave the Europeans in Kanpur a reason to feel confident that the mutiny might bypass them. In fact, Sir Wheeler was so confident that he sent his troops to Lucknow to meet the crisis and Kanpur was left with only around 300 European soldiers against 3,000 native sepoys. What Sir Wheeler did not realize at the moment was how useful the forces would have been to defend the siege of Kanpur in the days ahead.

---

[7]Taqui, Roshan, *Lucknow 1857: The Two Wars at Lucknow—The Dusk of an Era*, New Royal Book Co., 2001, p. 54.

The true bastion of the British in Kanpur was the magazine located in the northern part of the city. The thick-walled citadel was a warehouse of ammunition and contained a local treasury. General Wheeler relied upon Nana for the defence of the magazine and, ironically, allowed him to post his troop of 300 Maratha warriors and two cannons in front of the magazine.

Wiser sense prevailed at the last moment and Wheeler converted a military building located in the south of the city into a safe refuge for the Europeans. Nine barracks were being constructed on war footing with building materials already stored in the place. A 3-metre-high mud embankment was erected around the entrenchment.[8] Although no direct threat had yet occurred in Kanpur, European families were shifted in advance into the entrenchment.

In the wee hours of 5 June, three pistol shots signalled the onset of mutiny in Kanpur. Wheelers's apprehension came true. The sepoys began to burn buildings and plunder British bungalows. After a night of looting and destruction, the sepoys made off towards Delhi.

It took a long time for Sir Wheeler to fathom Nana Sahib's perfidious mind inside his colourful turban. On 5 June, Nana sent a letter to General Wheeler informing him to expect an attack the following morning at ten. Nana was a little late; at 10.30 a.m., his volunteers raided the magazine and plundered the treasury under the nose of two native infantry battalions supposedly loyal to Sir Wheeler. As the news of Nana Sahib's advances against the British garrison spread, several of the rebelled sepoys joined him. On 7 June, Nana Sahib and his army rounded up the entrenchment and the siege of Kanpur began. By 10 June, the Maratha chief was believed to be leading more than 12,000 native soldiers. On

[8]Malleson, G.B., *The Indian Mutiny of 1857*, Rupa Publications, 2016, p. 107.

12 June, Nana was informed that a party of European fugitives from mutiny-stricken Fategarh was sailing down the Ganges to drop anchor near Kanpur. Nana Sahib at once sent his troops and gunned down 126 unarmed European emigrants, mostly women and children. Two days ago, Nana's volunteers had gunned down an English lady and her four children who were travelling from North-West Province to Calcutta, unaware of the evil, landing up at Kanpur.[9] Nana's implacable demeanour was not true to his character; rather, his animosity towards the British was planted in his mind by his dewan, Azimullah Khan after his return from the Crimean war front.

Hazrat Mahal cheered the victory of Nana Sahib, running on blind faith, and was not much concerned about Nana's dubious role in the rebellion against the British. Mammu Khan's impression of Nana was mixed and he believed that the last Peshwa could not be trusted to lead the War of Independence in Lucknow.[10] Morality and honesty were ingrained in the hearts of the people of Lucknow. Hazrat Mahal argued that a lack of leadership would weaken the sepoys in front of the British canons. Nana Sahib had the ability and valour to bring them under one umbrella. However, Mammu had a different view.

On 9 June, a *parwana* (message) came from Bahadur Shah Zafar to one Mumtaz-ud-daulah, the brother of one of the former King's wives, Begum Shaida Mahal. The parwana summoned the Awadh force to join Emperor Bahadur in the holy war for freedom. The following day, a secret meeting was held in the kothi of Shaida Mahal to decide upon the spread of the mutineers in Lucknow.

[9]Ibid. 110–14.

[10]Qureshi, H.A. (trans.), *Qaiser-ut-Tawarikh of Kamal-ud-din Haidar,* Volume II, New Royal Book Co., 2008, p. 50.

The Begum's rebellious brother Mumtaz-ud-daulah was heading the session and trying hard to unite the discontented talukdars and zamindars for an all-out attack. Present at the conclave was the former King's elder brother Prince Mustafa, who was sitting in a corner and listening to the speakers carefully.[11] Rumours always seemed to follow him around. He was once the prime suspect of James Outram, who had confined him at the Residency. Later, he was found innocent and mentally unwell. He recuperated well under the supervision of Dr Fayrer and was released with an allowance for his living. Two days after the secret meeting was held at Begum's kothi, Major Banks raided Mustafa's house and the prince was arrested while he was offering his morning namaz. Mustafa Ali was imprisoned in a small room in Machhi Bhawan like a criminal.

The contents of the parwana were passed on to Khan Ali Khan, an ex-chakladar of Salon and *naib* (deputy) of Mahmudabad. Khan Ali promised to convince Raja Nawab Ali Khan of Mahmudabad, a powerful talukdar, to take the lead in the war against the British in Awadh.[12] The military police in Lucknow revolted and joined the rebels. There was another good news for the rebels—Moulvi Ahmadullah Shah, who was languishing in the jail of Faizabad, had managed to escape. On 8 June, the mutineers of Faizabad broke open the gates of the prison and Ahmadullah Shah was set free.

Moulvi showed his true colours and became the undisputed leader of the mutineers in Faizabad. Daleep Singh, the subedar of 22nd Oudh Infantry, broke away from the army and joined Ahmadullah Shah with his regiment.[13] On the other side, Raja

[11]Taqui, Roshan, *Lucknow 1857: The Two Wars at Lucknow—The Dusk of an Era*, New Royal Book Co., 2001, p. 81.
[12]Ibid. 80.
[13]Ibid. 81.

Nawab Ali Khan of Mahmudabad was the first talukdar of Awadh to show his solidarity with the rebel sepoys.

Meanwhile, Hazrat Mahal's fervour did not last long and, in fact, evaporated soon. Wajid Ali Shah was arrested in Calcutta on the charge of conspiracy against the British government and taken to Fort William.

eleven

...And the Struggle Begins

It was a bright and sunny Sunday morning on 14 June, like all other mid-summer days in Calcutta. The Europeans had returned home after the morning prayer in the church at Fort William and after a sumptuous Sunday lunch, they were turning in for a midday snooze. It was four o'clock in the afternoon when the sounds of trampling horses and rolling of carriages suddenly roused the peaceful Europeans in the British capital of India. Panic-stricken, in a bid to escape an unknown 'massacre', they tried to seek shelter inside Fort William, while others rushed to the docks on the eastern bank of Hoogly to board the ships before they sailed. Many houses in Chowringhee had been abandoned. The high officials had asked their families to board the ships.

In the suburbs, most of the houses belonging to the Christians were deserted. Horses, carriages, palanquins and vehicles of every sort were used to transfer the fugitives. Calcuttans first tasted the sting of the poignant tumult in 1857, which was certainly neither expected nor anticipated by the English masters. People had suddenly begun fearing a rebellion of potentially catastrophic dimensions after the news of armed mutinies and massacres in Lucknow, Kanpur, Benaras and Allahabad filled the air in Calcutta and added to the worry of the city's fragile safety infrastructure.

There was more than a grain of truth behind the alarm bells that rang on Sunday. Rumour had it that the native sepoys of

Barrackpore regiment had revolted. They had killed the Europeans in Barrackpore and Dumdum and were marching forward to Calcutta. The fervour reached a crescendo until it was confirmed that the native troops were disarmed in Barrackpore, Dumdum and Fort William and the state of affairs was under control.[1]

The night was terrifying and many Europeans posted sentries as safeguards or slept on the sofas with their pistols loaded beside them. Rumours flew thick and fast as the native servants filled the ears of their English masters. They were too scared of the final outcome.[2] The government enrolled corps of volunteers on horseback and on foot to patrol the streets and mounted guards at different points at night. Major General Sir Williams Cavanaugh of Fort William best describes the night of 'panic Sunday': 'I never saw Calcutta so quiet; now and then a figure clothed in white flitted past me and I met a patrol of volunteers; otherwise it was like a city of the dead.'[3]

The fight against an invisible enemy went on for a long time. Home secretary Cecil Beadon's words of assurance that 'everything is quiet within six hundred miles of the capital'[4] were found to be overstated, rather misleading to the government. J.P. Grant, a member of the Supreme Council, expressed his apprehensions, and warned by saying, 'In reality as well as in appearance we are weak here [Calcutta].'[5] It was not the native infantry; rather, Grant worried that he had no idea about the

[1]Malleson, George Bruce, *The Mutiny of the Bengal Army: An Historical Narrative Part 2,* Adegi Graphics LLC, 2005, p. 105.
[2]Blanchard, Sidney Laman, *The Ganges and the Seine: Scenes on the Banks of Both,* Chapman and Hall, 1862, p. 34.
[3]Cavenagh, Sir Orfeur, *Reminiscences of an Indian Official,* A.H. Allen & Co. London, 1884, p. 217.
[4]Malleson, George Bruce, and John Kaye, *Kaye's and Malleson's History of the Indian Mutiny of 1857–8,* Volume 1, Cambridge University Press, 2010, p. 1.
[5]Ibid. 9.

number of armed men at Garden Reach under the tutelage of the king of Awadh in exile.

Rumours were thick that the former King's men had begun to plunder the supposedly protected suburb and had turned the English into pitiable incumbents. The tone of the native sepoys had changed after the Meerut outbreak. Governor General Lord Canning realized that the British capital of India was no longer a safe haven for his compatriots and desperately tried to summon a European regiment to Calcutta in early June. The Bengali gentries, the so-called *bhadralok* community, had just started to emerge into prominence and had never lived so peacefully before, thanks to their British dispensations. They were firmly with the Raj and presented a united front against the beastly sepoys and those who dared to question the rule of law set up by the Englishmen. The former King of Awadh had come to the city and taken away their peace of mind.

Grant's awful portrayal of the former King of Awadh as an impending threat to the peace and tranquillity of Calcuttans enervated the Governor General more than the incessant danger of the Native Infantry. There was a rumour floating around that on the outskirt of Calcutta, the former King had been training a band of militant warriors, who were consorting with the sepoys of their fraternity to revolt against the British. His realm at Garden Reach was impermeable to outsiders and shrouded in mystery. Lord Canning feared a disastrous upsurge, which could arise unnoticed from the eastern corner of his capital.

A wave of sympathy was blowing in favour of the former King in Lucknow and across the north of India. Lord Canning was convinced that the wind could be turned to their favour only by taking the former King into custody. The effect would be manifold. Firstly, if the former King was detained, his followers in Calcutta would not have a leader to rally behind. Secondly, the wave of public sympathy in favour of the dethroned King aroused in London by the Oudh Commission would lose its strength. Rather, it would strongly appear in British Parliament as a tactic adopted by the commission to gain public favour. And lastly, the revolt of Awadh could be averted.

Canning did not have to wait long before an opportunity came to him for which he was not prepared initially. An incident took place on 13 June, the night before 'panic Sunday', which gave enough reason to Canning to secure his front. Abdul Subhan, a young Muslim, was caught spying inside Fort William. On interrogation, he divulged that he was an agent of the former King and had come from Garden Reach. He revealed that he had been assigned the task of unravelling the relationship that existed between the Europeans and the native troops in the garrison stationed at Fort William.

Abdul aimed to bring the native troops in his fold, so that they would take the side of the assailants in the event of an attack. He further confessed that Bahadur Shah Zafar, in connivance with Wajid Ali Shah of Garden Reach, was preparing for a war to drive out the British from their capital in Calcutta.[6] It was also revealed from his deposition that apart from the sepoys of Calcutta and Barrackpore garrisons, 400 followers of the former King were prepared to sacrifice their lives in the war against the British in Calcutta.[7]

There was no point waiting further to face the brunt of a grisly bloodbath. Late in the night on 'panic Sunday', Lord Canning held a closed-door meeting with his confidants and finally signed the arrest warrant of Wajid Ali Shah. All preparations were kept

---

[6]'Minute by Lord Canning', Governor General of India, IOL/PS/5/230, 18 June 1857.

[7]Cavenagh, Sir Orfeur, *Reminiscences of an Indian Official*, A.H. Allen & Co. London, 1884, p. 213.

confidential, and at dawn of 15 June, Lord Canning ordered G.F. Edmondstone, secretary to the Government of India, to arrest Wajid Ali Shah and four of his close confidants. A team of about 500 men of 53rd Regiment under Colonel Powell, some from the artillery, bodyguard line of Governor General, along with Commander Foulerton's naval force, boarded the *Semiramis* and reached the Garden Reach early in the morning.

After a late-night majlis in his rented kothi, the former King woke up as usual before dawn for his early namaz. He was not prepared for the troupe of 500 armymen knocking at his doors. He had not taken his bath even. The former King was taken by surprise and all his efforts to plead innocence fell on deaf ears. His house and grounds were searched, and about 600 men and a thousand stands of arms were discovered and removed.[8] After recovering from his initial shock, Wajid Ali Shah realized that destiny was prodding him to face the second challenge of his life. The operation was so perfect and so abrupt that his followers had no option but to accept the happenstance as one ordained in their kismet.

Wajid Ali Shah was arrested on the charge of conspiracy against the government and instigating insurgency among his armed followers. Edmondstone assured the former King that for his safety and security, he would stay in Fort William for the time being and would again return to his kothi once the law and order situation of the country was restored. He was apparently accompanied by Mujah-i-daullah and Diwanat-ud-daullah in a horse-drawn carriage. Ali Naqi Khan, the King's confidant and the former prime minister in Lucknow, was also a detainee. As soon as the King's carriage disappeared into the horizon of Garden Reach, the seed of rebellion in Calcutta—had there been any—died down forever.

---

[8]Campbell, Sir Colin, *Narrative of the Indian Revolt: From Its Outbreak to the Capture of Lucknow*, George Vickers, London, 1858, p. 70.

A beleaguering episode in the life of the banished King began, although his characteristic dignified behaviour seemed unchanged. Wajid Ali Shah was left with no option but to surrender to his destiny. While making a strong demonstration of the iniquity shown by the British, he surrendered himself to go wherever the Governor General ordered him to, exactly the way he relinquished his crown to James Outram a year ago. The banished King drove in through Coolie Bazaar Gate of Fort William at eight o'clock but was detained until two o'clock before he was finally allowed to settle in his room, prepared at the last moment to maintain the confidentiality of the plan.[9]

Sir Henry Lawrence was exhausted by the continuous flow of disturbing news. His outposts in Faizabad, Sultanpur and Sitapur were falling one after the other. On 12 June, he wrote to the lieutenant of the northwest province, 'Every outpost, I fear, has fallen and we daily expect to be besieged by the confederated mutineers and their allies.'[10] He was suffering from hypertension, insomnia and was often unable to control his emotions, his rage. He was losing his calm and Dr Fayrer asked him to take complete rest. 'By the end of the second week of June,' wrote P.J.O Taylor, 'British authority had been wiped out in the whole of Awadh except Lucknow.' All other places in Awadh were lost either to

[9]Extracts from Khan Sahib Abdul-Walī's *Sorrows of Akhtar: An autobiographical account of the deposition and imprisonment of Sultan-i-Ālam Wājid Alī Shah, the last King in Oudh*, a translation of Wajid Ali's *Masnavi Husn-e-Akhtari*, published in 1925.

[10]Malleson, George Bruce, and John Kaye, *Kaye's and Malleson's History of the Indian Mutiny of 1857–8*, Volume 1, Cambridge University Press, 2010, p. 275.

the mutineers or the army of talukdars and landowners.[11]

The revolt was no longer limited to a mutiny of the sepoys; rather, the canvas widened after more people of Awadh joined the group. Emissaries of the sepoys from Banaras, Allahabad, Jaunpur and Faizabad entered the city of Lucknow, along with civilians from areas where revolution was brewing. Sir Lawrence, in a fit of rage, ordered to take into custody the crown jewels of the former King left in Kaiserbag in his absence. The chief commissioner organized a state-sponsored loot under Major Bank on the evening of 17 June. It took several days to load 23 boxes of jewels in carts and take them to the Residency.

The momentous blockade of Kanpur had reached its nineteenth day on 26 June. Casualties were increasing and General Wheeler was left with limited food supplies, which would hardly support them for a week. Ammunition stock had already dwindled to almost nothing. It was impossible to combat a severe attack launched by Nana Sahib's army on 23 June to commemorate the centenary of the Battle of Plassey.

Nana's secretary Azimullah Khan sent Mrs Greenway, the wife of a merchant, into the entrenchment with a piece of paper, asking the Englishmen to surrender. In the first instance, General Wheeler rejected the offer, as it was not signed by Nana Sahib.[12] On the following day, Nana Sahib signed a second note and sent it through another elderly captive lady.[13] In spite of knowing well that Nana Sahib was not to be trusted, General Wheeler fell into his trap.

---

[11]Taylor, P.J.O., *A Feeling of Quiet Power: The Siege of Lucknow, 1857*, Indus, 1994, p. 22; Taqui, Roshan, *Lucknow 1857: The Two Wars at Lucknow—The Dusk of an Era*, New Royal Book Co., 2001, p. 86.

[12]Gupta, Pratul Chandra, *Nana Sahib and the Rising at Cawnpore*, Clarendon Press, Oxford University Press, 1963, p. 101.

[13]Ibid. 116.

Wheeler negotiated an armistice on 26 June and Nana agreed to let them leave town for Allahabad down the river. On the following morning, after dawn, more than 450 people, including a large number of women and children, went down to Satichaura Ghat by indigenous mode of transport arranged by Nana Sahib. As the British assembled at the dock and steadily embarked on the flotilla of 40 native boats, Nana's people came out from their hiding place and fired indiscriminately at the hapless people. Boats loaded with passengers were enkindled in the middle of the river. There was no escape and defence was impossible.

Only one boat out of 40 could escape the wrath of the natives, which was oared by some English officers after the native boatmen fled. Only four men on the boat survived: Lieutenant Delafosse, Lieutenant Mowbray Thomson and their two privates, Murphey and Sullivan.[14] Wheeler, his wife and elder daughter were among those killed in the massacre while it is thought that his younger daughter Ulrica had been among the few to escape death. A native horseman abducted poor Ulrica and later she killed herself by jumping into a well to avoid being dishonoured.[15]

Apart from 120 survivors of Satichaura Ghat, around 80-odd captive women and children were brought into a dilapidated villa named Bibighar or 'house of the mistress'. Nana Sahib placed the survivors under the care of a cruel prostitute named Hussaini Khanum, who stripped down the captives, tortured them ruthlessly and put them to hard labour, like grinding corns under the scorching sun for 18 days.

Poor sanitation leading to cholera and dysentery had already reduced the number of the captives. Nana tried to use them as

---

[14]Shepherd, W.J., *A Personal Narrative of the Outbreak and Massacre at Cawnpore: During the Sepoy Revolt of 1857*, London Printing Press, 1879, p. 92.
[15]Yalland, Zoë, *Traders and Nabobs: The British in Cawnpore, 1765–1857*, Michael Russell Publishing Ltd, 1987, p. 76.

pawns to resist the aggression of the British army towards Kanpur, which was being led by Sir Henry Havelock and Colonel James George Neill. When his scheme failed, Nana's hostages became his burden and, as advised by Azimullah Khan and Tantia Tope, he ordered people to 'dispose of' the remaining captives. It was not Nana but his general Tantia Tope who ordered the soldiers to shoot at the captives or to have them face the gallows if they refused. The sepoys refused to fire on innocent women and children. Nana's household too protested the grisly order and went on a hunger strike to put pressure on their master to revoke his order, but to no avail.

Nana had put the responsibility on Hussaini Khanum to follow his orders. Khanum, in turn, called upon one of Nana's bodyguards, named Sarwar Khan, her paramour, who engaged a gang of butchers carrying meat cleavers. The slaughtering went on for the entire day on 15 July. By next morning, all the captives were found dead, except three women and three children who managed to survive by hiding themselves behind the mound of cadavers. They were pulled out and thrown alive into a dry well and buried under corpses.[16]

Following the Satichaura massacre, Nana received a gun salute as a conquering hero, after which he issued instructions to celebrate the grand moment. He proclaimed himself as supremo of the Maratha confederacy on 30 April with pomp and show at his palace in Bithoor.

When Kanpur was rejoicing the grand victory of the new Peshwa, a large group of rebels, around 7,000 of them, assembled around

[16]Malleson, G.B., *The Indian Mutiny of 1857*, Rupa Publications, 2016, p. 118; Gupta, Pratul Chandra, *Nana Sahib and the Rising at Cawnpore,* Clarendon Press, Oxford University Press, 1963, p. 140.

26 miles north of Lucknow at Nawabganj.[17] Inspired by the fall of Kanpur, the rebels were openly inviting the authority to large-scale warfare. The native army started to move towards Lucknow on 28 June under the leadership of Raja Jai Lal Singh, the Nazim of Azamgarh.

The revolt was no longer limited to mutiny of native troops but aggrandized as mass awakening of the people of Awadh and affluent talukdars. Sir Henry Lawrence came to know about the movement from his crafty spies, but his haughty confidence prevented him from paying too much attention to it. Yet, the chief commissioner, with all his sincerity, tried to intercept a well-organized force of mutineers on the hottest days of summer. The British were powered by foot soldiers of 32nd Regiment, European cavalry, some loyal soldiers of 13th NI and a Sikh cavalry.[18] The battle took place at Chinhat and the insurgents outnumbered the British army in a ratio of 10:1. Lawrence had to face an unexpected defeat.

Lawrence ordered his men to retreat and the English defence recoiled into the Residency. The British troops, civilians and all other Europeans residing in Lucknow swarmed inside the Residency for shelter as the administration of the state slipped from their hands. Battle of Chinhat compelled the British to stay within the Residency's compound. After the British defeat at Chinhat on 30 June when Henry Lawrence and his troops retreated to the Residency, the whole of Lucknow, with all the palaces, apart from the Machhi Bhawan, fell into Indian hands. The historic siege of Lucknow thus began on 1 July 1857, confining 3,000 Europeans within the precinct of 37-acre British Residency.

---

[17]Mukherjee, Rudrangshu, *Awadh in Revolt 1857–1858: A Study of Popular Resistance*, Orient Blackswan, 2002, p. 83.

[18]Verma, Hari Narain and Amrit Verma, *Decisive Battles of India through the Ages*, Volume 2, GIP Books, 1998, p. 204.

The momentous victory of the native army was likely to have delighted the Begum. She was apparently narrated every detail by Mammu Khan, who also brought the news that all the British in Lucknow were made to languish inside the boundary of the Residency. The city was under the dominance of the natives. Hazrat Mahal apparently admired Raja Jai Lal's valour and his command over the native army. He was a trusted commander-in-chief of her husband, and the Begum, too, seemed to have deep faith in him. The Nazim of Azamgarh had managed to unite the powerful talukdars against the British and their combined strength had outnumbered the British army. In due course of time, the rebels received large-scale reinforcements from the talukdars and by the middle of November, out of estimated 53,350 combatants, 32,080 soldiers were contributed by the landed gentries.[19]

However, the Begum was allegedly apprehensive of the former King's fate in Calcutta. The British were licking their wounds and would be malevolent beyond imagination. The recent loss of Kanpur and Chinhat was likely to have a deleterious effect on the former King who was still languishing in custody at the mercy of the angrez.

When Wajid Ali Shah had walked past the doors of Coolie Bazaar, little did he know that he would be doomed to the life of a prisoner for 25 long months before he could walk out a free man. The former King was confined in a dingy room at the centre of the fort, infested with insects and mosquitoes. He could barely see the light of the day; he could not ever meet his people. Ali Naqi Khan was possibly quartered elsewhere. The behaviour of the

[19]Mukherjee, Rudrangshu, *Awadh in Revolt 1857–1858: A Study of Popular Resistance*, Orient Blackswan, 2002, p. 94.

staff was atrocious. But his living state improved with the active intervention of Cavanaugh, the town major, who helped in making his life a little comfortable.

The horrific experience in a desolate milieu dredged up the literary side of the banished King. *Masnavi Husn-e-Akhtari* (literally meaning 'Sorrows of Akhtar'), his autobiography, was penned in the dark cell of Fort William. Of all his masnavis, *Husn-e-Akhtari* was one of the best pieces of literature and can be embodied as his versified autobiography. His 'sorrows' were genuine and not stimulated for the sake of writing. The book embodies a poignant narration of his misfortunes and a testimony of his life.

The success in the battle of Chinhat gathered momentum and the sepoys were on a winning spree. More natives joined them, and on 1 July, the sepoys captured and occupied the space between Machhi Bhawan and the Residency. Machhi Bhawan held a host of honoured members of the state, like Prince Mustafa, the King's elder brother; Nawab Rukn-ud-daula, younger brother of Ghazi-ud-din Haider; Mirza Muhammad Haidar Shikoh, a member of the royal family of Mughals; and others captive. Colonel Palmer pawned them to open a safe path to escape into the adjacent Residency.

At midnight, between 1 and 2 July, the British detained in Machhi Bhawan were allowed to come out with a cart-full of women and children. Colonel Palmer made no mistake in taking a cue from the carnage of Satichaura Ghat. He kept the royal captives in front of his convoy as a protective shield and started moving to the Residency in the wee hours. Before making a final escape, the British garrison blew up 250 barrels of gun powder.

A thunderous sound shook the city of Lucknow. Chandeliers began to rattle in the houses of the Chowk, as far as Imambara of Khuda Baksh on the southern extremity. The jangling of glassware was likely to have been felt by Hazrat Mahal in her kothi. Initially, she thought that the angrez must have had retaliated and blown up hidden mines. In the morning, Mammu was called to calm her jitters. It is assumed that Mammu had all the information with him and reported to his mistress the incident that had happened at Machhi Bhawan the previous night. The Begum learnt from Mammu that the escapees had pawned the royal prisoners for a safe pathway and driven them to British Residency. The death of Mirza Muhammad Haidar Shikoh must have been shocking. The Mughal prince, who was one of the royal detainees deported from Machhi Bhavan, had been shot dead by Major Banks. Charges were brought in against the Mughal prince for conspiring with the help of one of his servants named Syed.

On the night before the siege of Machhi Bawan, a high-powered steering meeting of the talukdars and leaders of the native army was held at the house of Sharaf-ud-Daulah, an ex-minister in the court of Awadh. Raja Nawab Ali Khan of Mahmudabad and Raja Jai Lal Singh had taken the lead. The attendees were honoured members of feudal clans who had overwhelming influence over the natives. Even then, the great feudal lords were discrete and lacked an undeniable central command under the sky of Awadh. The discussion converged to a vital point that without the King heading them, the movement could not sustain for long. Raja Jai Lal Singh, with some military wisdom, worth his salt, had remained subservient to the empire of Awadh for generations. Raja Nawab Ali Khan of Mahmudabad was bestowed the title of 'Raja' by none other than Wajid Ali Shah and, hence, the Raja felt indebted. Raja Nawab Ali Khan had reasons to believe that the people of Awadh revered Sultan-e-Alam as an incarnation of God on earth and would never hesitate to sacrifice their lives for the holy cause of freedom at his command.

Hence, Nawab Ali Khan preferred to have the former King's heir enthroned without any delay and to make the army move under royal command, lest it would be impossible to uphold the spirit amongst the sepoys and natives for long. Raja Jai Lal seconded the proposal of Nawab Ali Khan and he was supported by all the great feudal lords and army officers, except one—Iltifat Ahmed. The latter was a representative of Moulvi Ahmadullah Shah of Faizabad. The Moulvi purposefully avoided the meeting on the plea of his leg being injured. Being an arch opponent of the royal house of Awadh, the Moulvi of Faizabad was adamant not to acknowledge the throne of Awadh.[20]

The native army continued its bombarding from all sides of the British Residency in Lucknow. From the rooftops of few remaining edifices near the Residency and all available vantage heights, relentless firing by muskets and matchlocks poured into the Residency. The howitzers that the sepoys seized from Machhi Bhawan were fired and the shells burst open into the British bastion. Food supply cut off and Lawrence was forced to take austerity measures in providing ration.

For the entire day, Sir Henry Lawrence was making rounds from corner to corner of the Residency, holding meetings to draw a strategy for rationing of food. After the day's fatigue, he reclined on his bed in a special room at ground level from where he could watch the activities outside. He was talking to Captain Wilson and his nephew, George Lawrence, and was about to make his opinion when a shell from an 18 pounder hissed into his cabin and blasted. Everything went dark inside after an ear-deafening massive

---

[20]Taqui, Roshan, *Lucknow 1857: The Two Wars at Lucknow—The Dusk of an Era*, New Royal Book Co., 2001, p. 104.

explosion. The room was filled with thick smoke, and when it cleared, Sir Henry Lawrence was found fatally wounded lying in a pool of blood on his bed. The other two gentlemen sustained minor injuries and were saved. Lawrence was immediately shifted to the dispensary of Dr Fayrer, where he succumbed to his injuries on 4 July, mumbling the name of his wife for the last time.[21]

[21]Edwardes, Sir Herbert Benjamin, and Herman Merivale, *Life of Sir Henry Lawrence*, Smith, Elder & Co., London, 1872, p. 610; Taqui, Roshan, *Lucknow 1857: The Two Wars at Lucknow—The Dusk of an Era*, New Royal Book Co., 2001, p. 105.

twelve

Awadh Finds a New King

Malika-i-Kishwar, the dowager queen of Awadh, lived at her new address at Harley House in London for almost a year. The annual rent of £550, which she paid, went in vain. She was away from her country for more than a year but provided a decent living to all 140 people of her retinue. Lakhs of rupees were spent by her ever since the Mission had come to London. It was not easy to get the sympathy of the British press, which was trying its best to advocate that the Commission aimed to defame the colonial administration in India, and that the Queen Mother had come to England simply to defend her son's licentious lifestyle, whereas the British found it abhorrent.

Finally, the long wait for Wajid Ali Shah's envoy came to an end when Her Majesty, the Queen of England, admitted the dowager queen of Awadh to an audience on 4 July 1857. The British Queen courteously received the 'Queen of Oude' in Buckingham Palace and took her inside, where she arranged a special 'zenana durbar'. The Queen Mother of Awadh was veiled and wore a robe made of gold tissues. She shook hands with Queen Victoria and sat on a similar chair opposite her. Her son and Moulvi Masih-ud-deen accompanied Malika-i-Kishwar. From the English side, the delegates were Prince Albert, the prince consort; Vernon Smith, the president of the Board of Control; and Sir G. Clark, who was the interpreter. The English delegation entered from the back and stood at the rear end facing the back of the dowager queen of Oudh. Only Queen Victoria's eldest son, 16-year-old Albert Edward, was allowed to stand beside his mother. After the grand arrangement was over, the 'Queen of Oude' removed her veil and handed over a letter from Wajid Ali Shah and a handful of ornaments, including pearls and precious stones, to Queen Victoria. The British queen was extremely courteous in addressing Malika-i-Kishwar as the 'Queen of Oude'.[1] Her Majesty's reception was generous and benevolent enough for the dowager queen of a state that had long been abolished by Her Majesty's government.

The dowager queen opened the dialogue to prove the greed of the East India Company to confiscate her state on flimsy grounds. The dowager queen spoke in traditional Urdu, which was translated to English by Sir Clark. Queen Victoria listened to the interpreter mindfully without any expression on her face. The cordiality shown to the Indian emissary a moment ago seemed to have faded. Malika-i-Kishwar's argument had reasonable merit but failed to cut ice. Oudh had brought fortune to the British Empire. Queen Victoria had five million more subjects and £13 lakh more revenue than she had before. The fact could not be denied. It was ludicrous to think that the British Crown would recommend the Indian government to relinquish its claim over Oudh. The durbar was courteously adjourned and postponed till the next day.

The 'next day' was not destined to come. The unexpected news of Wajid Ali's arrest in Calcutta bewildered the emissaries and soon the Oudh Commission melted into obscurity. Queen Victoria could not warrant an audience to the emissaries of the King who had reportedly instigated his people to revolt against the British Crown. The British were shocked by the atrocity of mutiny

[1]Queen Victoria's diary, preserved at Windsor castle, Berkshire

and affirmed the arrest of Wajid Ali Shah at the right time. They lost their sympathy for the Oudh Commission. The last hope of the emissary was shattered.

A state of barbaric euphoria engulfed the city of Lucknow after the siege began. Euphoria led to violence and the insurgents sanctified vandalism in the name of freedom. The rebels resorted to looting and plundering on a large scale, not even sparing the native elites. Law and order in Lucknow had collapsed without the British cops or a native king. Shops were ransacked in the Chowk and houses of famous singers and musicians of Lucknow were plundered. Volumes of rare English books stocked in the royal library and in General Martin's College were indiscriminately torched to ashes and thrown into ponds. Raja Jai Lal realized that the ecstasy would soon evaporate and the rebel army would disintegrate unless the natives found a leader. The seal of a monarch would provide legitimacy and enable enforcement of law and order. He was inclined to crown one of the sons of Wajid Ali Shah.[2]

Wajid Ali Shah's first son Nausherwan Qadr was physically challenged since birth, his second son Falakh Qadr died at an early age, his third son was the heir apparent but he was in London. The King's fourth son was Birjis Qadr. Rumours soared high that the cavalry of the native army was planning to swear in Suleiman Qadr, the youngest son of Amjad Ali on the throne. Suleiman was the son of Amjad Ali's wife Malika Ahad who was a flower-girl during her maiden days.[3] But Raja Jai Lal was interested in putting up Prince Birjis Qadr on the throne and made the sepoys honour the code of his order. Birjis was then a lad of 12 and would require a

[2]Mukherjee, Rudrangshu, *Awadh in Revolt 1857–1858: A Study of Popular Resistance*, Orient Blackswan, 2002, p. 135.

[3]Santha, K.S., *Begums of Awadh*, Bharati Prakashan, Varanasi, 1980, pp. 229, 294.

regent to support. Of the King's wives, only Hazrat Mahal, with all her diplomatic prudence and impressive personality, could bring a placid equilibrium, explained the Raja.

On 2 July, the day when Sir Lawrence received his fatal wounds, Raja Jai Lal Singh and Raja Nawab Ali Khan of Mahmudabad probably asked Mammu Khan to arrange a meeting with the begums in Kaiserbag. The eunuch allegedly took the opportunity to suggest Birjis Qadr's name into the ears of the two Rajas.[4] A seasoned practitioner of shrewd politics, Mammu presumably knew that his fate was intrinsically tied to the Begum. The jenana meeting came as a surprise to the ladies. The begums were reluctant to nominate a person on the throne when the King was still alive. Out of their abiding loyalty to the King, the people of Awadh remained staunch in their belief that the sovereign would return to take his seat. Instead, the angrez might turn nasty to the King in Calcutta to avenge the trouble caused to them in Lucknow. The King was still in the clutches of British and the fact could not be ignored. Rather, it would be prudent for Rajasaheeb to take the lead since the soldiers selected him as their uncrowned King. In such a situation, the royal family of Awadh was ready to endorse his leadership and support him as well.

The two gentlemen took some time for the excitement to run its course. The angrez would never relinquish their claim on Awadh, Jai Lal retorted, nor would they guarantee their greatness by releasing Sultan-e-Alam from prison.[5] Nana Sahib had proved beyond doubt that the angrez were not invincible. Kanpur was successful because the native soldiers found a jingoist at the vanguard. The general uprising and fervour seen among

[4]Taqui, Roshan, *Lucknow 1857: The Two Wars at Lucknow—The Dusk of an Era*, New Royal Book Co., 2001, p. 106.
[5]Mukherjee, Rudrangshu, *A Begum & a Rani: Hazrat Mahal and Lakshmibai in 1857*, Penguin Allen Lane, 2021, p. 13.

the natives should not be allowed to peter out. The natives of Awadh still believed that Sultan-e-Alam was the incarnation of God and so was his family. If the throne remained empty and the loyalists failed to find a sovereign to galvanize them, they would be bewildered like a headless chicken. The begums allegedly remained engrossed in Raja Jai Lal's rhetoric till it ended but failed to respond. It was not so simple to propose a name since none of the begums were prepared to risk their sons' life. The war had started and the throne was not made of roses. The gentries were in a hurry and gave the begums two days to decide. The rajas left Kaiserbag for the day, leaving behind the King's jenanas in a state of complete pell-mell.[6]

Raja Jai Lal Singh and Raja Nawab Ali Khan were back in the courtyard of Kaiserbag on 4 July, two days after the first meeting. Meanwhile, Mammu Khan apparently had a confidential discourse with his mistress. His foresightedness was beyond doubt. Long after Mirza Hamid Ali was selected as heir to the throne of Awadh, Mammu had allegedly wondered that since Birjis was the fourth son of the King, in case of any adversity for Mirza Hamid, Birjis Qadr's fate would open up. Since Meerza Hamid Ali was out of the country, in order of age, Birjis was ahead in the power race. But Birjis was the only son of Hazrat Mahal, her only inspiration to live. The angrez were not only powerful but could be notoriously vindictive. If Raja Jai Lal's army won the war, the throne would be left to her husband, the present king. If Raja Jai Lal's army lost the battle, his son's death would be inevitable. Nonetheless, her mother's heart would prefer her son to live in peace rather than to risk his life as the surrogate king. Begum Hazrat Mahal, who was hitherto trying to consolidate her son's position as his

[6]Taqui, Roshan, *Lucknow 1857: The Two Wars at Lucknow—The Dusk of an Era*, New Royal Book Co., 2001, p. 106; Santha, K.S., *Begums of Awadh*, Bharati Prakashan, Varanasi, 1980, p. 230.

father's rightful heir, was not prepared to let her son hold the flag of mutiny and be remembered as a martyr.

A voice loaded with conviction was apparently heard from behind the purdah, pronouncing the name of Prince Nausherwan Qadr as the twelfth king of Awadh. Wajid Ali Shah's begums had chosen the name of the eldest son of Khas Mahal unanimously. Nausherwan Qadr was physically challenged by birth and was passed over by none other than Sultan-e-Alam. Had Nausherwan Qadr been made to ascend the throne, reign of governance would be in the hands of the begums who could pull the string from behind. But the ruse soon evaporated when Sultan-e-Alam's first son was spared from consideration as his mother did not give her consent. Khas Mahal was in Metiyaburj, Calcutta. Raja Jai Lal forthwith proposed the name of Birjis Qadr to draw an end to the argument. He asked concurrence of the begums as time was running out.

The proposal irked subtle contention among the women of Wajid Ali Shah. Insidious envy presumably prevailed upon the begums to accept the dominance of a mutah wife, whom Jan-e-Alam disowned as inauspicious and removed from his palace. The Begum had a murky past, but a twist of destiny had taken her on a different path of life. She was fated to enjoy the omnipotence of a regent queen, risking the life of her son. But Rajasaheeb had a towering personality and none of the ladies had the courage to oppose him. Hazrat Mahal knew well the need of the hour. Her mother's heart was likely to have felt a dull thud of emptiness. Like a seasoned practitioner of diplomatic relations, Hazrat Mahal proclaimed that her son belonged to the most coveted family of Awadh and was born to dedicate his life for the cause of his people. In the most crucial hour of his time, he would be proud to sacrifice his life for the freedom of his motherland. The situation was so compelling that when Rajasaheeb sought consent from the begums, they could not deny him.[7] The enthralling influence of Raja Jai Lal and Raja Nawab Khan carried the day. On behalf of the consortium of natives, the gentlemen pronounced the name of Birjis Qadr as the twelfth king of Awadh. The ceremony of coronation was to be held on the following day. Since Birjis Qadr was only 12 years old, Begum Hazrat Mahal would act as regent of the minor king till his adulthood.

As soon as the gentries left Kaiserbag, Nawab Fakr Mahal, Bandi Jan, Nawab Suleiman Mahal, Nawab Shikoh Mahal, Nawab Farkhunda Mahal, Yasmin Mahal, Mahbuba Mahal, Khurd Mahal, Sultan Jahan Mahal and some other begums of Awadh came to meet Hazrat Mahal.[8] They allegedly retorted that Hazrat had not only disowned the King but also ignored them. She had placed her son on the throne of Awadh when the King was still alive. She had not even taken consent from the King or the Queen Mother. She had risked the life of Jan-e-Alam since the British might hang him to death for instigating his wife and son to wage war against them. Nonetheless, she had not done justice to her only child by making him ride the tiger. Hazrat Mahal seemed firm in her conviction but remained courteous. She allowed the begums to ventilate their minds and leave her place once they became exhausted.

It was an arduous task for Raja Jai Lal to persuade the army commanders that no better option was available than to select the child for the throne. The commanders had enjoyed independent power so far and were the most powerful section of the native strength in the absence of a monarch to rein them. The leaders agreed only on the conditions that, firstly, Birjis Qadr would

---

[7]Taqui, Roshan, *Lucknow 1857: The Two Wars at Lucknow—The Dusk of an Era*, New Royal Book Co., 2001, p. 106; Santha, K.S., *Begums of Awadh*, Bharati Prakashan, Varanasi, 1980, p. 230.

[8]Narain, Kirti, *Participation and Position of Women Uprising of 1857*, Himalaya Publishing House, 2017, p. 4.

be subservient to the diktats of the Mughal emperor; secondly the leaders would have a hand in selecting the prime minister of Awadh; thirdly, their pay would be doubled; and lastly, they would retain exclusive right to punish traitors if found guilty in their eyes.

The coronation of Birjis Qadr as the king of Awadh was already approved by Bahadur Shah Zafar, granting him rights to rule over the province on behalf of the Mughal emperor. Although held by his supporters to have received recognition by the king of Delhi, Bahadur Shah seemed to have addressed him merely as Mirza Birjis Qadr Bahadur. Zafar diplomatically avoided the use of titles 'padshah', 'malik', 'nawab' or even 'shahzada'. Unlike his father, the crown of Birjis Qadr was not independent and he was only given the authority to rule Awadh by Emperor Bahadur Shah Zafar on his behalf. Consent was also obtained from talukdars and other landed gentry in the territory of Awadh. Yet Birjis Qadr remained as king because his forebears were kings.

It was raining torrentially on 5 July. Monsoon clouds were hanging heavily from the northern sky. Two regiments of sepoys, in full regalia, were waiting in the white marble-clad Chandiwali Baradari of Kaiserbag.[9] Tradition was broken by choosing Chandiwali Baradari instead of customary Lal Baradari for such a ceremony. Dignitaries and guests had all assembled. Present in the stand were Sharaf-ud-Daulah, General Barkat Ahmed, General Hisam-ud-daula, Raja Jail Lal Singh, Raja Nawab Ali Khan, Shihab-ud-din Khan, Umrao Singh, Raghunath Singh, Raja Balkishan, Raja Beni Madhab, Daroga Mir Wajid Ali and other dignitaries. Mammu Khan was there too. The talukdars and landed gentries came to

[9]Taqui, Roshan, *Lucknow 1857: The Two Wars at Lucknow—The Dusk of an Era*, New Royal Book Co., 2001, p. 107.

witness the great moment. It was however a dull gloomy day. The traditional orchestra was missing. Prince Birjis Qadr and his mother Hazrat Mahal reached Chandiwali Baradari by afternoon forming a *juloos* (procession).[10] From the noble gathering, Shihab-ud-din and Saiyid Barkat Ahmad—the Chinhat-famed risaldar of the 15th Cavalry[11]—went to the prince and placed a gold-stringed silk *mandeel* (cloth turban) upon his head.[12] Major Banks had looted the original crown of the former King. Sultan-ul-ulema conducted the ceremony. Twenty-one gun salute was fired by the artillery of Faizadabd commanded by Jahangir Baksh Subedar and Mir Kazim Ali in-charge of the magazine.[13] The clatter of the muskets reached the Residency a mile away, which roused hope for a moment to the besieged that relief had come from Calcutta to rescue them. Birjis Qadr was crowned as the twelfth Nawab of Awadh. His mother Hazrat Mahal was pronounced the Queen Regent of Awadh till the minor king reached his adulthood.

The swearing-in of the cabinet of Nawab Birjis Qadr was followed. Sharaf-ud-Daulah, a Kashmiri Sunni and a trusted minister in the court of Mohammad Ali Shah and Amjad Ali Shah, was appointed the *wazir* (prime minister).[14] Mammu Khan was made *dwaroga of dewan khana* (chief of the court of law), which was a much-weighted position, superior to many in the cabinet. Although he was not above the chief minister,

---

[10]Ibid.

[11]Rizvi, S.A.A., and M.L. Bhargava, *Freedom Struggle in Uttar Pradesh*, Volume 1, Uttar Pradesh Publications Bureau, 1957, p. 103.

[12]Rizvi, S.A.A. and M.L. Bhargava, *Freedom Struggle in Uttar Pradesh*, Volume 2, Uttar Pradesh Publications Bureau, 1957, p. 103; Santha, K.S., *Begums of Awadh*, Bharati Prakashan, Varanasi, 1980, p. 231.

[13]Taqui, Roshan, *Lucknow 1857: The Two Wars at Lucknow—The Dusk of an Era*, New Royal Book Co., 2001, p. 54.

[14]Pemble, John, *The Raj, the Indian Mutiny and the Kingdom of Oudh, 1801–1859*, Oxford University Press, Delhi, 1960.

the eunuch became the power centre of Awadh. He maintained his unchallenging sway over the regent Queen. The next most prominent minister was Raja Jai Lal Singh. He played a dual role of the chief of council of state and collector of the army.[15] The council was a powerful body of about 20 army officers and civilian ministers. The role of the council at the moment was to enforce the siege of Residency and to arrange funds for maintaining the native army. Raja Jai Lal Singh was a courageous soldier and spirited man. His eloquence was apparently well cherished by Hazrat Mahal, who trusted his leadership in the battle against the angrez. Hisam-ud-daula was nominated as General of Royal Army, Raja Balkishan was made the finance minister as he was during Birjis Qadr's reign, and Thakur Dayal was sworn in as the private writer to the nawab.

Hazrat Mahal was given the authority to act as regent of the minor king by oath. She was bestowed the titles of 'Rajmata' by the Hindus and 'Janab-i-Aliya' by the followers of Islam. Covered by her veil interwoven with gold strings, Hazrat Mahal stood up to address the audience. Although she had no experience in public address, she spoke eloquently like a seasoned envoy of the people. She urged the audience to stand united and take an oath to drive out the angrez from the country. The talukdars, risaldars and native army, wielding unquestioned authority in the absence of the King, frowned at the audacity of a muta wife who was a mere dancer in her past. Raja Jai Lal could sense the imminent danger brewing. He had already perceived the mind of haughty army commanders whom he had met a couple of days back. But the sepoys and common natives of Awadh were in the mood to hail their new king. No matter how old he was, he was the son

[15]It was the responsibility of the collector to recover money from rebellious subjects.

of Sultan-e-Alam and hence an embodiment of Lord Krishna!

After a lacklustre coronation, the Rajmata and nawab left the place, making their way through the elated crowd before the last rays of sun disappeared. William Howard Russell, the Irish War correspondent with *The Times*, was then in India to cover the mutiny. Russell, who was renowned for his dispassionate journalism, complimented Hazrat Mahal by saying,

> The Begum exhibits great energy and ability. She has excited all Oude people to take up the interest of her son and the chiefs have sworn to be faithful to him. We affect to disbelieve his legitimacy but the *zamindars* who ought to be better judges of the fact, accept Birjis Qadr without hesitation.[16]

When the new king sat on the *masnad* (throne) of Awadh amidst a throng of the hailing crowd, a deep mourning and low chanting from the Holy Bible gloomed the air inside the Residency, a mile away from Chandiwali Baradari. The dead body of Sir Henry Lawrence was resting in peace inside a coffin, awaiting interment in a small graveyard behind the Residency. His epitaph would bear his own words: 'Here lies Henry Lawrence, who tried to do his duty. May God have mercy on him.'[17]

Signficantly, on that very day, the news of Wajid Ali Shah's arrest reached the English shores and drove the final nail in the coffin of the Oudh Commission.

---

[16]Russell, William Howard, *My Diary in India: In the Year 1858–9*, Volume II, Routledge, Warne and Routledge, p. 274.

[17]Kaye, Sir John William, *Lives of Indian Officers: Major D'Arcy Todd. Sir Henry Lawrence. General Neill. General John Nicholson*, David Bogue Publisher, 1880, p. 195.

The path of Hazrat Mahal was not free of barbs. She had her hour of glory and found herself installed as the de-facto empress of Awadh. She could hardly have been happy with the state of affairs. A conscientious person could not live in comfort with a crown of thorns. She was heading a precarious coalition of sepoys and native gentries lending support from outside. But on the inside, she had more enemies than friends and sorting out the heterogeneities within her people was indeed an arduous exercise. Some of the begums were in league with the British officers and were trying their best to diffuse the attack on the Residency. Miftah-ud-daulah, the wise and trusted courtier since the time of her husband, warned her that the stellar constellation was not favourable for her son. When Birjis was crowned before sunset, the moon was in the constellation of Scorpio. The astrologers of Awadh predicted that the time was not auspicious and his regime would not last long.[18] The prophecy was disheartening for the mother of an only child. But she had chosen her path, being aware of the dangerous consequences. Destiny had ordained for her a belligerent and peripatetic existence.

After ascending the throne, the Begum issued a proclamation under the seal of Birjis Qadr with a small prefatory note saying that the proclamation was to be circulated among the Hindus and Muslims largely. The proclamation also carried a pamphlet called *Fateh-i-Islam* and instructed that all men and women, whether Hindus or Muslims, should be ready to destroy the English for defending their own religion. There were instructions regarding the strategy to fight the British once they entered the city. The pamphlet instructed that people should remain in their houses with doors locked from inside and all the men, women, children and even slaves ought to put the English to death by firing guns,

[18]Santha, K.S., *Begums of Awadh*, Bharati Prakashan, Varanasi, 1980, p. 256.

carbines and pistols, shooting arrows and pelting stones, bricks and earthen pots from the terraces. It had the potential to incite violence against the Christians and the sepoys were assured that they would not commit sin if they kill the English in the holy war. Although the proclamation was undated, scholars[19] believe that the document was prepared sometime between 5 July and 17 July 1857, the period when Moulvi Ahmadullah Shah was most active.

While most of the King's wives acknowledged the sovereignty of Nawab Birjis Qadr by offering *nazr* (tribute to a superior or the payment of a fee to the Lordship) of gold coins, a section of royal women acidulously resisted the ascendency of Janab-i-Aliya from the beginning. Some also refused to acknowledge the sovereignty of Birjis Qadr. In the hour of crisis, Shahensha Mahal appeared to have lent her helping hand, trying to spread her influence over the King's women to accept Hazrat Mahal and her son. But the same lady joined the camp of Mir Wajid Ali to rescue the besieged incumbents from the Residency for which she was rewarded.[20]

Shifting allegiances was an old practice among the talukdars of Awadh, which Hazrat was likely to be scared of. Indeed, it was an onerous task to rein the people and sort the wheat from the chaff. Aspirants to the throne of Awadh were many. Barkat Ahmad supported Suleiman Qadr. Daroga Mir Wajid Ali betrayed the queen, shifted to the other side, and helped the British in their rescue operation; General Outram also awarded him. Only Mammu Khan stood by her side all along. Thwarting the general belief that the Queen was not much more than a marionette in the hands of Mammu, William Russell maintained that Hazrat

---

[19]Mukherjee, Rudrangshu, *A Begum & a Rani: Hazrat Mahal and Lakshmi Bai in 1857*, Penguin Allen Lane, 2021, p. 93.
[20]Santha, K.S., *Begums of Awadh*, Bharati Prakashan, Varanasi, 1980, p. 256.

Mahal was 'ardent, intriguing, subtle, courageous and devoted to her son'.[21]

But the arch-rival of the Begum, Moulvi Ahmadullah Khan, was possibly licking his wounds in a silent corner. The Moulvi of Faizabad and his followers could not accept the ascendency of a mutah begum to the pinnacle of power. He was a strong claimant to the Awadh throne. Furtively, he kept himself away from the crowning ceremony of Birjis Qadr, making the excuse of a war-inflicted wound. He was taking his time to recuperate from his virtual defeat. After the battle of Chinhat, the Moulvi developed a sense of invincibility and deep arrogance. His conceit deluded him into believing that shaping the destiny of Awadh was his prerogative. His arrogance did not rise in a vacuum. Indeed, the Moulvi's chivalry was praised by his enemies. The British considered him a great warrior and an implacable enemy, so much so that Brigadier Thomas Seaton, who fought for Lucknow's relief, described him 'as a man of great abilities, of undaunted courage, of stern determination and by far, the best soldier among the rebels'.[22] The British found him a dervish in name only; in reality, he was a prince in disguise and was preparing the masses to wage war against the government. The colonial rulers were so afraid of Moulvi that a reward of ₹50,000 was declared for capturing him alive and the mutineer who would bring him alive would be pardoned. Nonetheless, the Begum and the Moulvi had a common enemy and a mission. Their ambition was to set Awadh free from British hegemony.[23]

---

[21]Russell, William Howard, *My Diary in India: In the Year 1858–9*, Volume II, Routledge, Warne and Routledge, p. 337.

[22]Malleson, G.B., *The Indian Mutiny of 1857*, Rupa Publications, 2016, p. 17.

[23]Santha, K.S., *Begums of Awadh*, Bharati Prakashan, Varanasi, 1980, p. 231; Qureshi, H.A. (trans.), *Qaiser-ut-Tawarikh of Kamal-ud-din Haidar*, Volume II, New Royal Book Co., 2008, p. 275.

To counter the ascendency of Hazrat Mahal, Moulvi Ahmadullah and his followers started to hold regular strategic meetings at Taron Wali Kothi. The old observatory building became the seat of Ahmadullah Shah. The Moulvi sent a message to the Begum through Mammu Khan demanding four guns and ₹5,000 as an homage to prove his autonomy. The Begum consulted her advisors and rejected his offer.

Hazrat Mahal, with her son, shifted her residence to Chowlakhi Kothi,[24] which was the favourite summer residence of Aliya Begum. The palace was owned by Wajid Ali Shah's barber Azim-ullah Khan. While making Kaiserbag palace complex, the King had acquired the building at a fabulous price of ₹4 lakh and had made it a part of his palace complex. On 7 July, two days after the coronation, the Begum first summoned a durbar with her son seated on the throne. The assembly took place in Kothi Mirza Wala, which was part of Chowlakhi Kothi. She appeared on the stage with her son preceded and surrounded by her Turkish guards. She was dressed in her traditional garara interlaced with gold strings and ornamented with pearls. For the first time in public, she wore only a light, almost see-through veil, to cover her face.

Tough days were ahead for the Begum and it was not the time to rejoice. On the first day of her durbar, Raja Jai Lal rang the alarm that ammunitions were running short since the war of Chinhat. The British blasted their ammunition depot at Machhi Bhawan before they left, leaving no scope for the natives to collect. A large number of sepoys from Lucknow had gone to Delhi, reducing

---

[24]Taylor, P.J.O., *A Companion to the 'Indian Mutiny' of 1857*, Oxford University Press, 1996, p. 82. Chowlakhi Kothi is a palace in Lucknow closely associated with the name of Begum Hazrat Mahal, who is said to have taken many vital decisions regarding the independence of Awadh in this kothi. It was one of the ill-fated structures that were razed to the ground by the British force.

the strength of the native alliance. Relief force from Calcutta was expected to arrive shortly to challenge the combating natives. The British soldiers were well equipped with Enfield rifles with shooting range four times that of the outdated Brown Bess of the natives. The Enfield rifles could be the sole deciding factor in the war. The Howitzers were no match to the native cannons. Had the sepoys mutinied after accepting Enfield rifles, history would have been written differently.

The Begum made a vital announcement under the seal of Birjis Qadr: all foot soldiers, horsemen, gunners and the officers of the former King who were thrown out of employment would be brought back to service again. The durbar was attended by some of the English soldiers who remained outside the Residency. They promised to shift their allegiance too.[25] Hazrat Mahal was considering setting up factories for the supply of ammunitions but all that would require money. Major Banks, in his state-sponsored loot, had confiscated the wealth of the King less than a month ago. Hazrat Mahal depended on Raja Jai Lal for arranging funds. Apart from his military assignment, the Raja was also the collector of the state. Hazrat Mahal was also aware of the former King's private treasure, which was hidden secretly under safe custody of Hisam-ud-daulah and Miftah-ud-daulah. The wealth could be sufficient to pull her out of crisis and there could be no better way to spend the money than for the country. Meanwhile, the Begum also started to strike coins in the name of her son, imitating early Awadh currencies from the Muhammadabad Mint near Banaras under the province of Bengal.

Hisam-ud-daulah and Miftah-ud-daulah were summoned on 8 July, the following day. The two gentlemen were subservient to the

---

[25]Taqui, Roshan, *Lucknow 1857: The Two Wars at Lucknow—The Dusk of an Era*, New Royal Book Co., 2001, p. 110.

former King. The trusted confidants of the former King refused to disclose the existence of any such treasure. On the same day, keeping faith in the queen, Raja Gurbaksh Singh of Ramnagar, with 12,000-foot soldiers and the Afridi Pathan warriors who came to settle in Malihabad during the time of Nawab Shuja-ud-daula, joined Oudh force under the tutelage of Begum Hazrat Mahal.[26]

On 9 July, a heavy attack was planned by Moulvi Ahmadullah to intensify the siege of the Residency. Under his leadership, the Residency was attacked from all three sides. Raja Jai Lal with his royal soldiers attacked the Residency from the eastern side; the newly joined force of Raja Gurbaksh Singh and Afridi Pathans attacked from the western side; and Beni Madhab and the Moulvi himself raided from the southeast. Beni Madhab was appointed as the administrator of the Jaunpur and Azamgarh regions by the Begum. There was panic all around the Residency and European families were forced to take shelter in the basement. The Baillie Guard located at the southeastern corner of the Residency was broken by the Awadh force and the sepoys advanced further into the territory of the Residency. Still, the siege could not be held longer as the soldiers had to retreat with the setting sun. The gun powder and ammunitions had fallen short.

Intelligence reports from the battlefield reached the Begum in her palace and that made her upset. Nothing could be salvaged without money. The Begum once again called the custodians of the former King's treasure. After an initial rejection and much hesitation to disclose its existence without the consent of the former King, Hisam-ud-daulah and Miftah-ud-daulah agreed to hand over the treasure to the Regent Queen by explicit order of

---

[26]Mukherjee, Rudrangshu, *Awadh in Revolt 1857–1858: A Study of Popular Resistance*, Orient Blackswan, 2002, p. 109; Taqui, Roshan, *Lucknow 1857: The Two Wars at Lucknow—The Dusk of an Era*, New Royal Book Co., 2001, p. 111.

Nawab Birjis Qadr. One of the caskets was opened by breaking the royal seal, to find gold and silver worth several lakh rupees. The treasure was some relief in the time of crisis.

The meteoric ascent of Mammu Khan ruffled the feathers of the enemies as well as allies of Hazrat Mahal. He was an ordinary eunuch who had earned a bad name that he was an omen of doom for his masters. He was rejected by all the peace-loving begums in the jenanas, till he joined the service of Hazrat Mahal after the birth of Prince Birjis. Her well-wishers had allegedly cautioned the Begum that the eunuch would bring her bad omen in life. Mammu was an unimpressive, stunted, dark-complexioned man, timid in nature but overly intelligent. However, he gained the sympathy of his mistress soon. Since 12 years before the coronation, Mammu had been serving the Begum, and remained subservient to her till the end of his life. Hazrat Mahal seemed to be solely dependent on her eunuch's extraordinary diplomatic acumen and his impeccable network of intelligence. Mammu Khan always remained obedient to his mistress and never attempted to delude her. Although looked down upon by the Begum's other cohorts, Mammu was never spurned by his mistress.

A twist of fate raised Hazrat Mahal to the seat of power and by virtue of that Mammu Khan became the most powerful person in her kingdom. Hazrat paid him for his loyalty by making him the Dwaroga of Dewan Khana. The regent Queen was unbending in fulfiling her desire, despite dissenting murmurs from Raja Jai Lal. Raja was an arch-enemy of Mammu since both of them were jostling with each other to get the Begum's favour. Although not even a minister by his position, Mammu became more significant than prime minister Sharaf-ud-Daulah. Hazrat Mahal's soft corner for Mammu was openly circulated by the British who took advantage of the Queen's generosity to spread smutty rumours about illicit affairs.

Shortly after her emergence, Hazrat Mahal blossomed forth as a remarkable organizer who could move her people with her magical appeal. Her cabinet of astute advisors were seasoned practitioners of statecraft and they made their best attempt to manoeuvre her in the right direction. She was energetic and held meetings every day in the morning with her wazir Sharaf-ud-Daulah and ministers of her cabinet to keep herself abreast of the stately affairs. Raja Jai Lal kept her informed about military activities on a daily basis during his visit in the afternoon. Mammu remained her sentinel against all adversities. Hazrat Mahal returned all landed properties that had been confiscated by the British to the talukdars. Taxes were abolished to lessen the burden of the subjects and she also issued edits through her son to crack down on food hoarders. She had no wish to remain a marionette of her army commanders or to conduct herself according to the wishes and directives of the feudal lords. Her fight against the foreign confiscators continued and she had a long way to go.

thirteen

Paree Turns Warrior

The cloud of fear and uncertainty hanging over the capital city of Calcutta was now settling down. Wajid Ali Shah cried for justice, testifying his innocence and loyalty towards the British. He wrote several letters to Canning pleading for his release. Finally, his appeal to Lord Canning bore fruit. In July, he was removed from his cell and housed in the erstwhile Governor House built inside the fort in 1802 while Ali Naqi Khan was accommodated in the Royal Barrack—both guarded by the European sentries.[1] Canning, in a letter, explained to Wajid Ali that arrangements were being made to protect him from the 'insurgents'. However, the government would make all provisions at its own cost for His Majesty's comfort. To ensure security, the government would look for a safer residence as soon as the turbulence was over. Till then, he would live in the fort with complete dignity and comfort, free from anxiety. Canning did not give false assurance. Wajid Ali's life did become smooth and easy. He was allowed to have food brought from his residence, even though under strict vigil. Wajid Ali wrote that he was given a pulling fan in his room and ice was supplied in the summer months to keep his room cool. Servants were provided to take care

---

[1]Augustine, M.L., *Fort William: Calcutta's Crowning Glory*, Prabhat Prakashan, 1999, p. 159; Malleson, G.B., *The Mutiny of the Bengal Army, by One Who Has Served Under Sir Charles Napier*, Oxford University Press, 1857, p. 106.

of his personal needs and their conduct was watched closely.

Before entering his cell in Fort William, Wajid Ali Shah had deposited his jewellery and valuables in the safe deposit of the Company's treasury.[2] He was allowed to spend his money in custody to meet his obligations and to pay his attendants. He was committed to supporting his emissaries and his family in England. However, his resources were dwindling and were soon reduced to only a lakh of rupees. He admired his people and their faithfulness amidst the unbearable misery. However, his romantic pursuit went on.

The news of Akhtar Begum giving birth to his son was a harbinger of ecstasy. This second wife of Wajid Ali Shah was the daughter of Ali Naqi Khan. The former King was eloquent to describe her mesmerizing beauty in his Masnavi and bewailed her absence. A contemporary Scottish daily elucidates the King's daily life in custody:

> He spent most of his time in writing poetries and letters to his begums who lived in Lucknow and in Garden Reach. He would love to send valuable souvenirs to his begums. He was fond of toys and spent much money on them. Nothing could give him more pleasure than to sit and watch the circular movements of automatic toys set in motion by him. He was particularly very sceptic of being intruded upon and Colonel Cavanaugh was extremely rigid in allowing anybody, no matter his rank, to enter into his room or in any other way to disturb him. Ali Naqi Khan was less comfortably situated. He was always reserved and devoted most of his time in reading Koran.[3]

---

[2]Llewellyn-Jones, Rosie, *Engaging Scoundrels: True Tales of Old Lucknow*, Oxford University Press, 1999, p. 150.

[3]*The Caledonian Mercury and Daily Express*, 6 September 1859, No. 21824.

While Wajid Ali was fiddling with his toys, trying to set those in motion, one of his begums in his native country had put the entire bastion of his tormentors in a simmering vortex. While in custody, he came to know about the great mutiny. *Masnavi Husn-e-Akthari* proudly extolled his 14-year-old son Birjis Qadr and his valiant mother, the Regent Queen of Awadh, for leading the great war of freedom against the British. Begums from Lucknow were writing letters to Jan-e-Alam, which were mostly informal. In one such letter, Janjan Begum wrote to her husband that Hazrat Mahal had volunteered her only son for the noble cause. Yasmin Mahal wrote, 'When I feel depressed I go to look upon Birjis Qadr. He resembles you...it brings some solace to my heart. His mother is kind to me and makes me welcome when I go.'[4]

No stone was left unturned to keep the detained King in a jovial mood, yet, a deep-rooted sorrow was locked in his bosom, not for the subversion of his power but for the ball and chain they placed heartlessly to thwart his mind. He could not write his poems; there was no music in his life and no romance with his begums. His 'sorrows' were full of sombre tributes: 'My health is giving up, my hairs are falling, my eyes remain laden with tears and my mind is becoming restless. I have lost all my power and cannot take food in my hands...'.[5] These lines in *Husn-e-Akhtari* lamented the pangs of separation. His heart burnt and his eyes wept. He sadly remembered the sweet memories of Khas Mahal and his other consorts, Begum Malka-e-Mulik, Begum Mahbub-e-Khas, Begum Jaane Jaan, Begum Mumtaz Alam, Kaiser Begum and Begum Khujista Mahal, who stayed back in Lucknow. He

---

[4]The letter (originally in Urdu) is a part of *Begamat-i-Awadh ke Khatut*, p. 46. See Santha, K.S., *Begums of Awadh*, Bharati Prakashan, Varanasi, 1980, pp. 231–2.

[5]Abdul-Walī, Khan Sahib, *Sorrows of Akhtar: An Autobiographical Account of the Deposition and Imprisonment of Sultan-i-Ālam Wājid Alī Shah, the Last King in Oudh*, 1925.

was madly in love with Zafri Begum as much as he loved his favourite poems of Firdausi! She would send him paan in the jail as a token of her love, but her devotion did not last forever. Khujista Mahal too left the King to marry a man in Calcutta and later left for Lucknow. Kaiser Begum went back to Lucknow. Wajid Ali reconciled with his destiny as his begums left him one by one. It was only Begum Khas Mahal who remained with him till the end with loving care. She never missed to send him his meals and five pieces of paan in prison. Wajid Ali Shah, being a prolific writer, composed a small masnavi about his wives. Internal evidence shows that it was composed in Fort William. It is titled *Masnavi Bahr-e-Mukhtalif.*

Wajid Ali Shah was preoccupied with his romantic sorrows, evoking memories of his sweet days with the begums. The struggle of Lucknow and the heroic role of Hazrat Mahal could not make a dent in his heart. He was never a warrior, nor did he ever have the fervour of an aspiring king. His diaries of prison life were full of pangs of alienation from his womenfolk and protest against his claustrophobic incarceration. His concerns were snugly intramural and devoid of diplomatic dexterity. He sobbed alone in the darkness of his cell but never attempted to vilify his tormentors. He had lost his seat of power a year back, along with fighting for his rights in England, and yet his masnavis remained too frigid to lament over his lost kingdom. He had renounced his throne prophetically and accepted his fate with dignity. *Masnavi Husn-e-Akthari* proudly extolled his 14-year-old son Birjis Qadr and his valiant mother for leading the great war of freedom against the British but urged them to stand down. His compromising ethos kept him away from confrontation with the British in Lucknow. The former King found it increasingly difficult to get his crown back, which he had handed over to James Outram. Rather, he would have preferred to stay back in the fringes of Calcutta and to recreate his kingdom of passion.

In Calcutta, he would have set himself free from his unpleasant responsibility of governing his people; instead he would have time to nurture his desire, his poetry and his music. The struggle of independence led by one of his wives, who had been all but dissociated from him long ago, did not evoke any patriotic emotion.

Wajid Ali Shah's romanticism was reflected in his letters of love that he wrote to his Begum Aklil Mahal in Lucknow from his cell in Fort William. The begum was a good singer and in many of his letters, the King sent her his gazals to sing.

When Wajid Ali Shah was deeply absorbed in writing ghazals for Aklil Mahal, the native force under Raja Jai Lal was fighting tooth and nail to reconquer Farhat Bakhsh Palace and the Chatter Manzil from the British. It was on 15 July when the natives won, and both historic edifices came under their control. Farhat Bakhsh Palace was the birth place of Wajid Ali Shah and the place where he was coronated. The holy palace was converted into a kennel and a stable by Coverley Jackson. When the native force was struggling to capture Farhat Bakhsh Palace and Chatter Manzil in Lucknow, the ghastly mass homicide of British women and children was taking place at Bibighar in Kanpur.

The consequence of the Bibighar massacre was the emergence of a sudden fit of anger, which turned the British soldiers brutal and they torched houses of the natives and firing on every native citizen they encountered. Nana Sahib did not take any chance to fight back but fled from the territory and sunk into oblivion. The embittered British troops continued unchallenged carnage for two days, and on 19 July, they stormed the palace of Nana Sahib in Bithoor, which was destroyed by canons. His 14-year-old daughter was among many other hapless women and children who were burnt alive.

On 16 July, when British troops were storming the alleyways of Kanpur, Hazrat Mahal called a crucial durbar at Kothi Mirza Wala in her Chowlakhi palace. Raja Jai Lal Singh, Wajir Sharaf-ud-Daulah and Mammu Khan were present, among others. Raja Jai Lal reported the capture of Farhat Bakhsh Palace and Chatter Manzil by the combatant native force. He also informed that Nana Sahib had escaped from Kanpur and had gone underground. Conversely, spies of the native army were working well inside the Residency, mapping important hideouts and also the houses where the chief commissioner was moving into furtively. They also located the site where Indian princes were incarcerated.

After giving a patient hearing, Hazrat Mahal advised Raja to start laying underground mines around the Residency. Bande Hasan, who was an expert in laying mines, was summoned and assigned the job. He had a stronghold on the Pasis, an ancient Dalit caste expert in drilling underground tunnels and laying mines.

A fierce attack was launched early in the morning on 20 July by a native force assembled near river Gomti and led by Moulvi Ahmadullah Shah. The baton of command was passed on to Colonel Sir John Inglis of 32nd Foot after the death of Sir Henry Lawrence, while Major Banks succeeded as the chief commissioner.[6] With the sudden impact of the attack, John Inglis, who had so far maintained a successful defence, went haywire and was almost about to give up the post. The network of mines planted underneath the buildings of the Residency caused panic among the civilians. Ladies started to hear strange clatters beneath the ground and assumed that mining had reached below their bedrooms and could pop up at any moment from under a table!

It was 21 July. The siege of Lucknow had been going on for 21 days. The British force was outnumbered by Indian soldiers,

[6]Malleson, G.B., *The Indian Mutiny of 1857*, Rupa Publications, 2016, pp. 205–6.

who were attacking the bastion from all directions. The combatant force within the Residency was not more than 1,700, while the rest were civilians. The whole command was now in the hands of Colonel Inglis.

During one of his evening briefings, Raja Jai Lal informed the Begum that her old enemy James Outram had been summoned from England by the British authority to rejoin as chief commissioner of Lucknow. Raja Jai Lal had no doubt that shortly the British would consolidate their force by infiltrating more soldiers from outside to rescue the European civilians locked inside the Residency. Not much time was left for the natives to triumph over the angrez, the Begum pondered. Side by side, the torment meted out to the commoners of Lucknow in the name of jingoism had become counterproductive and therefore had to be stopped. She issued a stringent order through her son to stop the plundering of native properties and to increase vigilance against hoarders and black-marketers of foodstuff who were responsible for the inflation of food prices. She distributed grains and cereals to the suffering population. Enforcement of the law was tightened and rigorous punishment to the offenders was imposed.

Shelling on the Residency as well as placing of underground snipers by Bande Hasan and his gang of Pasis under the Begum's leadership further alienated the entrapped individuals at the Residency. On 25 July, Colonel Inglis received communication from Havelock through a trusted messenger named Angad that the rescue army would arrive in Lucknow within five to six days.[7] News had come that the relieving army was fighting the native combatants at Unnao, some 40 miles away from Lucknow.

In the evening briefing, the Begum came to know from Raja Jai Lal about the cruelty meted out to the natives by the British

[7]Malleson, G.B., *The Indian Mutiny of 1857*, Rupa Publications, 2016, p. 208.

in Kanpur. Nana Sahib and his close associates had fled from the city to escape barbarity. There was a rumour that he had taken refuge in a jungle in Nepal. The Begum was allegedly shocked and stood aghast for a moment. She surely would not have liked to be remembered in the pages of history as a fugitive like the Maratha Peshwa, whom people of Lucknow once idolized.

Hazrat Mahal had passed on a clear message that the throne of Awadh had no enmity with innocent women and children, that she would not tolerate any indignity shown to the European civilians and that helpless ladies should be given shelter and protection. Hazrat Mahal had given safe refuge to many womenfolk who had lost their husbands in the battle. She reprimanded Raja Lone Singh of Metauali, who had allegedly kept some English civilians imprisoned in his custody. The Begum instructed them to bring them safely to Lucknow.[8]

Not 'five to six days' but a month had passed since Havelock had promised Colonel Inglis to relieve them from the Residency. The latter was at the brink of his patience. Havelock had not managed to move beyond Unnao, as the villagers fought fiercely against the British army. It had been raining heavily for some days and the countryside was in a deluge. Cholera became an open menace to the army men. The loss to the British side was heavy and the British general knew well that if the situation continued for some more days, he would lose all his men before reaching Lucknow.

Havelock had asked for more forces from Calcutta, but Lord Canning was reluctant to deplete his defence. Colonel Inglis had lost many of his wounded men in the exchange, despite the relentless endeavour of the surgeons to save them. The food

---

[8]Taqui, Roshan, *Lucknow 1857: The Two Wars at Lucknow—The Dusk of an Era*, New Royal Book Co., 2001, p. 154.; Fremont-Barnes, Gregory, *The Indian Mutiny 1857–58*, Bloomsbury, 2014.

storage, too, was dwindling fast. Inglis was fighting with only 350 European soldiers and 300 natives of which many of them were wounded. Cholera inside the Residency was wreaking havoc.[9]

Raja Jai Lal believed that he must hit the iron when it was hot and urged the Begum to call a durbar before the opportunity was missed. His army was prepared to strike the final blow. Bande Hasan's labyrinth of underground mines had left the Residency standing on a volcano. Most of the areas inside the 37-acre Residency were not found safe by the residential engineers. The work progressed silently but promptly as desired by the Begum. Hazrat Mahal gave a clarion call to head for the final attack and named it 'Operation Sawan'.[10]

It was raining heavily since the previous night; it was a new moon day in the month of Sawan. It rained all day on 18 August. The siege of the Residency fell on its forty-ninth day. The occupants in the Residency suddenly woke up to an ear-splitting sound of a massive explosion, which shook the bungalows in the compound. From five o'clock in the morning, blasts continued successively for an hour or so. The intensity was so high that Captain Alexander Orr and Lieutenant Mecham, along with two sentries who were standing on the roof of Johanna's building, were blown away and killed. It was a complete solar eclipse, which started at eleven in the morning. The attack stopped since then as the sepoys had taken a break for religious reasons. After a day's break, Operation Sawan continued on 20 August under the leadership of Commander Yusuf Ali Khan of the former King's army. The shelling went on heavily on the eastern side of Residency and the Water Gate of Bailey guard. Combatants crept up the gate and set fire by igniting

---

[9]Wilson, Thomas Fourness, *The Defence of Lucknow: A Diary by a Staff Officer*, Smith, Elder and Company, 1858.

[10]Taqui, Roshan, *Lucknow 1857: The Two Wars at Lucknow—The Dusk of an Era*, New Royal Book Co., 2001, p. 138.

a large number of combustible materials piled up on the gate. On that day, a large portion of Mons de Prat's house fell in. A shell exploded inside the staircase of the main building. Further adding to the misery, an unknown fever prevailed upon the incumbents, which led to a significant number of deaths in the Residency. Foodstuff was running short and ration was reserved only for the sick and wounded. Evereyone in the Residency started panicking, as the last defence was crumbling. The final blow came the next day following an explosion of a heavy mine with heavy casualties. Johanna's House was completely ravaged to the ground. Almost all Europeans residing outside the Residency in the territory of Awadh were killed and the country was on the verge of expelling the white interlopers.

The Begum's strategy resulted in a grand success that went beyond her imagination. She had good news. The delay in sending troops from Calcutta had forced Havelock to retreat. Two-thirds of the Bengal army had joined the rebellion, yet they could not be smug at this time. The Begum called a durbar on 21 August with her comrades, including Raja Jai Lal, Raja Nawab Ali Khan, Mir Mehdi, Bande Hassan, Raja Balkishan, Yusuf Ali Khan and, last but not the least, Mammu Khan. She announced the strategy of her next assault, which she named 'Operation Muharram'. There was little space for complacency. Raja Jai Lal had already informed them that the Residency was surrounded by a six-metre deep trench, 18-feet wide and fortified with Howitzer cannons. Much of the firing was launching from the rooftop of the main building. The Begum conveyed that the only chance to win was to dig tunnels and place mines. The explosions would create a breach in the trench through which her soldiers could pass through. Raja Jail Lal liked her idea of tunnel warfare.

The following day, 22 August, was the first day of Muharram, but the city was not prepared to mourn. No one was in the mood to take out the age-old Tazia and wax Zari Mubarak lying ready in the Imambara of Asaf-ud-daulah. Hazrat Mahal had no option but to depend on the trustworthy Raja Jai Lal and Rana Beni Madhab. It was finally under their supervision that the age-old procession came out from Asafi Imambara and reached Hussainabad Imambara—its final destination.[11]

Hazrat Mahal had risen to her position out of nothing but had a steep political ambition to set her kingdom free from usurpers. The Regent Queen of Awadh was a great renouncer and renouncers are fated to enjoy such omnipotence. For the sake of her country and to win the holy battle, it would not be prudent for her to stave off Moulvi Ahmadullah Shah when both were striving for the same goal. It might not have been possible for her to win the laurel without his help. Moulvi Ahmadullah came from Faizabad, the erstwhile capital of Awadh, and was well within her domain. He was not only a great warrior and an irrefutable leader in his field, but, in the end, he was also her subject. The Begum found no match for him in Awadh to take her dream project forward. But Moulvi continued to boycott a woman-driven government. He was the arch-enemy of the Begum and reproached the Begum for remaining unveiled in the company of men and smoking hookah at her leisure. He claimed himself as a prophet of God. He was an extremely intelligent person, very shrewd and cunning, and had the uncontested skill of gathering people.

The Begum was in an awkward predicament and apparently called her saviour Mammu Khan to arrange a meeting with the Moulvi. Time was running short and Calcutta would soon dispatch new reinforcements. Raja Jai Lal was not in favour of the Begum's submission to Ahmadullah Shah, as the Moulvi was

---

[11]Taqui, Roshan, *Lucknow 1857: The Two Wars at Lucknow—The Dusk of an Era*, New Royal Book Co., 2001, p. 141.

always trying to undermine the throne of Awadh and throwing his weight around. He was too ambitious and had his eyes on the throne of Awadh at the dispensation of some talukdars. The Moulvi was not only the enemy of British, but he could also turn against the Begum once the usurpers left the country. Ahmadullah Shah's followers declined to accept Hazrat Mahal, a 'former concubine', as regent of their king when Sultan-e-Alam and the Queen Mother both were alive. Significantly, skirmishes between Ahmadullah Shah and Mammu Khan were apparently not unusual and often ended with injuries. It went to such an extent that Begum once had to send Rana Beni Madhab to calm them down.[12] Yet, his mistress was stubborn and Mammu had to call upon Moulvi Ahmadullah Shah.

The Moulvi, often called Danka Shah by his followers, was a multi-faceted person and more talented than any of the Begum's men in Awadh. Moulvi was a Sunni who belonged to the family of affluent armymen. After getting his traditional Islamic education, Moulvi got his training in warfare as well. Unlike the Begum's war cohorts, Ahmadullah accrued experience from England, Russia and the Middle East, and had good command over English.[13] It was therefore difficult for the Begum to ignore his presence in the crisis when the ball started rolling in her favour.

Moulvi came to Chowlakhi Kothi to meet the queen on 22 August, paying her due respect and courtesy. He was extremely cautious but agreed to the proposal of Begum. She appointed him in-charge of 'Operation Muharram'. Ahmadullah accepted the responsibility but with a grain of salt. He would not take any order from Mammu Khan. On his return, Shah called a meeting in his place at Taron Wali Kothi, which was attended by his war

---

[12]Ibid. 146.

[13]Kumari, Rashmi, *Maulavi Ahmad Ullah Shah and Great Revolt of 1857*, Manjari Srivastava (trans.), National Book Trust, 2016.

cohort Raja Durg Jai Singh and his followers, his risaldars and the in-charges of his regiments. The Begum's proposal of Operation Muharram was passed.

The following day, on 24 August, Raja Durg Jai Sigh heavily shelled the Residency from the western side, incurring fresh panic among the incumbents. The native soldiers, however, gave time to the Europeans to surrender before storming the Residency. There were more than 500 women and children locked inside and more than a hundred injured who had no other choice but to pray to God to save them from their predicament. The incumbents were not prepared to surrender and rather preferred to accept their ill-fated destiny. The memory of Satichaura still haunted them.

On 6 September, Operation Muharram reached its pinnacle after the Chinhat-famed Syed Barkat Ahmad came to lead the army of 8,000-strong infantry, 500-strong cavalry and a team of skilled Pasis. Syed Barkat Ahmad had seen success once again after Chinhat. The day could have been the last day of the war had he not refrained himself from committing a brutal crusade. Around six in the morning, a mine explosion breached a portion of the northern wall and the troop led by Barkat Ahmad entered the Residency. Barkat asked them to surrender and waited till dusk. When the inhabitants ended up trapped and endured deep mental anguish on the brink of meeting an inevitable end, Syed Barkat Ahmad called back his army. It was beyond his ethics to take up arms against defenceless people.[14]

---

[14]Taqui, Roshan, *Lucknow 1857: The Two Wars at Lucknow—The Dusk of an Era*, New Royal Book Co., 2001, p. 146. We have also seen counterstatements that the native combatants failed to break the wall but placed tall ladders to cross the barrier. They were successfully shot down by guards from the inside, resulting in heavy casualties. See Wilson, Thomas Fourness, *The Defence of Lucknow: A Diary by a Staff Officer*, Smith, Elder and Company, 1858.

It was not until 23 September 1857 that the rebellion first heard the cracking of gunfire on the other side of Lucknow, and two days later, the first rescue operation led by Sir Henry Havelock as chief commander and Sir James Outram broke all barriers and entered the Residency by nightfall.[15]

The most trusted name in the British army of India, Sir James Outram, was called from England after he returned from the Anglo-Persian War. Sir Outram, who was by then knighted, was summoned by Lord Canning with a brief but significant annotation, 'Write to Sir James Outram that I wish him to return to India immediately. We want all our best men here.'[16] On his joining, he was asked to proceed to Lucknow without delay. James Outram left Calcutta on 25 August and marched towards Awadh. Lucknow was his old place and the turning point of his career and future of the Raj. Sir Outram was made the chief commissioner of Lucknow on 11 September, the post he had left 15 months ago. A combined British force of 3,000 army men under General Havelock and James Outram crossed the mile-long pontoon bridge over river Ganga on 19 September under the cover of Colonel Vincent Eyre's heavy guns, entering the territory of Awadh.

On the evening of 22 September, amidst torrential rains and thunderstorm, the British force captured Alambagh Palace. Set amidst a beautiful garden fortified by high walls some five miles away from Lucknow, it was an ideal place for the army to reside. Alambagh Palace was a country-house, which was built by Wajid Ali Shah for his first wife Alam Ara Begum. It rained incessantly outside and the army decided to halt at the palace.

---

[15]Brock, William, *A Biographical Sketch of Sir Henry Havelock, K.C.B.*, Oxford University, 1858, p. 223.
[16]Forrest, George William, *Sepoy Generals: Wellington to Roberts*, Cambridge University Press, 2011, p. 290.

A day after the British force reached Unnao, the news came to the Begum. She was busy reading the letters written by her subjects. Even in her busy schedule, Hazrat Mahal made it a point to read the host of daily mail received from her subjects carefully. The mail carried more pieces of information than the reports brought to her by her informers. Hazrat Mahal called her advisors, rajas and the regiment heads for an emergency meeting at Chowlakhi Kothi. In the meeting, all their rage turned on the incumbents locked inside the Residency. Many of her confidantes advised her to crush the incumbents inside the Residency and evacuate the premises before the rescue army arrived. The idea did not excite her as she was not in favour of shedding the blood of innocent people. However, the progress of the army needed to be stopped before they entered the city unchallenged. Raja Jai Lal was asked to proceed to Alambagh and prevent the British force from moving forward.

Although the rebels outnumbered the British combatants four to one, it was the lack of a unified and concerted attack that prevented them from flanking the last post of the Residency. Yet, the British force under Sir Outram, Sir Havelock and Brigadier General James Neill encountered a tough battle in Alambagh on 23 September 1857.[17] The casualties were heavy and the colonial force lost 196 lives; out of the 2,000 men, 535 soldiers left the field wounded on that eventful day.[18] Brigadier General Neill, who captured the city of Kanpur, was beheaded. Havelock's son too was injured in a fierce encounter.[19] The soldiers were exhausted as they had been fighting incessant battles for months. Havelock himself was almost worn out in the mêlée at Kanpur. Nevertheless, the

---

[17]Malleson, G.B., *The Indian Mutiny of 1857*, Rupa Publications, 2016, p. 238.
[18]Ibid. 245.
[19]Edwardes, Michael, *A Season in Hell: The Defence of the Lucknow Residency*, Taplinger Publishing, 1973, p. 217.

ravage of cholera incapacitated more than 240 people!

When Hazrat Begum was trying to find consolation at the end of a stormy day, a messenger from Delhi came to meet her, only to add further despair. On 14 September 1857, after a four-month-long siege, Delhi fell into the hands of the British. On 17 September, when the titular king of India, Bahadur Shah Zafar, left the Red Fort to avoid further bloodshed, there was panic in the city. Finally, he was taken into custody on 20 September by Major William Hodson from his hideout at Humayun tomb, some six miles away from Delhi. He was brought back to Delhi as a prisoner. His sons were shot dead by Major Hodson and their decapitated heads were shown to the old king placed on a platter. The barbarity shook Hazrat Mahal deeply. She was losing her steam.

The battle of Alambagh failed to hold the spirit of the native combatants. Despite significant catastrophe, the British soldiers finally overwhelmed the native barricade and marched into the city and entered the Residency.

Although Havelock and Outram fought their way through to the Residency, they could not release the detained civilians; rather, they got trapped and remained besieged in the Residency. The first relief of Lucknow virtually failed at the cost of several lives, the only consolation being recapturing of Chatter Manzil, Farhat Bakhsh palace and Alambagh from the clutches of the mutineers.[20] Supply lines were cut off and the air inside was laden with the agony of wounded defenders.

The catastrophe was equally appalling on the other side, as more than 5,000 rebels had been either killed or wounded in encounters.[21] This finds a mention in Outram's diary, 'We are now regularly besieged again, with no chance of getting out with

---

[20]Malleson, G.B., *The Indian Mutiny of 1857*, Rupa Publications, 2016, p. 245.

[21]Mukherjee, Rudrangshu, *Awadh in Revolt 1857–1858: A Study of Popular Resistance*, Orient Blackswan, 2002, p. 91.

500 women and children, besides wounded.'[22] The inclusion of the army men in the Residency only added hungry mouths.

A large number of native fighters streamed in from different parts of Awadh to lend hands in the battle. At times, it became difficult for the Regent Queen to provide them with their wages and ration. Raja Jai Lal had to struggle hard to wrench funds from the affluent landlords. Gold and silver ornaments from the Begum's depository were liquidated to pay the troops.[23] One morning, while Hazrat Mahal was taking daily notes in her room, she was informed by the guard that a troop of Abyssinian women, 25 to 30 in number, was urging to meet her. These women had been engaged as a special force by her husband and disbanded after Awadh was annexed. Since then, the women had been unemployed, living in wretched conditions at Moosabagh. Hazrat Mahal ordered for them to be enlisted on a payroll and deployed at strategic locations in a bid to call for full-scale guerrilla warfare against the angrez. Additionally, a group of 16 Sikh soldiers changed camps and swore allegiance to the Begum. The Sikhs promised to bring over all the other Sikhs working for the British force into their fold if they were allowed to retain their arms and looted wealth. The Gwalior Contingent, which revolted against Maharaja Schindia's British appeasement, also swore allegiance to Hazrat Mahal.

As the siege of Delhi was cleared off, rebels swarmed into Lucknow in response to the appeal of Begum Hazrat Mahal in the name of *khuda* (god). The soldiers, who fought for Bahadur Shah in Delhi, turned to the second seat of power. An infantry regiment of 300 sepoys, called Jahangiri, joined the Begum from

---

[22]Outram, James, *My Dairy of Mutiny*. See Taqui, Roshan, *Lucknow 1857: The Two Wars at Lucknow—The Dusk of an Era*, New Royal Book Co., 2001, p. 161.
[23]Rizvi, S.A.A. and M.L. Bhargava, *Freedom Struggle in Uttar Pradesh*, Volume 1, Uttar Pradesh Publications Bureau, 1957, p. 172.

Delhi. The sepoys were proficient bridge makers and, within no time, erected a boat bridge over Gomti near Farhat Bakhsh Palace. The regiment was posted in Alambagh to defend fresh entry. By November, Begum was joined by another 200 soldiers who were proficient snappers and miners. Eight cannons had also arrived from Delhi.[24]

Outram had to pay heavily for his miscalculation. The first relief of Lucknow was no relief. The incumbents of the Residency were still under siege. The arrival of Outram and Havelock in Lucknow in no way could dampen the spirit of the native sepoys. Instead, the combatants intensified their effort to expel the white raiders en masse. Outram, who had come to relieve the besieged, was captured like a mouse caught in a trap. Chatter Manzil was stormed by Raja Jai Lal, slaying 15 English sentries.

The first relief was a draw, if not a loss to the British. The Begum knew well that this would not continue for long. With the restoration of British power in Kanpur and Delhi, the Governor General was likely to concentrate all his strength in Lucknow. Hazrat Mahal had to prepare to withstand yet another assault very soon. She had never been *pardanashin* (veiled) and traversed the territory of Awadh extensively, talking personally to the talukdars to bring them into her fold. She was prepared to waive their taxes for five years, if needed, to lure them.[25] The landed gentries were mostly fence-sitters, and after the failure of Havelock and Outram's army, many of them switched sides and owed their allegiance to the Begum. The talukdars paid her loyalty or *nazranaa* (token) of their allegiance. Hazrat Mahal almost single-handedly collected

---

[24]Taqui, Roshan, *Lucknow 1857: The Two Wars at Lucknow—The Dusk of an Era*, New Royal Book Co., 2001, p. 185.

[25]Rizvi, S.A.A. and M.L. Bhargava, *Freedom Struggle in Uttar Pradesh*, Volume 3, Uttar Pradesh Publications Bureau, 1957, p. 232.

₹5 lakh and rallied 180,000 soldiers to fight the battle.[26]

However, bad news was in the offing for the Begum. Jung Bahadur, the prime minister and the de facto ruler of Nepal, joined hands with the British after much negotiation. He was allured with a portion of the northern territory of Awadh adjoining his kingdom of Nepal. The Begum had mistaken Jung Bahadur as her trusted ally in the war. She had not thought of Bahadur's long-cherished dream to usurp the sub-Himalayan territory of Awadh. He had allegedly hinted about his ambition to her many times, but the Begum had failed to interpret the meaning of his words.

Hazrat Mahal was in a crisis and Miftah-ud-daulah, the custodian of the royal treasury, reported that the treasure was running dry. The Begum levied war tax upon the wealthy classes and members of royal families who had made a significant fortune during the heydays of the empire. The war tax levied on the rich varied from ₹500–20,000. The response among the latter was mixed. Many of the royal members, like Nawab Taj Mahal, the widow of Nasir-ud-din Haidar, refused to pay. In contrast, others clamoured against forceful extortion of money; blame was apparently pointed squarely at Mammu Khan. There were also exceptions like Niger Mahal. She joined Hazrat Mahal in her cause and donated generously from her coffers.

The peril of the incumbents in the Residency went on till November 1857 when a second relief was attempted by the British with Lieutenant General Sir Colin Campbell at its helm. Outram was firm in his belief that re-establishment of the British rule would remain a dream till the capital of Awadh remained in the

[26]Santha, K.S., *Begums of Awadh*, Bharati Prakashan, Varanasi, 1980, p. 237. See also Qureshi, H.A. (trans.), *Qaiser-ut-Tawarikh of Kamal-ud-din Haidar*, Volume II, New Royal Book Co., 2008, p. 238.

hands of rebels.[27] Symbolically, Lucknow emerged as the only seat of rebels after the relief of Delhi and the imprisonment of Bahadur Shah Zafar. The rebel forces swelled to more than 180,000 but still lacked a unified leadership to organize them to fight unitedly.[28] On the other hand, Campbell was left with 5,000 soldiers at best.[29] A Scottish Army general, who was in England after his retirement, he had been summoned to India at the behest of Lord Palmerston when he was 65 years old. Campbell arrived in Calcutta in August and was given charge for the second relief of Lucknow, which his younger predecessors had miserably failed in doing.

On 10 November, heading an army of 4,500 soldiers and fortified with 49 years of impeccable war experience, Campbell reached Alambagh.

When he arrived at Alambagh on 12 November, he had a total force of 4,500 men and 42 guns.[30] By 14 November, his strength with reinforcements rose to 5,000 men. Sir Campbell made extensive use of semaphore in maintaining communication with Outram in the Residency.

Learning from the mistakes of the British army in the first relief, Campbell carefully avoided the tortuous lanes following Charbagh Bridge and won over Dilkusha Park, rebels at La Martiniere College and finally Secundrabagh, which was surrounded by strong masonry walls. British artillery guns faced a tough battle at Secundrabagh before the native army was routed and Secundrabagh captured.

---

[27]Outram's telegram to General Lord Canning, 17 September 1857. See also Mukherjee, Rudrangshu, *Awadh in Revolt, 1857–1858: A Study of Popular Resistance*, Orient Blackswan, 2002, p. 90.

[28]Mukherjee, Rudrangshu, *Awadh in Revolt 1857–1858: A Study of Popular Resistance*, Orient Blackswan, 2002, p. 94.

[29]Malleson, G.B., *The Indian Mutiny of 1857*, Rupa Publications, 2016, p. 318.

[30]Amin, Major Agha Humayun, 'Sir Colin Campbell's Final Relief and Evacuation of Lucknow Residency Garrison-November 1857', *Defence Journal*, Vol. 3, No. 10, 2000.

The British force marched to its next destination at Shah Najaf on the road to the Residency and faced hitherto the toughest resistance. Shah Najaf was the mausoleum of Ghazi-ud-din Haidar and his wives, built by the king himself. By the time the Imambara came under British control, it was dark and Campbell decided to take a break. Campbell's last resistance was at Moti Mahal. The British troops stormed Moti Mahal on the morning of 17 November 1857, captured some adjacent houses and brought them under control. After repeated efforts, the defenders—led by Havelock and Outram—and the relievers—led by Campbell–joined hands.

The British triumph over Lucknow was a watershed moment in India's history of freedom struggle, which re-established the British rule once again in India. The second relief of Lucknow produced 24 Victoria Cross winners on 16 November 1857, the largest number won in a single day.[31]

The evacuation started on 20 November 1857. Lucknow was as calm like never before. The natives were watching the subsequent move of the English rescuers patiently. At midnight of 22 November, finally a long column of European soldiers and civilians came out of the Residency with nearly a thousand injured people. James Outram made a chain of his Indian servants serving in the Residency, tied their hands and made them walk in front of the column as a security shield for the Europeans against native attacks. The angrez, amidst a dreadful crisis, made no mistake to carry with them the treasures looted from the former King's palace. Twenty-three camels and 18 elephants were loaded with the King's jewellery, gold and silver worth ₹80 lakh and cash worth ₹23 lakh. The loot was safely escorted to Kanpur.[32]

---

[31]Malleson, G.B., *The Indian Mutiny of 1857*, Rupa Publications, 2016, pp. 332–3.

[32]Taylor, P.J.O, *A Star Shall Fall: India: 1857*, Collins, UK, 1995, p. 336; Taqui, Roshan, *Lucknow 1857: The Two Wars at Lucknow—The Dusk of an Era*, New Royal Book Co., 2001, p. 199.

It took four days to shift the non-combatants from the Residency to Dilkusha Park. On the morning of 24 November, Henry Havelock, who was down with dysentery in his camp for the past four days, breathed his last in the arms of his eldest son. The British column left Dilkusha Park for Alambagh, carrying with them the dead body of Sir Henry Havelock. He was interred just outside the Alambagh fort with full military honour. Thus ended the battle and Campbell succeeded in saving his countrymen in India at the cost of 536 lives.[33]

It was a new day for Lucknow on 23 November. The Awadh army gave a gun salute of 101 gun fires, announcing victory. Hazrat Mahal had turned her debacle into an opportunity. What her in-laws could not do, she had done it. The angrez were driven out and Lucknow was free from the British! The last European in the city dumped their belongings and set fire to them before deserting their places. An errie silence prevailed over the Residency. Chatter Manzil, Moti Mahal, Kursheed Manzil, Farhat Bakhsh Palace, Qadam Rasool—all were deserted by the British and came under the possession of the Begum's army. The people of Lucknow rejoiced the victory brought in by the Begum. The unwarranted Europeans were all driven out. Nevertheless, complacency had no place in the Regent Queen's mind. She would not end her struggle till the last angrez in the kingdom of Awadh was driven out and Sultan-e-Alam Wajid Ali Shah regained his lost glory.

Without wasting time, the Begum called a meeting of her military council on 23 November and expressed her desire to include army commanders of Delhi in her council, against the

[33]Amin, Major Agha Humayun, 'Sir Colin Campbell's Final Relief and Evacuation of Lucknow Residency Garrison-November 1857', *Defence Journal*, Vol. 3, No. 10, May 2000.

wishes of some commanders in her regiment. There was a serious complaint from her artillery commanders that a large quantity of bullets failed to go off during the vital crossfire. The Begum's men identified some unscrupulous workers in her ammunition factory who had adulterated cartridges with rice bran and saw dust just to make money. Mammu Khan's brother was apparently one of the five kingpins of the racket. The Begum hanged all of them to death.

Although Outram was waiting in the wings to recapture Lucknow, Campbell had to rush to secure the British possession of Kanpur. Tantia Tope, a personal adherent of Nana Sahib, routed the British-reoccupied Kanpur with the help of Gwalior Contingent and forced General Windham to retreat from the city. Sir Campbell rushed to Kanpur from Alambagh while the Europeans moved away to Allahabad and other safer places. Awadh was now virtually free from Europeans and Begum's dream was fulfilled. Furthermore, the victory of Tope added to her strength. But all was not well in Awadh. Dotted in the garden of Alambagh fort were 4,000 British army men parading to guard their last garrison under the indomitable general, Sir James Outram. The chief commissioner of Oudh was licking his wounds in a dark corner of the deserted fort of Alambagh, waiting for a favourable time to come.

With the departure of the angrez from Awadh, thousands of soldiers, officers and civilians poured into the territory of Awadh in search of greener pastures, and the Begum faced the challenge to feed all the mouths. Law and order of the city were put at risk and she had to impose more responsibility on the city *kotwal* (police authority) Ali Riza Khan. There was an acute shortage of funds and again the Begum had to struggle to make ends meet like a proficient wazir. The British deserted Awadh but discrete skirmishes went on in various pockets. Moreover, the British force was garnering support from outside to increase its strength for launching a second attack. On 29 November, news came to the Begum that the combined force of Gwalior Contingent and British army from Delhi under Major William Hodson was marching towards Lucknow and halted at Unnao to join Sir Colin Campbell. Hazrat Mahal was prepared to face her final destiny with an unflagging strength of mind and a vast regiment of combined native force.

With the fall of Delhi and Kanpur, Lucknow was swarming with fighting men. Talukdars were still on the field, under Man Singh—with 4,000–5,000 men—and Raja of Amethi—with 3,000 men and four guns. Hazrat Mahal expected that the British would come back shortly with further reinforcements to take over Lucknow. The soldiers in Alambagh were short of ration and no grain dealer or vegetable vendor came forward to continue the supply of ration. Outram's garrison of 4,000 soldiers was made practically inert. The anti-British sentiment was running high and people had a feeling that the British were on the losing side and not worthy of any help or respect.

fourteen

The Begum Fights the Last Battle

Hazrat Mahal used every bit of strength to confront a further fortified British army in the final battle of Lucknow, with one lakh native soldiers at her beck and call. She summoned her military council and ordered them to engage Bande Hasan and his gang of Pasis to lay mines at strategic locations in the city.[1] She sold her jewellery and valuables worth ₹5 lakh to erect bulwarks all around the town, engaging thousands of labourers who worked day and night. Trenches were dug around Kaiserbag and filled with water channelled out from the Gomti. Hazrat Mahal toiled from dawn to dusk and made her presence felt on all fronts—from providing food for her people to arranging funds to buy ammunition.

There were stumbling blocks everywhere. Begums of Kaiserbag ganged up against her for allegedly squandering the royal treasury. Valuables of the mahals who went to Calcutta with the King were sold to meet expenses.[2] Funds were needed to run the newly opened arms factory, which had cast four new cannons by indigenous methods. Moulvi Ahmadullah Shah was constantly plotting against

---

[1]Taqui, Roshan, *Lucknow 1857: The Two Wars at Lucknow—The Dusk of an Era*, New Royal Book Co., 2001, p. 207.

[2]Rizvi, S.A.A. and M.L. Bhargava, *Freedom Struggle in Uttar Pradesh*, Volume 2, Uttar Pradesh Publications Bureau, 1957, p. 268.

her and resisting the leadership of a matriarch in warfare. He garnered a section of talukdars who switched sides and became his followers. Mammu Khan seemed to be the Moulvi's arch-enemy as the latter could not accept a eunuch in the seat of the Dewan-e-Khas of the Regent Queen. Whispers were thick in the air that Daroga Mir Wajid Ali was conniving with the British and fanning rebellion in the jenana against Hazrat Mahal. Raja Man Singh of Mehdona estate in the district of Faizabad was maintaining his alliance with Outram. The Raja was the most powerful of the talukdars; he held the largest army of 7,000 native warriors and was paying the highest revenue, amounting to nearly ₹1.5 lakh a year. Many of the talukdars had invested in East India Company's securities and had nothing to gain from the war.[3] Moreover, the King in Calcutta, who was contemplating compromise with the British government to cut his days in the murky cell short, admonished the conduct of his wife for siding with the rebels and using his son to wage war against His Lordship.[4]

Meanwhile, Sir Colin Campbell was advancing from Kanpur to attack Lucknow. Jung Bahadur was also on the move to join the angrez. The strength of the rebels in Lucknow was swelling but could not dislocate the garrison of Outram at Alambagh, even by an inch. The native army was not prepared to go for direct attack against the British and commence a mopping-up action.

Hazrat Mahal was losing her patience. On 22 December, Hazrat Mahal called an urgent meeting of her military council and lent a piece of her mind. 'The whole army is in Lucknow, but it is without courage. Why does it not attack the Alumbagh?

---

[3]Taqui, Roshan, *Lucknow 1857: The Two Wars at Lucknow—The Dusk of an Era,* New Royal Book Co., 2001, p. 209.

[4]Letter issued by Cecil Beadon, Secretary to the Government of India, to Major C. Herbert, 26 September 1859. See *Accounts and Papers of the House of Commons*, Volume 46, Great Britain Parliament, London, 1862, p. 39.

Is it waiting for the English to be reinforced and Lucknow to be surrounded? How much longer am I to pay the sepoys for doing nothing? Answer now, and if fight you won't, I shall negotiate with the English to spare my life.'[5]

Time was running out and Hazrat Mahal and Moulvi Ahmadullah Shah emerged as parallel powers. Rumours were buzzing in the air that Moulvi was planning to take over the throne of Awadh. Division amongst the landed gentries was widening and the rift was becoming perceptible in the native army. Hazrat Mahal used her diplomatic finesse and invited Moulvi Ahmadullah through Mir Mehdi, the intelligence head of the council of the newly annointed Birjis Qadr.

The Moulvi had a second meeting with the Begum on 21 December at Chowlakhi Kothi, annotated with a precondition that Begum would not allow Mammu Khan and Wazir Sharaf-ud-Daulah to stay in the room. His undue stipulation was tolerated and Begum received him with warm greetings. Her face was unveiled. She had all respect and praise for him as a holy man. The ice melted and Moulvi pledged to fight for the cause, leaving aside personal enmity in the hour of crisis. Begum urged him to defend the border of Awadh and to check the entry of gurkhas under Jung Bahadur. The meeting ended in peace and the following day, Moulvi sent 12 of his regiments to stop the advance of gurkhas from the north near Gorakhpur. Raja Man Singh of Mehdona was bestowed with a Khilat,[6] which made him feel obliged to stay by the Regent Queen's side.

There was an old saying about Outram, 'A fox is a fool and a lion a coward by the side of Sir J. Outram.' When combined forces

---

[5]Mukherjee, Rudrangshu, *Awadh in Revolt 1857–1858: A Study of Popular Resistance*, Orient Blackswan, 2002, p. 103.

[6]*Khilat* is a loose, long-sleeved silk or cotton robe that was given to an individual by the king or queen as an honorific award.

of Moulvi and Begum pledged to fight till the end, Outram cast his lethal dice. The chief commissioner spread rumours through his stooges in the native army, resorting to forged letters in the name of Moulvi, that Hazrat Mahal and wazir Sharaf-ud-Daulah were playing tricks to stave him off from Lucknow into the remote borders, so that they could negotiate with Outram and give up Lucknow on terms favourable to them.

Outram's stratagem worked well and resulted in a fierce fight between the followers of the two groups on 7 January on the verge of Outram's final attack. The coalition built by Hazrat Mahal with Moulvi Ahmadullah Shah was ruined forever. The rebels streaming from Delhi were wayward and outrageous. Unlike the disciplined Awadh soldiers who were dedicated to their motherland, the outsiders coming from Delhi and Kanpur were riotous and had no one to command. At times, they turned out to be counterproductive to Begum's war strategy.

The confidence of the British suffered a breach when, on the morning of 14 January, Outram's camp at Alambagh was attacked by one of Hazrat Mahal's followers, a fanatic Hindu named Barke Das, alias Hanuman. Outram escaped narrowly with only a scratch from Hanuman's sword. Sir Colin Campbell was upset and advised his authority to leave aside Lucknow and subjugate other areas of the province. 'Subjugation of the province [Oudh] will follow the fall of Lucknow as surely the conquest of France would follow the capture of Paris,' he deemed.[7] Governor General Lord Canning was nervous by the alarm raised by one of the most trusted servants of the Empire and resorted to the path of reconciliation.

---

[7]Letter by F.H. Cooper to G.F. Edmonsdstone, 18 January 1858. See Taqui, Roshan, *Lucknow 1857: The Two Wars at Lucknow—The Dusk of an Era*, New Royal Book Co., 2001, p. 229.

On 24 January, when Hazrat Mahal was taking daily notes in her room, she was informed by the guard that an angrez sepoy had come to meet her. The white man had come from Alambagh with a proposal in his hand from Sir James Outram, who, on behalf of Lord Canning, had sent her a draft treaty to call off the battle, in lieu of which East India Company promised to grant her peaceful living in Lucknow at her palace and a pension amounting ₹1 lakh per annum. When the Begum read out the content of Outram's proposal before her close confidants, Raja Jai Lal was astonished and Mammu Khan irritated. The angrez were not only ruthless but also shameless. She would not fall into the trap and lose her claim to the throne. The Begum handed over the paper to Khan Ali Khan to throw away in the fire. Sir H.W. Russell, in his applausive words, complimented the Begum's subtle diplomatic finesse, 'She declined to tactically renounce the rights of her son by accepting a British pension. She was a better man than her husband and lord.'[8]

The last chance of reconciliation had failed and the East India Company found it crucial to strike an agreement with Jung Bahadur, the prime minister and de facto ruler of Nepal, to support them in the war. The Nepali gurkhas were competent shooters and excelled in close combat with traditional Khukri knives.

When Bahadur was asked by the British to lend a helping hand against the native force in Awadh, he demanded a refund of the revenue Nepal had lost since the British confiscated a portion of Nepalese territory following the Treaty of Sugauly in 1815. When the loss of revenue was determined, Bahadur asked for additional reparation from the Governor General. Lord Canning was left with no other option than to promise him to return Kailali, Kanchanpur, Banke and Bardia after the mutiny. Jung Bahadur

---

[8]Chitkara, M.G., *Women and Social Transformation*, APH Publishing, 2001, p. 403.

was apparently lured by the promise made by Lord Canning. The Begum was informed about the deal made by Kunwar Singh of Bihar, who was a wise man of 80 and a great supporter and admirer of the Begum. On his advice, the Begum made a counter offer promising Jung Bahadur to confer not only the revenue of Gorakhpur but also that of Azamgarh, Arrah, Chhapra and the province of Banaras if he was willing to join her.[9]

The Begum's proposal was rejected by Jung Bahadur, as he had already struck a deal with the British. Another source said that two spies in the disguise of Qalandar Fakir were sent by Hazrat Mahal to Jung Bahadur, carrying her proposal. On their way to Gorakhpur, where Bahadur was temporarily stationed, the spies were caught by British sleuths and sentenced to death. The source believed that Begum's proposal did not reach Jung Bahadur.[10]

The war preparation was in the final stage. The Begum was however at a disadvantage, as many talukdars had switched sides at the last moment. This was a spin-off of the growing influence of Moulvi Ahmadullah Shah. It was difficult for the Begum to determine who was Moulvi's inveterate enemy—the angrez or the Begum herself. Brushing aside all cynicisms, she called for a meeting of the royal military council at Chowlakhi durbar on 23 February 1858. But Begum was not happy to see that many talukdars were missing in attendance. Moulvi Ahmadullah's invisible hand had inflicted conspicuous damage. Hazrat Mahal finalized her war strategy and the distribution of her force. She divided her army into four divisions under four *salars* (army chiefs). The Delhi force was under Muzaffar Jahan; the Maghribi or western force under the command of Raja Jai Lal; the Battalion of Najeeb under

---

[9]Rizvi, S.A.A., and M.L. Bhargava, *Freedom Struggle in Uttar Pradesh*, Volume 2, Uttar Pradesh Publications Bureau, 1957, p. 268.

[10]Taqui, Roshan, *Lucknow 1857: The Two Wars at Lucknow—The Dusk of an Era*, New Royal Book Co., 2001, p. 230–31.

Hisam-ud-daula; and finally, the artillery force under Bahadur Ali. Hazrat Mahal finally announced that she would lead the army at Alambagh front, keeping the minor king Birjis Qadr behind her seat.[11] This was an unusual happenstance in the royal court of Awadh.

Significantly, the founder of the Nishapur dynasty, Burhan-ul-Mulk, was a great warrior and fought on behalf of Mughal emperor against the Persian marauder, Nadir Shah. Burhan-ul-Mulk's nephew and his successor Safdar Jung was a militant person who was the vanguard of the Mughal Empire against Ahmad Shah Abdali, the Afghan warrior-king in 1748. Safdar Jung's son Shuja-ud-daula fought the momentous Battle of Buxar, in a consortium with the Mughal Emperor and Nawab of Bengal. Shuja-ud-daula suffered a crushing defeat, which coerced him to surrender before the British force. Since then, traditionally, the Nishapur dynasty of Awadh preferred to remain happy-go-lucky, often giving up part of their territory to buy peace. The nawabs and kings resorted to peaceful cohabitation with the enemies instead of fighting battle, only to add further to territorial expansion or quelling insurgencies.

Wajid Ali Shah was no exception; he was not particularly interested in ruling the country. Hazrat Mahal was the first amongst begums of Muslim dynasties in India who had shown indomitable courage to remove her veil and look into the eyes of her enemies. To embolden the spirit of her people against the mighty British army, Hazrat Mahal picked up the sword to lead the army of one lakh native soldiers in the battlefield. Sir W.H. Russell, the war correspondent for *The Times of London,* who was in Lucknow at that time, wrote in his eyewitness account acknowledging Hazrat Mahal's gallantry: 'This Begum exhibits great energy and ability.

---

[11]Ibid. 240.

She has excited all Oude to take up the interests of her son and the chiefs have sworn to be faithful to him... The Begum declares undying war against us.'[12] The same journalist was critical of the former King who was in captivity in Calcutta as a 'sensualist', 'half-idiotic' who 'has neither consented to his deposition nor taken one farthing of the annuity which the Company settled on him, nor has he given the least ground for believing that he has participated in the mutiny and rebellion'.[13] The statement reveals that the English had realized that the former King of Oudh could not be linked to the upheaval in Lucknow and in all respects, the insurgency can be attributed to Begum Hazrat Mahal only. Karl Marx, who was keeping a close watch on the eventualities of the war in his late 30s, acknowledged that 'Hazrat Mahal, Begum of Oudh, during the national liberation uprising of 1857–59 in India headed the rebels'.[14]

Meanwhile, Raja Balkishan, who had been serving as finance minister in the court of Awadh since the time of Wajid Ali, passed away due to a severe heart attack. Bad luck continued to haunt the Begum as six successive attempts to dislodge Outram's garrison from Alambagh failed miserably from the end of November 1857 to February 1858. On 25 February, the Begum mounted an elephant and led the native soldiers in one of the several attempts to win over Alambagh. She was desperate to get her kingdom back and if she had to learn to fight to do so, so be it. Sayada Begum wrote to Sultan-e-Alam from Lucknow, saying, 'Hazrat Mahal showed such courage that the enemy was terrified. She has

---

[12]Russell, William Howard, *My Diary in India: In the Year 1858–9,* Volume II, Routledge, Warne and Routledge, London, 1860, pp. 274–5.

[13]Ibid. 226.

[14]Marx, Karl and Friedrich Engels, *The First Indian War of Independence 1857–1859*, Foreign Languages Publishing House, 1960, p. 242.

brought the name to the Sultan Alam.'[15] Begum Sarfras wrote to Akhtar Mahal in Calcutta: 'I did not know Hazrat was such a brave lady. Seated on an elephant, she led her troops against the English without any fear.'[16] The English garrison was attacked by a force led by Moulvi Ahmadullah Shah and by Raja Man Singh from another side, but rebel forces failed to dislodge the British. Kamal-ud-din Haidar, a minister in Awadh court, blamed the army as indecisive and indiscipline.[17]

On 1 March, huge columns of British soldiers, under the command of Sir Colin Campbell, marched down from Kanpur and reached Sir Outram's garrison at Alambagh. The strength of the British army, which brought the final relief to the besieged troops in the Residency, was not strong enough to quell the rebellion in Lucknow. Therefore, Lord Canning summoned British troops afresh from England, Burma, Ceylon and Persia and even the troops that had been on a sea expedition to China.

The final destination of the British soldiers was Kaiserbag, the Regent Queen's abode, and Campbell had chalked out his strategy accordingly. The British General had three pawns to play—Sir James Outram, Brigadier Thomas Franks and Jung Bahadur. Sir Campbell remained the supreme commander of the battle. The largest congregation of a British force under Sir Colin Campbell and Sir James Outram started its journey from Alambagh at the crack of dawn on 2 March and captured Dilkusha Bag. The Begum was upset at the death of Wajid Ali Khan Resaldar, Jahangir Khan and Captain Umrao Singh in the battlefield of Dilkusha. For that day, the British force remained stationed at Dilkusha Kothi.

---

[15]Jain, Simmi, *Encyclopaedia of Indian Women through the Ages: Period of Freedom Struggle*, Kalpaz Publications, 2003, p. 20.
[16]Ibid. 20.
[17]Qureshi, H.A. (trans.), *Qaiser-ut-Tawarikh of Kamal-ud-din Haidar*, Volume II, New Royal Book Co., 2008, pp. 245, 258.

Colonel Robert Napier, Campbell's trusted chief engineer, suggested that a wing of the British army should operate north of Gomti to outflank the defences of Lucknow. Napier proved himself a game-changer. He recommended that Lucknow should be attacked from the east because the approach to Kaiserbag was shorter from there and the positions were better known. The weakest part of the native defence was on the north and Campbell should take that advantage, Napier suggested.[18] Campbell accepted his suggestion and gave Outram the command of the northern force. Campbell had enough soldiers in hand to create two wings. He decided to send all his guns to the north, so that Outram could place artillery points at the northern bank of Gomti. It would be easier for Sir Outram to continue heavy firing to the south, which was otherwise difficult to approach. Colonel Robert Napier took only two days to construct two pontoon bridges over Gomti. He started the construction on 4 March and by the evening of the next day, a smooth passage for Outram and his garrison was ready.

Meanwhile, on 4 March, Brigadier Franks, who had been operating in eastern Awadh, joined Campbell's force at Dilkusha Bag with his troops and 3,000 Nepali gurkhas sent to him by Jung Bahadur as a token of appreciation. Thus, Colin Campbell was fortified with a total strength of 25,000 soldiers and 5,000 horsemen with the joining of Brigadier Franks.

From Dilkusha Bag, Sir Campbell and Outram got separated. On 5 March, Campbell and Brigadier Franks moved west towards Kaiserbag while Outram marched towards the north. On 6 March, before dawn, Outram crossed Gomti and moved north till he reached Faizabad Road. From there, he reached Machhi Bhawan on his way to Kaiserbag.

[18]Malleson, George Bruce, and John Kaye, *Kaye's and Malleson's History of the Indian Mutiny of 1857–8*, Volume 4, W.H. Allen & Co., 1889, p. 256.

On his way, Colin and Franks ran over the mutineers gathered at La Martiniere College. Meanwhile, Outram placed his batteries on the opposite bank of Gomti and heavily shelled on La Martiniere. The native army contested for two days before they gave up on 9 March. A thousand native sepoys sacrificed their lives. The army moved towards Begum Kothi, the last palace before Kaiserbag. Before approaching Begum Kothi, Colin Campbell re-stormed Secundrabagh—the place where he faced the toughest challenge during the final relief of Lucknow. The army also occupied Kadam Rasul and Shah Najaf on their way and both places were found abandoned.

Misfortune seemed to follow the Begum. Raja Man Singh knuckled under and gave in to the British. From his Shahgunj Fort, Man Singh expressed his regret through a personal letter to Outram for supporting the natives and called for a truce. During the first relief of Lucknow, the raja contested against Havelock and Outram, but his vacillating role raised doubts in the Begum's mind. Being the holder of one of the largest taluks, he was often wooed by both camps. But, he carefully avoided his commitment to either side. Even while fighting with the sepoys six months earlier, Man Singh continued inconclusive correspondences with the British. He apparently waited only to see which way the wind was blowing. Had the rebels been victorious, he would have most likely tried his best to prove his loyalty to the Begum. The raja was asked to deposit ₹3 lakh as nazrana to the Begum, four months of pay to the rebels, 15 guns and mark his presence with the rebel army as the cost of his betrayal. Man Singh was agreeable to all the terms of the sepoys, except the last one.[19] Hazrat Mahal confiscated his property out of sheer vengeance and the sepoys besieged him

[19]Mukherjee, Rudrangshu, *A Begum & a Rani: Hazrat Mahal and Lakshmi Bai in 1857*, Penguin Allen Lane, 2021, p. 43.

in the fort of Shahgunj. Therefore, it became necessary for him to seek British help.[20] Similarly, the estate of Rustam Sah of Dera in Sultanpur was confiscated by order from Hazrat Mahal for siding with the British. Similar treatment was meted out to the talukdars who had shown loyalty to the British and allowed their estates to get plundered by the rebel army.[21]

Mammu Khan, the ever-loyal commentator of the Begum, apparently brought the news that Major William Hodson, who had killed the Mughal princes, was proceeding to Lucknow along with Sir Campbell from the southeastern corner. Mammu's words seemed to have ignited the fire of vengeance in the Regent Queen. She ordered her eunuch to prepare her war elephant. She would not have liked to miss the chance of leading her army against Major Hodson and take revenge. The Begum announced a death sentence for Hodson and Campbell, and declared awards for the slayers of the British generals.[22]

It was 11 March 1858, an eventful day when Sir Colin Campbell and the battalion under Brigadier Franks pounded the sepoy garrison of 5,000 rebel soldiers at Begum Kothi by heavy shelling throughout the day. Campbell's strategy of bifurcating the army worked exceptionally well and helped him win the battle of Begum Kothi. Outram constantly gave support to Campbell by firing and pouring shells from the opposite bank of Gomti. The Kothi was captured after a tough fight and 800 dead bodies of

---

[20]Mukherjee, Rudrangshu, *Awadh in Revolt 1857–1858: A Study of Popular Resistance*, Orient Blackswan, 2002, p. 118.

[21]Mukherjee, Rudrangshu, *A Begum & a Rani: Hazrat Mahal and Lakshmi Bai in 1857*, Penguin Allen Lane, 2021, p. 43.

[22]Taqui, Roshan, *Lucknow 1857: The Two Wars at Lucknow—The Dusk of an Era*, New Royal Book Co., 2001, p. 255.

the native sepoys were counted inside.[23] The corpses were rolled into a ditch nearby. On the same day, Major William Hodson, the slayer of the last Mughal princes, was paid his dues when a lethal splinter pierced his chest. His last words were, 'I hope I have done my duties.'[24]

On that day, 11 March 1858, the British strength was further reinforced when the Nepali gurkha contingent, under the leadership of Jung Bahadur, joined the British army. Jung Bahadur was given a guard of honour amidst the fluttering Union Jacks and melodious tune of the bagpipers of 93rd Highlanders.

The British would not have succeeded had it not been abetted by the combined forces of the gurkhas and the Sikhs. The Nepalese gurkha contingent, led by Jung Bahadur with 9,000 army men and 2,870 horses, was slowly making their way to Lucknow from Gorakhpur via the Faizabad road.[25]

The following day, on 12 March, Campbell's army raided and captured Sibtainabad Imambara, the eternal resting place of Wajid Ali Shah's father, which was only a mile away from Campbell's final destination, Kaiserbag palace. By the evening of 12 March, all great edifices on the eastern side of Kaiserbag up to Sibtainabad Imambara were confiscated by Colin's army.

The army was stationed just a mile away from Kaiserbag—the abode of Begum Hazrat Mahal, their ultimate destination. Raja

---

[23]Thomas, Roy Digby, *Outram in India: The Morality of Empire*, Author House, 2007, p. 237; Watson, Bruce, *The Great Indian Mutiny: Colin Campbell and the Campaign at Lucknow*, Praeger Publishers, 1991, p. 89.

[24]Amin, Major Agha Humayun, 'Sir Colin Campbell's Final Relief and Evacuation of Lucknow Residency Garrison-November 1857', *Defence Journal*, Vol. 3, No. 10, May 2000.

[25]Malleson, George Bruce, and John Kaye, *Kaye's and Malleson's History of the Indian Mutiny of 1857–8*, Volume 4, W.H. Allen & Co., 1889, p. 271; Taqui, Roshan, *Lucknow 1857: The Two Wars at Lucknow—The Dusk of an Era*, New Royal Book Co., 2001, p. 253.

Jai Lal and his native army were there in full strength to defend the last bastion. For reasons best known to him, Sir Campbell halted at Sibtainabad Imambara till the morning of 14 March but continued shelling heavily on Kaiserbag from its eastern side. Outram reinforced the northern bank of Gomti opposite to Kaiserbag with heavy artillery, prepared to fire on Kaiserbag.

Finally on 15 March, Colin's army, led by Franks and Napier, made a forward march to Kaiserbag. Outram was instructed to move on to Lucknow and join Campbell at Kaiserbag. James Outram and his garrison arrived at Kaiserbag on 16 March, crossing Gomti by a bridge near Chakar Kothi or the king's racecourse. All roads led to Kaiserbag, the abode of Hazrat Mahal.

Sir Colin Campbell, a bona fide bachelor of 65 years, had been enjoying his retired life with a hefty annuity of £2,000 per annum from East India Company after 49 years of relentless military service. He was personally requested by Lord Palmerstone, the then leader of opposition in British Parliament, to take up the baton of India since Awadh, the prized possession of the century-old British colony, was at stake. For the first time since the initiation of East India Company on Indian soil, the British realized that the sun was setting on the British Empire. James Outram made it clear in a letter to Governor General by saying, 'The moral effect of abandoning Lucknow will be very serious against us; the many well disposed chiefs in Oudh and Ruhelkhand, who are now watching the turn of affairs, would regard the loss of Lucknow as the forerunner of the end of our rule.'[26] Sir James was summoned to join the army in Lucknow by

[26]Inclosure 83 in No. 4, Further papers (No.4) p. 245, Papers Relating to Indian Mutiny. See Mukherjee, Rudrangshu, *Awadh in Revolt 1857–1858: A Study of Popular Resistance*, Orient Blackswan, 2002, p. 90.

British Parliament. Never in the British colonial history of India was Britain so proactive to recover their losses as they were in Awadh. A veiled Mussalman wife of a conservative native king, a mere woman of unknown heritage in her mid-30s, had shaken the British Indian Empire to its foundation and rolled the heads of colonial heavyweights.

Successive triumphs over Indian states since the Battle of Buxar had goaded the British military generals into the belief that the British on Indian soil were invincible, that they had the perpetual authority over the omnipotent native kings. Confiscation of the kingdom in Awadh was a bloodless exercise as the monarch Wajid Ali Shah preferred to relinquish his turban than to take up arms. The offer of the landed gentries to build a consortium of armed forces and fight against the British was found immoral by the King, which is why it was turned down abruptly. Lucknow had once put down the sword after a staggering defeat in the Battle of Buxar nearly a century back. Now, Wajid Ali Shah was rather looked down upon by the angrez as someone who would rather send his crown for display at the Crystal Palace exhibition of London than suffer the weight of the crown on his head. But the British made a mistake in underestimating Hazrat Mahal. They were not the one to be reproached alone. Hazrat Mahal was after all none other than one of the innumerable courtesans in the King's harem. She grew up in the house of Lucknow courtesans and made her way into the royal harem. Nevertheless, she broke away from her husband after she gave birth to her only child. She was labelled as inauspicious and ostracized in the jenanas after the King went into self-exile, and was left with her only support, Mammu Khan.

Yet, destiny had ordained for her an audacious existence. In 1857, the Begum came out from her shell at the behest of her most trusted feudal head Raja Jai Lal to teach a lesson to the 'till-then-all-conquering' East India Company. Heterogeneous elements from the territory of Awadh and the province of Bengal had already united and were on the verge of expelling the white interlopers. Unprecedented in the history of India, not less than one lakh native sepoys and volunteers rallied behind Hazrat Mahal, ready to sacrifice their lives for the sake of their motherland.

Hazrat Mahal was the sole power-centre of Awadh and had a bewitching influence over native soldiers and war volunteers numbering over a lakh. Awadh was becoming increasingly centralized with the advent of the Queen, and the role of feudal lords was trivialized. Though Mammu Khan and Raja Jai Lal remained rivals to each other, both thwarted the talukdars who challenged the authority of the Queen when Sultan-e-Alam was alive. The question was also asked by the begums of the King's jenanas. Moulvi Ahmadullah Shah refused to accept the leadership of a woman who was a nautch-girl in her past. Covetous talukdars frequently resorted to treasonous conspiracy against the Regent Queen.

The clarion call of British Parliament that 'we want all our best men here' (in Lucknow) only echoed their crumbling confidence before the grit of an unyielding woman. The British generals had taken no chance and summoned their best regiments. No battle fought by the army of East India Company hitherto had such a congregation of army-men with a single-point agenda—to hound the Begum and sentence her to death. The Governor General of East India Company summoned the ablest regiments of armed forces to move down to Lucknow from all corners of the country. The net effect was a congregation of 57,840 foot soldiers, 11,677 horsemen and 132 guns being contributed by Sir Colin Campbell, Sir James Outram, Brigadier Thomas Franks and Jung Bahadur from Nepal.[27] In the history of East India Company, the

[27]Taqui, Roshan, *Lucknow 1857: The Two Wars at Lucknow—The Dusk of an Era*, New Royal Book Co., 2001, p. 242.

magnificence of the British army on the Indian soil was largest. All roads were leading to Chowlakhi Kothi, the abode of the Regent Queen of Awadh.

When the combined British force reached the boundaries of Sibtainabad Imambara on 13 March, close to a mile from the Chowlakhi Kothi, Begum Hazrat Mahal was found restless, moving to and fro in the durbar room with a sombre face. She was keeping herself abreast of the situation from Mammu Khan, Daroga Mir Wajid Ali, Raja Jai Lal and a few other lieutenants in her kothi. The Begum was determined to fight till her last breath. Her only request to the courtiers was to remove Birjis Qadr to a safer place. Hazrat Mahal was warned by Mammu Khan and Jai Lal that the British were planning to besiege the palace, which would make it challenging to retaliate with her inside. Instead, it would be prudent for her to leave Kaiserbag and fight against the British from a safer place. The begums residing in the jenanas of Begum Kothi, Moti Mahal, Khursheed Manzil and Kaiserbag had been already shifted to safer places. More than 35 women were detained at Begum Kothi by Brigadier Frank's regiment and their fate could not be traced. Yet, Hazrat Mahal refused to accept an inglorious exit and was determined to face the challenge head-on. She would have undoubtedly preferred to see her son in safer custody but would not have hesitated even to sacrifice him for the sake of his motherland. She was destined to be a crusader in the war of independence. Unlike Jan-e-Alam, she remained resolute in her determination to not leave Lucknow till her last breath. Had Jung Bahadur been convinced to join the Begum and had the vacillating Man Singh not changed sides again, one wonders if things might have been different.

The night of 14 March was dreadful. Lucknow had never witnessed such a ferocious battle where savagery and chauvinism coalesced. Kaiserbag was smeared with the blood of more than

2,000 martyrs. About 9,000 Nepalese gurkhas had wreaked havoc. The sepoys fought till the last drop of blood was bled to save their Regent Queen. Mammu Khan, her closest confidant during hard times, requested the Begum to leave Kaiserbag, taking Birjis along. Finally, in the wee hours of 16 March 1858, Begum Hazrat Mahal, with a few of her belongings and ornaments, crept out the doors of Chowlakhi Kothi of Kaiserbag with her only son and faded into the darkness.

fifteen

The Chauvinist and the Loyalist

In the wee hours of 16 March 1858, the Begum left Chowlakhi Kothi with her son, glancing through the pillars of Kaiserbag once and forever. She left Lucknow just as the former King had exactly two years earlier. Circled by a band of Abyssinian women guards, she came out from the western gate of Kaiserbag with four vaults full of *ashrafis* (royal gold coins). The Begum and Birjis entered a palanquin, and Mammu Khan was riding a horse. Mir Mehdi, Ahmad Hussain, Hakim Hasan Raza, Miftah-ud-daulah, Qasim Ali Khan and Sharaf-ud-Daulah were on foot. She reached the house of Sharaf-ud-Daulah, stayed there for the night and then moved for 3 miles to the palace of Daulat Khana in Husainabad. Sharaf-ud-Daulah, Miftah-ud-daulah, Qasim Ali Khan and Mammu Khan moved with her.

Like her husband, the Begum too had options. James Outram's offer of truce was still open and the Begum could have retained her title and palace and enjoyed an allowance of ₹1 lakh per annum. She could have lived peacefully in Lucknow for the rest of her life. Outram's endeavour to restore peace continued till the last day of battle, enticing the Begum with alluring offers that could perhaps have provided comfort to her for the rest of her life. But unlike the former King, Begum Hazrat Mahal was neither an ambassador of culture nor a veiled member of the jenana who lived only for her husband. The uncompromising Begum would settle for nothing short of complete freedom for the entire country. Rather, she spurned the offer with disdain.

Mammu had informed that the army of Outram and Colin had taken possession of Kaiserbag and resorted to rampant looting. Meanwhile, a messenger named Naeem came and met the Begum at Daulat Khana with a letter from Outram. For the last time, the chief commissioner requested the Begum to cease the battle and surrender, in lieu of which she would be paid an allowance and peaceful living at Lucknow. Notwithstanding the peril she was facing in exile, the Begum rejected the offer. The messenger rode away, making the Begum suddenly conscious that her hideout was no longer secure and was rather exposed to the British spies. In the late afternoon, on the same day, as the sun was setting on the horizon, the Begum left the place. She was hoping to come back soon with a mightier army to combat the enemy.

From Daulat Khana, the Begum moved to a safer custody at Ghulam Raza Khan's house, where she stayed till late evening. In the darkness of night, the Begum once again started her journey, this time to Mahmudabad, the domain of Raja Nawab Ali Khan, one of the most powerful talukdars to take the lead in the war.

As soon as the Begum deserted Kaiserbag, the British soldiers ran amok and rampantly plundered the palace, only leaving behind such items as marble statues, furniture, massive jade bowls that the soldiers found difficult to move. Even *The Times* famed journalist W.H. Russell confessed that he could not restrain his greed and grabbed a portrait of Wajid Ali Shah mounted on a wall and carried it off on his return to his country 'as a small bit of loot of very little value'.[1] Hazrat Mahal, anticipating the British vandalism,

---

[1]Russell, William Howard, *My Diary in India: In the Year 1858–9*, Volume I, Routledge, Warne and Routledge, London, 1860, p. 317.

took along with her as much of the royal jewellery and ornaments as she could. Nevertheless, it was not the loot that damaged the palace as much as the Britons' vicious attempt to demolish Wajid Ali's dream abode. Begum Hazrat Mahal's Chowlakhi Kothi was amongst one of the many ill-fated structures that were plundered at the hands of the British. The death sentence of the last dream of the King was written the day the secretary to the governor of India said, 'As to buildings in Lucknow, the only one that I think it might be well to level to the ground is the Kaiserbag as that is the palace where our chief enemies have resided during the rebellion.'[2] By the end of June 1858, the value of the plunder estimated by *The Times* was no less than 1.5 million pound sterling, indeed a prodigious sum in those days.[3]

The departure of the Begum from Lucknow was a clear indication to the British that they had finally gained their much sought-after victory. The final nail in the coffin of the rebels was driven in the grim battle, which took place at Musa Bagh on 19 March where the British army routed the 7,000 native sepoys. Sir Colin repented that he missed capturing any of the kingpins who led the rebellion at Musa Bagh. 'Sir Colin possibly fancied, he might be fortunate enough to catch the Begum, the Moulvie, or some other great leader,' ridiculed William Howards Russell.[4]

But the question remained as to why the British intelligence failed to spot the Begum and her people leaving Kaiserbag in a long convoy under the nose of Sir Campbell, Sir Outram, Brigadier Franks and Jung Bahadur. Was it not that James Outram wanted to do a favour to the Begum by keeping her

---

[2]Llewellyn-Jones, Rosie, *A Fatal Friendship: Nawabs, the British, and the City of Lucknow*, Oxford University Press, 1986, p. 194.

[3]Taylor, P.J.O., *A Star Shall Fall: India: 1857*, Collins, UK, 1995, p. 105.

[4]Russell, William Howard, *My Diary in India: In the Year 1858–9*, Volume I, Routledge, Warne and Routledge, London, 1860, p. 353.

out of sight of the rebels? The conditions of the begums in the King's jenana at Kaiserbag was pitiable, and falling back to Russell's diary, the plight could be ascertained: 'We found them (begums) all in one, large, low, dark and dirty room, without windows, on the ground floor.'[5] The plunder of Lucknow went on for a month, turning the city of gold and silver into ghastly ruins where vultures scavenged for corpses.

Hazrat Mahal decided to leave Mahmudabad and shift her base to Baundi. Her journey was well narrated by Kamal-ud-din Haider, a minister in Awadh court. On her way, she visited some of the powerful territories of Awadh to pool their support. She did not receive a warm welcome in all places and faced many acrid situations from the landlords who were changing their colours quickly. After their defeat in Musa Bagh, many of the rebel sepoys fled from Lucknow and joined the Begum en route. The exact date when the Begum reached Baundi is not known, however it appears from various records that her caravan reached Baundi in late April 1858.

The Begum crossed the river Gogra and shifted her base to the fort of Baundi in the district of Bahraich—an almost mythological, thickly forested area on the bank of holy river Sarayu. It was here the Begum endured her life's biggest challenge, which she fought almost single-handedly from May to December 1858. The fugitives from Musa Bagh joined her in few days and rallied behind her with an army of 6000 soldiers. A retinue of followers, attendants, begmats and mahlats, nobles and subjects joined her one by one. Kamal-ud-din Haidar informed that most of the talukdars and landlords continued paying their taxes to the Begum. The Begum was successful in racking up the embers in the heart of her myriad followers.

---

[5]Ibid. 357.

The dream of coming back was enlivening. In the decisive moment, the Begum was likely to have missed her closest lieutenant Raja Jai Lal who was busy fighting his last combat in Lucknow. The Begum was only left with Mammu Khan, her true trusted companion. Head-on confrontation with the enemy was not the choice of day as warned by Jai Lal. The Begum resorted to guerrilla warfare to harass the British from all the sides and to keep them in distress without respite. The British army was stronger in power and weaponries. They could only be defeated by resorting to every tactic in the Begum's arsenal. She had taken her new strategy to prepare her army for a secret battle.

British intelligence report had it that Nana Sahib, who was untraceable till March 1858, joined the Begum with his brother Bala Rao and was staying in the district of Bahraich close to Baundi. The Begum had built her territory in the trans-Gogra region. The whole of Gonda and Bahraich, where Begum was most active, remained outside the British gaze. Colin Campbell was concentrating more to consolidate his position in the south and central part of Awadh before taking up the northern part and therefore leaving the trans-Gogra region out from their immediate attention.[6]

Hazrat Mahal and Birjis Qadr were ensconced in the fort of Baundi, strongly supported by the rajas of Churda and Payagpur. The Raja of Baundi was the head of the Raikwar clan and was devoted to the cause of Begum Hazrat Mahal. Her fort was encircled by a force of 15,000 to 16,000 sepoys and followers at all times. There were 1,500 cavalries, 60 to 70 camel corps, 500 foot soldiers and 17 canons in a standalone army of which 13 were placed outside the fort.[7] Although a relic of her durbar at

[6]Chitkara, M.G., *Women and Social Transformation*, APH Publishing, 2001, p. 402.
[7]Forsyth to Edmonstone, 3 July 1858, for Department Secret Cons., 27 August 1858. See Mukherjee, Rudrangshu, *Awadh in Revolt 1857–1858: A Study of Popular Resistance*, Orient Blackswan, 2002, p. 126.

Chowlakhi Kothi, the Begum started holding her camp functional as the nerve centre of the last vestige of the rebel army. Mammu Khan became her minister-in-charge. She had, by then, been more avenging and ordered her followers to plunder the talukdars who were proved to be stooges of the people's enemy. Plans were chalked out to coordinate the massive movement of rebel forces from the northern side of the territory in September as more combatants were joining the Begum's army every day.

The blazing ember was still alive in her heart and the Begum aspired to strike back from her exile.[8] The period witnessed a series of sporadic outbreaks by the sepoys of talukdars and other feudal lords, all united under Begum Hazrat Mahal. The Begum's patriotic fervour inspired eminent revolutionaries of 1857, such as Nana Rao, Bala Rao, Moulvi Ahmadullah, Beni Madhab to fight back. The turbulence went unchallenged till the scorching heat of summer finally slackened.[9]

As time passed by, the British regiments steadily pressed down on the native combatants. The defeat in the battle of Shahjahanpur on 20 May challenged the supremacy of Moulvi Ahmadullah's leadership over the sepoys of Awadh. Despite unleashing a band of the best intelligence sleuths, the British could never succeed in capturing Moulvi alive and declared a bounty of 50,000 silver coins for anybody who'd bring his head. Nevertheless, the spiritual leader of Faizabad and the preacher of jehad—Moulvi Ahmadullah Shah, who was equally respected by the British raconteurs, was beheaded on 15 June 1858.[10] The Moulvi was treacherously killed

[8]Baundi is located at Bahraich district. See Hashia, Haseena, *Muslim Women in India since Independence: Feminine Perspectives*, Institute of Objective Studies, 1998, p. 42.

[9]Forbes, Archibald, *Colin Campbell, Lord Clyde*, BiblioBazaar, 2008, p. 198.

[10]Guha, Ranajit and Gayatri Chakravorty Spivak, *Selected Subaltern Studies*, Oxford University Press, 1988, p. 169.

by Jagannath Singh—a local raja of Shahjahanpur and his brother. They carried the severed head of Moulvi to the District Magistrate to collect the official reward.[11] Three days after the tragic death of Moulvi, news came to the Begum that Rani Lakshmi Bai of Jhansi was killed in a battle in Kotah-ki-Serai near Gwalior. Begum felt trepidation in her heart as the never-to-compromise Rani was nearly of her age and died the death of a true martyr for the cause of her motherland.

The British waited till the middle of October when the crackdown began under Lord Clyde (Sir Colin Campbell was by then promoted to Lord Clyde of Clydesdale). The British army stormed the rebels from the south and swept them to the north in Nepal where the army of Jung Bahadur was waiting in their wings. Steadily, the British force intensified in the northern territory of Awadh, bursting into action under Lord Clyde in the middle of October 1858, to mop up the last rebel of the state. The talukdari bastions started to dwindle, as the British crackdown was hard to challenge. More feudal lords surrendered before British supremacy.

Although the rebellion was quelled, 1858 marked the eclipse of the East India Company. An Act was passed in the British Parliament in August 1858 under which the government of the East India Company in India was terminated. The Company's possession in India was thenceforth vested on the Queen. A proclamation from Queen Victoria was read out by Lord Canning in a durbar in Allahabad on 1 November 1858 in the presence of high British civil and military officials and hardly any representative from the native Indians.

The proclamation was ingrained with offers of amnesty to incite the warmongers to change sides. Queen Victoria guaranteed

[11]Ibid. 169.

truthful compliance of all treaties and complete abeyance from territorial aggression. Most importantly, the proclamation promised clemency to all offenders except to those who had directly taken part in the murder of British subjects. The proclamation reminded Hazrat Mahal of Raja Jai Lal's caution—not to trust the words of the British. From the fort of Baundi, Hazrat Mahal challenged the proclamation and issued a counter proclamation in the name of his son Nawab Birjis Qadr. The counter proclamation urged the people of Awadh not to fall into the trap of the British, for it was an unfailing custom of the English never to forgive a fault, be it great or small. Had it been so, then why was the King, who had never been disloyal to the British, still languishing in the English jail, she argued. If the Queen of England denied territorial ambition, then why was Her Majesty not taking initiatives to restore the country to the people who deserved it?

Notwithstanding the Queen's proclamation, Lord Clyde was waiting in his wings for a winter campaign to crush the rebel troops congregated in the northern territory of Awadh and push them to the Nepal frontier where they would die of privation and diseases in the fever-infested terai forest. Meanwhile, Jung Bahadur who was still showing his allegiance to the British, was putting pressure on the Begum to surrender before Sir Robert Montgomery, the chief commissioner of Awadh after Outram, and to lead a peaceful life. The British strategy worked well. The raja of Amethi, Lal Madho Singh, who was one of the Begum's most loyal allies, surrendered before Montgomery and retained his possession.

Lord Clyde crossed the Gogra from Faizabad and entered Bahraich on 17 December 1858. Begum Hazrat Mahal was determined not to surrender to the British and left the fort of Baundi in December with some of her faithful followers and took refuge in the foothills of Himalaya.

Meanwhile, Nana had his base at Bahraich, with an army of 3,000 trained soldiers. When Lord Clyde entered Bahraich, Nana fled further to a place called Churda. When the British army chased him to Churda, he moved further north to Banke in Nepal. Nana offered his last resistance at Banke with his remaining soldiers before he fled further north, crossing the river Rapti and sought refuge in the jungle of Terai. Bala Rao fled to Tulsipur when chased by the army of Brigadier Hope Grant and finally disappeared into the jungles of Nepal.

By the end of 1858, Hazrat Mahal had lost most of her supporters. Rohila chief Khan Bahadur Khan and Mammu Khan were still by her side. The dying ember had not extinguished. She was still hopeful about reorganizing the native army far from her hideout inside the impenetrable forest of the sub-Himalaya. Finally, on 7 January 1859, on a frosty winter day, with enemies hounding her, Hazrat Mahal with her allies crossed the river Rapti to take refuge in the terai of Nepal. She was accompanied by Mammu Khan, Khan Bahadur Khan, Ganga Singh, Umrao Singh, Khan Ali Khan and others. Rana Beni Madhab joined the Begum on her way to Nepal. Although debatable, the number of followers remaining with the Begum was not less than 4,000.[12] Jung Bahadur returned to Nepal from Lucknow in March 1858 and continued to aid the British in mopping up the rebels who sought refuge in Nepalese terai. Being a trustworthy ally of the British government and knowing well the consequences that might result from it, Jung Bahadur took calculated risks of housing Begum Hazrat Mahal, Birjis Qadr, Nana Sahib and his brother Bala Rao as political émigrés in Nepal from time to

[12]Sen, Surendra Nath, *Eighteen Fifty-Seven-1857*, Ministry of Information and Broadcasting, New Delhi, 1957, p. 367.

time.[13] The British troops forced the rebels out of the Indian territory.

The Begum lived a nomadic life for a year in the dense jungle of terai. The dream of regaining the kingdom which her in-laws had nurtured for a century was fading fast. Her only ray of hope in the despair was her son Birjis Qadr, who was now a youth of 14. It was he who would take up the baton in the future.

From her exile, Hazrat Mahal came to know that Tantia Tope was hanged at Shivpuri on 18 April 1859. Tope was allegedly betrayed by his trusted friend Raja Man Singh of Narwar[14] who handed him over to the British in return for his life and protection of his family from his enemy. After parting ways with the Begum from Daulat Khana, Sharaf-ud-Daulah went to Dargah Hazrat Abbas, where Moulvi Ahmadullah had pitched his garrison of the native army. In a ghastly fight with the British, Sharaf-ud-Daulah was martyred. Rana Beni Madhab died while fighting the gurkhas in November. Nana Sahib disappeared in the jungle of Nepal and his fate was never known. Jung Bahadur reported that he succumbed to fever in the terai jungle of Dang district in Nepal in September 1859. However, there were different opinions that Jung Bahadur had arranged secret asylum for Nana Sahib and his associates for a massive sum of money. He spared Nana from prosecution because he was a Brahmin.[15] But the most dreadful news came to Hazrat Mahal while she was wandering in the jungles of terai. Raja Jai Lal Singh, her mentor and her most trusted commander-in-chief was hanged by the British in Lucknow in September 1859 from a

[13]Tyagi, Sushila, *Indo-Nepalese Relations: 1858–1914,* DK Publishing Company, 1974, p. 82.

[14]Not Raja Man Singh of Mehdona estate in the district of Faizabad. Narwar was an estate in Shivpuri, presently in Madhya Pradesh.

[15]Gupta, Pratul Chandra, *Nana Sahib and the Rising at Cawnpore,* Clarendon Press, Oxford, 1963, p. 176.

tamarind tree.[16] Miftah-ud-daulah was caught by the gurkhas and handed over to the British army. He was escorted to Faizabad where he was tried rigorously and tortured to write a letter to the Begum asking her to come back to Lucknow since the Queen of England had granted amnesty to all and agreed to give her a good pension if she desired to settle in Lucknow. As expected, the letter found no reply from the recipient. On a later date, Miftah-ud-daulah was released, but his properties were confiscated. He moved to Calcutta.[17]

But not all was dreary for the Begum. After an excruciating incarceration of 25 long months, Jan-e-Alam was set free from his prison in Calcutta.

Unlike the other days, 9 July 1859 carried a different meaning for the exiled King—it was a red-letter day for him. He had his lunch and his long evening prayer. It was not before half-past five, when he, bathed in the rays of the evening sun, walked out of his cell and upheld his oriental ethos—conveying thanks to the government for allowing him to join his family.

At last, he was released from his austere cell of Fort William after 25 long months of excruciating imprisonment. His liberation was announced by Colonel Cavanaugh and Major Herbert with much delight and courtesy. An open horse carriage, which was waiting at the Coolie Bazar gate since evening, drove him off to Metiyaburj. Major Herbert accompanied him while the retinue followed behind.[18] The news of his release was sent to London by the Indian government. Ali Naqi Khan was conditionally

[16] *Gazetteer of the Province of Oudh*, Oudh Government Press, 1877, p. 80.
[17] Qureshi, H.A. (trans.), *Qaiser-ut-Tawarikh of Kamal-ud-din Haidar,* Volume II, New Royal Book Co., 2008, pp. 140–1.
[18] *The Caledonian Mercury and Daily Express*, 6 September 1859, No. 21824.

released from imprisonment at the same time.[19]

In the backdrop of trials and tribulations, Wajid Ali had come to realize that his loyalty to the Crown had been baseless and futile. A twist of destiny had changed his path and taken him away from the lap of luxury and put him on the stage of austerity. He had no better option than to strike a favourable deal with the Governor General. The British force won the epic battle under Lord Clyde and released Lucknow from the clutches of the rebels. With the capture of Lucknow and defeat of the native army in March 1858, the British reinstated their position in India but with a change. Britain had realized that it was much too risky to leave the affairs of this prized possession to the care of a freewheeling mercantile body of men. The Empire of India was ushered in, the empress being Queen Victoria. On 1 November 1858, the famous proclamation in the queen's name was issued and the immediate sovereignty was transferred from the Company to the Crown. Lord Canning, the first viceroy of India under the British government, could have found no better opportunity to kill two birds with one stone—deal with the native rebels and their idol Wajid Ali Shah.

The 25-month-long rigorous incarceration had put to test the banished King and blotted his last hope of getting back his lost empire. He was thrown into stark misery, leaving behind several mouths to feed. Returning to Lucknow to see the eclipse of a century-old heritage would have been a pointless attempt. A crisis due to the depletion of funds was bound to besiege the

---

[19]Letter issued by the secretary to the Governor General of India to Major C. Hebert, 6 September 1859. See *Accounts and Papers of the House of Commons*, Volume 46, Great Britain Parliament, London, 1862, p. 37. The translated version of the letter from Wajid Ali Shah to Lord Canning, 5 October 1859 and Canning's reply on 17 October 1859, etc. See Azhar, Mirza Ali, *King Wajid Ali Shah of Awadh*, Volume 2, Royal Book Company, Karachi, 1982, p. 2.

King sooner or later. His followers, who had their own agenda, persuaded him to accept the British terms and live happily. His extraordinarily imaginative mind would indeed find a new home in Calcutta.

Of all the King's men, the King's emissaries in London met the most despairing end. Canning had taken a calculative risk by putting the banished King behind bars and spreading the rumour that Wajid Ali Shah had instigated the sepoys, and was reasonably responsible for the mutiny against the British government. He was, indeed, lucky. The effect was instantaneous. The British public had rebuffed Oudh's sentiment as the mutiny of 1857 broke out. The Governor General was able to invalidate the British sentiment that had been in favour of the former King. As it so happened, the mutiny was at its peak in April 1857 and Canning got a golden opportunity to accuse Wajid Ali Shah in Calcutta as an accomplice to the great misery caused to the British citizens living in India. The complete volte-face by the British public in England after the mutiny came as heaven-sent for Lord Canning. The all-powerful British government did not feel that it had any obligation to prove the King guilty or even to admit the petition filed by the King for justice.

The Oudh Commission, as a last resort, had submitted an appeal titled 'Petition from the Queen and Princes of Oude to Parliament', which was presented before the House of Lords by Lord Campbell on 6 August 1857. Digressing from the commission's fundamental claim of reinstating the confiscated kingdom, the Oudh royal family had spent more time proving the King's innocence in the recent mutinous outbreak.

The appeal was justified in the eyes of the law. Still, Lord Campbell had refrained from submitting the petition before the Lords for consideration, since the pleas of the royal family of Oudh were rejected on the flimsy ground that the word 'humble' had been omitted throughout.

The austerity of penury had struck the hapless emissaries in London. Funds had started dwindling since the last support of £4,783, which the King arranged to send in October 1856 while in prison, was almost exhausted. The appeal for a grant made to the directors of the East India Company had been rejected for obvious reasons. Soon, the royal family found itself spiralling towards debt, which further splintered them. The family vacated the 'inauspicious' Harley's house and a small country home was rented for the queen Mother. The retinue started to scatter. Finally, a sum of £7,156 came from Wajid Ali Shah in January 1858 and the entourage breathed a sigh of relief. Meanwhile, internal conflicts were brewing. The disheartened Queen Mother left London for Calcutta via Paris and wished to visit Mecca on her way.

The Queen Mother went to Paris where she breathed her last on 24 January 1858. A month later, Prince Mirza Sikandar Hasmat, Wajid Ali's brother, died in Paddington, London, on 25 February. His body was taken to Paris and laid beside his mother. Moulvi Masih-ud-deen eventually settled in Britain and married an English woman. Rose Brandon and his wife sailed off to New Zealand and spent the rest of their lives there. Major Bird stayed back in England. Heir Apparent Mirza Hamid Ali Bahadur sailed off from London to reach India via Marseilles and Alexandria. He would come to stay with his father in Metiyaburj.

Wajid Ali returned to Metiyaburj after 25 months. He stepped out of the horse-drawn carriage and walked into his riverside palace that he had rented from Maharaja of Burdwan. While in incarceration, Wajid Ali Shah had already made up his mind to settle in Metiyaburj and to start a new life after his release. He dreamt of building his 'kingdom' of passion in the style and spirit of Lucknow. But Wajid Ali was in penury, trying to meet the expenses of 140 members of the Oudh Commission staying in England for two years. Further, his courtiers, his begums and their attendants in Metiyaburj were more than 500 in number. The wealth that he had carried from Lucknow was dwindling fast. A twist of destiny had changed his path and taken him away from luxury to austerity. He was keen to come to a settlement with Lord Canning to make ends meet. He was ready to annul his claim to Awadh's throne in London in lieu of his monthly allowance of ₹1 lakh as promised by the government, which was to be paid retrospectively from the date of annexation.

At the outset, he begged pardon for the conduct of his wife Hazrat Mahal for taking sides of the rebels and for using his son Birjis Qadr[20]—a complete volte-face of his earlier soliloquy in *Husn-e-Akhtari,* where he hailed his wife and son for their relentless struggle for freedom. Moulvi Masih-ud-deen pleaded before Parliament that Waid Ali had been coerced to accept the truce under pressure in detention and hence the settlement should be ignored. On hearing this at Metiyaburj, Wajid Ali was annoyed with his emissary and announced that he had consented willingly in a sound state of mind only after his release; and saying so, he immediately dismissed Moulvi Masih-ud-deen from his position of power.

Lord Canning was waiting for this opportunity. The appeasing words of Wajid Ali Shah in his letter to Canning, dated 5 October 1859, greased Lord Canning's ego. The Viceroy accepted his proposal but decided to disburse his allowance from the prospective date of his release from custody. The delay in accepting the British proposal in time and losing a large portion of revenue

---

[20]Letter issued by Cecil Beadon, Secretary to the Government of India, to Major C. Herbert, 26 September 1859. See *Accounts and Papers of the House of Commons,* Volume 46, Great Britain Parliament, London, 1862, p. 39.

from Awadh during the period of mutiny from which the stipend was supposed to be paid was enough ground for the government to curtail his allowance from a retrospective date. Moreover, the government bargained to drop the annual allowance of ₹3 lakh, which was the promise for the upkeep of his retinue. Wajid Ali also accorded a personal right to retain his title as long as he would live; consequently, the title would cease and the pecuniary allowances would not continue on their present scale after his death. Also, it was officially intimated that separate provisions would be made for the King's wife Hazrat Mahal and his son Birjis Qadr, in the event of their surrender. Lord Canning instructed to release his monthly stipend from 9 July onwards, the day when Wajid Ali was released from imprisonment.[21]

After his release, Wajid Ali purchased a large riverside estate at Metiyaburj in the south-eastern fringe of Calcutta, with the permission of the British government.[22] Step by step, he started to construct a city that would one day be an extension of Nawabi Lucknow. He spent lavishly out of his income of ₹1 lakh per month and continued to live in an extravagant fashion. A beautiful township sprawled in Metiyaburj that had often been described as Chota Lucknow. His own memories of Lucknow were fading fast. The Hooghly had entwined his heart with deep and enduring bonds, which appeared to him familial and destined to grow further. Gomti had been replaced by Hooghly in his life. Calcutta was new to him and so was the culture of Bengal. The King's Chota Lucknow was the apple of his eye—his pride and ego and his success in shaking the arrogance of the snooty bhadraloks of Calcutta. With the giant shadow of Anglicism looming large on the horizon of Calcutta, Wajid Ali Shah's fervour of traditionalism

[21]Ibid. 41.

[22]Ibid.

remained unwavering and steadfast. He continued the tradition of holding durbars in Mughal style in a remote corner of Calcutta. Metiyaburj had replaced Lucknow in his heart.

When he was lavishly spending from his income to recreate Lucknow in Metiyaburj, Begum Hazrat Mahal was wandering in the thick jungle of the sub-Himalayan terai with a handful of 1,500 faithful followers, 'half-armed, half-fed and without artillery', relentlessly hounded by the British soldiers.[23]

[23]Taylor, P.J.O., *A Companion to the 'Indian Mutiny' of 1857*, Oxford University Press, 1996, p. 44.

sixteen

The King's Days in 'Chota Laknau'

Wajid Ali Shah was busy in recreating Lucknow on the banks of Hooghly. He did not hesitate to spend copious amounts of his wealth to keep the glitter of Lucknow alive on the banks of Hooghly. There were same bustling activities, the same language spoken, the same style of poetry, the same conversation, same wit, same cock-fighting and opium. Even the shopkeepers and moneylenders were from Lucknow. People could freely stroll around the parks and zoo; often a lucky one would catch a glimpse of a charming lady peeping from the windows or would hear a recital of an eloquent shayari. The *tazia* of Muharram was never so enchanting as it was there.

Moulana Abdul Halim Sharar was only nine years old when he came to live in Metiyaburj in 1869, a decade after Wajid Ali had started building up Chota Laknau. His narrative is a testimony of the former king's opulent life in Metiyaburj. The King started living in his original mansion called Sultan Khana, which he, in all likelihood, bought from the maharaja of Burdwan. He had apparently also bought two more mansions that he later named as Asad Manzil and Murassa Manzil. Sharar was inclined to believe that all three mansions were gifted to him by the British government. Nonetheless, Sharar's assumption could not be justified by contemporary records.[1]

The former King, who was in an innovative spree, constructed several beautiful mansions planned to house not only his entourage but also his innumerable womenfolk. Beautiful gardens and lawns surrounded the edifices. Several beautiful houses were also built surrounding Sultan Khana for his wives.

Gardens and lawns were maintained and designed in various geometrical shapes to give them an aesthetic appeal. Beautiful shops were set up for about a mile along the road for his employees to earn their livelihood. A guardhouse was built near the gate of Sultan Khana where drums were beaten to mark the hours. The flag of Awadh was flying high in the sky of Metiyaburj. The symbol of the Nawabs was a pair of fish, which all the houses in Metiyaburj bore. In his kingdom of Metiyaburj in Calcutta, the splendour of Wajid Ali's flag was fluttering higher than the Union Jack.

The King's memories of Lucknow were fading fast. The opulence of Lucknow could not match the novelty of Metiyaburj. However, peace prevailed in the enforced solitude. The throne was lost and with it also his commitments. The story could have ended there, but it did not. Prudence urged him to accept his destiny. And a new life unfolded. He spent his time in the menagerie and in writing poetry. The King's menagerie in Metiyaburj was a paradise for the people of Calcutta as well as for the visitors and painters who came from abroad. His evenings were enchanting, spent in the company of notable singers and dancing girls. No wonder the King lived a blissful life with his family of 39 mahals, 100 begums, 31 sons and 25 daughters.[2]

The King was reckless in spending to fulfil his desire and his monthly allowance often fell short. He had to squander the

---

[1]Sharar, Maulana Abdul Halim, *Lucknow: The Last Phase of an Oriental Culture*, Oxford University Press, 1994, p. 17.

[2]'A Retired King', *The New York Times*, 11 November 1874.

reserve that he had brought from Lucknow. *Husn-e-Akhtari* reveals that 5,000 people were living in Metiyaburj before the mutiny, and with more emigrants coming in from Lucknow in search of greener pastures, the population swelled to 40,000 after the mutiny.[3] And it was the responsibility of the banished King to provide for them all.

One would wonder how opulent the King was during his heydays. While vacating the Residency after the final rescue, the Europeans carried with them 23 camels and 18 elephants loaded with the King's jewellery, gold and silver worth ₹80 lakh in addition to ₹23 lakh in cash.[4] By the end of June 1858, the value of the plunder of Kaiserbag after Hazrat Mahal left was estimated by *The Times* as no less than 1.5 million pound sterling.[5] While leaving Lucknow in a wretched condition, Hazrat Mahal carried with her immense wealth, which helped her to support 10,000 supporters in exile. The wealth brought by the former King to Calcutta provided not only his retinue but also his emissaries staying lavishly in London for two years. The deposed King maintained his opulence almost in the same fashion as he did in Lucknow. Nonetheless, Lord Dalhousie's sarcasm that with the annexation of Oudh, his gracious queen had 1.3 million pounds more revenue than she had before was not hyperbole.[6]

---

[3]Sharar, Maulana Abdul Halim, *Lucknow: The Last Phase of an Oriental Culture,* Oxford University Press, 1994, p. 74.

[4]Taylor, P.J.O. *A Star Shall Fall: India: 1857,* Collins, UK, 1995, p. 336; Taqui, Roshan, *Lucknow 1857: The Two Wars at Lucknow—The Dusk of an Era,* New Royal Book Co., 2001, p. 199.

[5]Taylor, P.J.O., *A Star Shall Fall: India: 1857,* Collins, UK, 1995, p. 105.

[6]Baird, J.G.A., *Private Letters of the Marquess of Dalhousie,* William Blackwood and Sons, 1910, p. 369; Dalhousie's letter dated 8 February 1856.

seventeen

Begum's Life in Exile

Before leaving Kathmandu for India on 10 December 1857, Jung Bahadur, the de facto ruler of Nepal, gave a speech to his people to explain the reason for his desperate venture. He cited three motives behind his mission. Firstly, he wanted to show that the gurkhas were prepared to shed blood for allies who treat them with respect and trust them. Secondly, being aware of the power and strength of the British, he would not try to ruffle their feathers and provoke them to turn against the gurkhas and annihilate them. And lastly, to form an alliance with the British by helping them restore their authority on Indian soil. If the war was won, the British would be obliged to return the terai areas which the Nepalese lost to the Company by the Treaty of Sugauli.[1] But what Jung Bahadur had purposely concealed was his apparent lust for the King's treasure in Lucknow.

Hazrat Mahal was ignorant about Jung Bahadur's agendas, otherwise she would not have tried to form an alliance with him. Jung Bahadur returned to Kathmandu triumphantly in March 1858, carrying with him several wagons of the King's treasure looted from Kaiserbag and a promise to get back the lost terai.

Almost 10 months after Jung Bahadur returned to his capital, Hazrat Mahal and her allies crossed the river Rapti and took refuge

[1]Tyagi, Sushila, *Indo-Nepalese Relations, 1858–1914*, DK Publishing Company, 1974, p. 80.

in the terai of Nepal. She traversed through the dense jungle, swamps and terrains around 150 miles and reached the mountains of Bhutwal. Jung Bahadur's 'faithfulness' to the British continued after his return to Kathmandu and on Canning's pressure, the gurkha chief appeared to be desperate to drive out the Indian fugitives from Himalayan foothills of his territory.

When Hazrat Mahal was wandering with her troop in the wilderness of Sunari, she came across a messenger of Jung Bahadur named Captain Niranjhan Manjhi who was carrying with him a letter written to Begum Hazrat Mahal, a week after she intruded the territory of Nepal. The letter was an explicit warning to the Begum asking her not to seek refuge in Nepal with her force, and that she should end her animosity with the British and make peace with them. The Begum must have appreciated that Jung Bahadur was treaty-bound to take the side of British and expel her from Nepal if she intruded his country without his consent. Mammu Khan came forward in her rescue and gave a haughty reply that the Begum would neither take any help from Jung Bahadur nor surrender to her arch-enemy.

The sum and substance of Jung Bahadur's intimidation might not be a true reflection of his heart. His mind was ripped into two. It would seem that he could not turn hostile to the British, nor could he afford to miss the chance of milking the opulent fugitives from Awadh. Begum Hazrat Mahal was a golden goose and it would be sheer stupidity to force her to leave his country. A letter, dated 1 February 1859 and bearing the signature of Birjis Qadr, reached Jung Bahadur; the tone of the letter was submissive. Qadr desired to meet him and unveil the real face of the British. Qadr wanted to continue his journey only to meet him. The Nepalese de facto leader softened his stand and allowed the Awadhi queen and her associates to move to Chitwan.

A letter written by Jung Bahadur on 23 February bears

testimony that the Nepalese chief commander was still in a dilemma. Bahadur had issued a final warning to the Begum to leave his country within 10 days from receipt of his letter or prepare to face death at the hands of the gurkhas. The Begum would not be given refuge even if she disarmed her people or offered to pay money for her shelter. Bahadur's general advisory to the war fugitives who had not taken part in the carnage of Europeans was to surrender before the British officer residing at Sagauli in response to the general amnesty declared by the Crown. They would be allowed to return to their houses in Awadh peacefully.

Meanwhile, Jung Bahadur's fidelity instilled confidence amongst the British that formed the base of the Anglo-Nepalese friendship that lasted for a century. But the swarming of rebels in the Nepal terai for safe refuge was becoming a matter of growing discontent to the Raj. Newly designated Viceroy Lord Canning was putting pressure on Jung Bahadur for his reluctance. But to maintain fidelity in the new friendship, the British refrained from intruding the Nepalese border to smoke out the rebels; instead, they repeatedly requested Jung Bahadur not to give asylum to the rebels in his country. The rebels were trying to organize an army in the deep jungle of terai and made vigorous attempts to entice Jung Bahadur to join them for a large sum of money. Begum Hazrat Mahal, Raja Ganga Dhar Rao and Bala Rao issued a communiqué to Bahadur, appealing him to join their cause for his benefit.[2]

Excesses committed by the gurkha brigade as well as the British army sharply swung public sympathy of the commoners in favour of the Begum and her associates. The fact was not unknown to Lord Canning and therefore, the Viceroy never attempted to hunt the rebels inside the territory of Nepal, nor did he put pressure on

---

[2]Letters from the rebels to Jung Bahadur and the latter's reply. See Tyagi, Sushila, *Indo-Nepalese Relations, 1858–1914*, DK Publishing Company, 1974, p. 80.

Bahadur to hand them over to him. The Viceroy only urged him to seal the border and turn down the rebels from seeking refuge in Nepal. Jung Bahadur, who was still jostling for power in his territory, was facing a dilemma. Bahadur once confessed before the Resident Surgeon in Nepal, Dr Henry Oldfield, that he was apprehensive that his troops might be reluctant to obey his order to expel the rebels by force. Bahadur's confession was exaggerated. Dr Oldfield revealed Jung Bahadur's interest in retaining the rebels in a letter written on 21 March 1859. 'I have strong ground to believe that the real motive of the trip was some business,' the surgeon said claiming that Bahadur had shortly visited the terai to supply victuals against heavy price.[3] He allegedly had an eye on the immense wealth being carried by the rebels from Awadh. Rumours had it that the fugitives had paid Jung Bahadur a lofty sum to buy peace.

Three months had passed since Hazrat Mahal had received the ultimatum from Jung Bahadur to leave his country. She had taken refuge at Naikot. It was a gruelling test of endurance for the Begum. She remained busy, nursing her ailing son Birjis Qadr who was down with severe bouts of unknown fever, which was endemic in that part of the country. She could not reply to Jung Bahadur's letter. Hazrat Mahal was in deep trouble. She had undertaken a terrifying journey from Sunari to Naikot to shift her base. Passing through the unknown ravines had been a dreadful experience and she had lost most of her cavalry, horses and camels in the unaccustomed hilly tracts. Hundreds of beasts of burden and horses had died, falling from heights. Many of her people had deserted her in favour of amnesty. The Begum was uncertain about her son's life. Birjis was getting treated using indigenous herbal medicines and his fate was left in the hands of Allah. After much coaxing, she replied hastily to Jung Bahadur, asking him

[3]Ibid.

for some time since the survival of her only son was in question. Finally, the Begum gave her reply stating precisely that she had no intention of surrendering before her arch-enemies, nor was she ready to leave Nepal.

It was not difficult for the British to decode the real Jung Bahadur under his military garb. A letter written by Major George Ramsay, the British Resident in Nepal to Cecil Beadon, secretary to the Government of India in the foreign department posted at Fort William on 13 June 1859, testifies the British outlook.[4] The letter specified that Jung Bahadur had expressed his desire to invite the Begum to Kathmandu where he, jointly with the Resident, would try to convince her to accept the amnesty being offered by the British government. The Resident was inclined to believe that Jung Bahadur was playing for both sides and refrained from sending a force against the Begum. The gurkha chief once had expressed his desire to give asylum to Hazrat Mahal and his son if need be. Bahadur gave an impression to Ramsay that the Begum was unbending in her decision and would resort to taking poison if forced. Whether out of conviction or for reasons of strategy, Jung Bahadur decided to opt for a U-turn, which also led the British to review their existing options once again.

In a communiqué with the English Resident, Jung Bahadur wanted to know what treatment the government would levy on the Begum, if she was made to surrender. On 19 August 1859, Jung Bahadur was assured by the Resident that, 'The Nepal Government will, however, bear in mind that there is no intention on the part of Governor-General to deny to the Begum an unmolested residence in India and a maintenance as soon as she shall have made submission,' and also 'Begum Hazrat Mahal will receive all

[4]Rizvi, S.A.A., and M.L. Bhargava, *Freedom Struggle in Uttar Pradesh*, Volume 2, Uttar Pradesh Publications Bureau, 1957, p. 610.

the consideration which is due to her as a woman and a member of a Royal House, political power she shall never have and she will do wisely to secure by prompt submission a generous treatment and an honourable position for the rest of life.'[5] The assurance sounded like empty promises to Jung Bahadur. The Begum could not be handed over to the British.

The memories of mutiny were fresh in their minds and the British would simply not give further chance to the Begum to organize an armed upsurge. The government would have no objection in allowing the Begum to stay in Nepal as long as Jung Bahadur would not facilitate her to take up arms. The stone-hard stubbornness of the Begum coerced the government to soften their stand and to maintain a placid equilibrium. The government informed her: '...to remain in Nepal in the position of a private individual under a written pledge that she shall hold no communication with the rebel leaders or with their troops, or with the people of Hindustan'.[6]

After much vacillation and a failed attempt, Jung Bahadur made up his mind and invited Begum Hazrat Mahal and his son to Kathmandu in September 1859 to give them a patient hearing. His first attempt to call the Begum ended up failing in May when acrid criticism in *Friend of India*[7] on 26 May badly hurt his confidence

---

[5]Foreign Department Political Consultations, No. 183-184, 19 August 1859. See Santha, K.S., *Begums of Awadh*, Bharati Prakashan, Varanasi, 1980, p. 248.

[6]Rizvi, S.A.A. and M.L. Bhargava, *Freedom Struggle in Uttar Pradesh*, Volume 2, Uttar Pradesh Publications Bureau, 1957, p. 611; Santha, K.S., *Begums of Awadh*, Bharati Prakashan, 1980, p. 247.

[7]*Friend of India* was one of the oldest newspapers of India that began publishing in the early nineteenth century from Serampore Press in today's Hooghly district of West Bengal every Thursday. By the second half of the 1800s, it had become a popular journal of Indian and world affairs. *Friend of India* later became a daily and adopted the title *The Statesman* and continues to be one of the leading newspapers even today.

and made him roll back his decision. Soon, he again became adamant about giving the Begum her due recognition.

Bahadur's decision of inviting the Begum was instantly informed to Lord Canning by Robert Ramsay. However, the Viceroy was reluctant to show any interest in Begum's asylum in Nepal as long as no allowance had to be given from his side. He considered her a war fugitive taking asylum outside India, and therefore not entitled to get any pension. Therefore, he was happy as long as the Begum or his son did not claim any compensation or allowance for their livelihood. However, he would consider paying her allowances if she surrendered to the Indian government and retired to Lucknow on his dictated terms.

Nevertheless, Hazrat Mahal was fully aware of the judicial enquiry being held in Lucknow under Chief Commissioner Charles Wingfield to prove her guilty of murdering European citizens in the mutiny, directly or indirectly. The British authority was sorting out the wheat from the chaff to fix charges on the Begum for 'murders' committed in the war situation, while conceding to the fact that she had personally prevented many atrocities, especially on women, withstanding the demand from her commanders. Yet, their attitude was hostile and retaliatory. Wingfield described her as 'a woman of savage disposition who delighted in the blood of Europeans and therefore little likely to have raised voice on the side of mercy in killing of Europeans'.[8] However, he admitted that he could not collect a single witness to testify the Begum's direct involvement in the carnage of Europeans.

Jung Bahadur shared an enigmatic relationship with the Begum, which was viewed by different authorities from different perspectives. It is indeed difficult to decipher the man behind his

---

[8]Rizvi, S.A.A. and M.L. Bhargava, *Freedom Struggle in Uttar Pradesh*, Volume 2, Uttar Pradesh Publications Bureau, 1957, p. 103.

dark goggles, which he habitually liked to wear. His conviction was neither trusted by the British nor was he believed by the rebels from India. Jung Bahadur Rana, who was by that time given the honorific title of 'Rana'—bestowed upon him by King Surendra—was convinced that the Begum's legitimate rights would be denied by the British, who would try her arbitrarily for 'murder' and make her suffer the consequences. Jung Bahadur's apprehension intensified when Cecil Beadon, the foreign secretary of the Government of India, directed the Resident of Nepal to produce before Jung Bahadur copies of letter written by Wajid Ali Shah to Lord Canning, where the former King had condemned the conduct of his wife against the British and declaimed any sympathy for her.

Beadon tried to frustrate Jung Bahadur, yet, the Rana's mind was completely made up about Hazrat Mahal. Considering the traditional amiability between the gurkhas and Awadhi kings, Jung Bahadur decided to not let Hazrat Mahal die an ignominious death since she deserved fair treatment, at least from him, in Nepal.

British authorities tried to prove that Rana's veracity was not all just black and white; there were also shades of grey. Both contemporary and succeeding English authorities firmly believe that Jung Bahadur was selective in bequeathing his benevolence to the Indian fugitives and measured them by the yardstick of immense wealth they had brought from India. Nineteenth-century English traveller and commentator Perceval Landon claimed that Jung Bahadur Rana favoured Hazrat Mahal and Nana Sahib in exchange for a huge sum of money. Rana bought their coffers at a meagre price and arranged for their settlement in Nepal. Nitpickers believe that Jung Bahadur spread a rumour that Nana Sahib had been killed by the gurkha army while arranging his hideouts in Nepal to escape the British. Similarly, Hazrat Mahal and her son received asylum in Kathmandu at a heavy price. Robert Ramsay once reported that a jeweller was summoned from Delhi by Jung Bahadur to make a valuation of the jewellery of Nana Sahib and the Begum.[9]

After 11 months of excruciating hardship in the thick terrains of sub-Himalayan terai, Begum Hazrat Mahal and Birjis Qadr entered Kathmandu on the evening of 8 February 1860, guarded by an army of gurkhas from Naikot. For the first time since she had crossed the border of Nepal, she came in full public gaze. A palatial house called Barf Bagh, belonging to former minister Bhimsen Thapa in the palace complex of Thapathali Durbar, was arranged and furnished by Jung Bahadur for her immediate possession.[10]

The Begum and his son were allowed to bring with them only 28 people, including eunuchs as bodyguards, attendants, cooks, palanquin bearers, water carriers and hookah bearers for the Begum.[11] Rana had posted Nepalese servants and guards at the queen's service. He sent his best hakims to check the health of Birjis Qadr who recovered from an unknown fever; he wanted to avoid being blamed if something went wrong with the young nawab. Jung Bahadur conferred to her a decent allowance of ₹400 per month.[12] But Hazrat had to pay dearly for Rana's 'generosity'. Little is known in history to ascertain whether Begum's residence at Barf Bagh was temporary or permanent. There are conjectures to confirm that she shifted from Barf Bagh to a new residence, which she had built on her own. Yet, the reason for such benevolence on the part of Jung Bahadur remained obscured and invited enough British wrath. Rana was conscious not to stir the imperial ego and, therefore,

---

[9]Rizvi, S.N.R., and S.Z.H. Jafri, *The Great Uprising of 1857: Commentaries, Studies and Documents*, Anamika Publishers, 2009, p. 104.

[10]Foreign Department Political Consultations, No. 243–255, 1860, Volume 13. See Santha, K.S., *Begums of Awadh*, Bharati Prakashan, Varanasi, 1980, p. 250.

[11]Ibid. 266.

[12]Foreign Department Political Consultations, No. 264, 1879.

allegedly made it clear that none of the Begum's associates, not even Mammu Khan, would be allowed to enter Kathmandu.

As the months passed, the Begum apparently became increasingly cynical about Mammu's allegiance towards her. The Begum was seemingly losing faith in her closest cohort, suspecting him to be working hand-in-glove with her enemy. She, therefore, allegedly dismissed Mammu Khan, who served her faithfully for 14 years for want of 'courage and devotion'. Mammu stayed back at Sunari with his fragmented army, still hoping to restore his image and to get a call from his mistress. He apparently started losing patience and decided to follow the Begum. On his way, according to Kamal-ud-din Haider, his path was blocked by Bam Bahadur, the brother of Jung Bahadur. Mammu Khan was captured and handed over to the British commanding officer. With Mammu's arrest, the last remnants of the native army disintegrated. Most of them went back to Awadh and surrendered in return for amnesty.

Mammu came back to Lucknow in handcuffs and passed through the doors of prison on 17 December 1859 at Farhat Bakhsh Palace, the place where he had dominated for years. His protracted argument to prove him a saviour of the whites, especially the women imprisoned in Kaiserbag and Taron Wali Kothi, from the hands of the rebels did not hold water. Mammu Khan was tried for a long period and was sentenced to be hanged. His appeal was heard by George Campbell, the judiciary commissioner who annulled his death sentences and ordered deportation to the Andamans. On his way to the Andamans, Mammu Khan allegedly escaped. He was again arrested and awarded life imprisonment. His reason of death in the Andamans remains obscure.[13]

Meanwhile, after helping the Begum and her son to settle down in Kathmandu, Jung Bahadur marched with his army to

[13]Qureshi, H.A. (trans.), *Qaiser-ut-Tawarikh of Kamal-ud-din Haidar,* Volume II, New Royal Book Co., 2008, pp. 135–6.

Surhi Khola to disperse the rebels. The gurkhas rounded up 23,000 insurgents and disarmed 11,000 sepoys. After hair-splitting trials, the sepoys who took part in the grisly killing of European citizens were chaffed out and deported to Lucknow under armed guards and the rest were set free.[14] Around 300 fugitives settled in the terai of Nepal, taking up agriculture to earn livelihood. Several others, after undergoing trials and tribulations, could get through the territory of Awadh and returned home.

The landscape of Lucknow had changed beyond recognition. British had set free the 'garden, granary and the queen province of India' from the tradition and ethos of the nawabi era, which enthralled the kingdom for the past 136 years. They had re-established their authority once again. Wajid Ali's favourite Kaiserbag was fragmented and bought by several opulent gentries and talukdars in piecemeal. Hazrat Mahal's habitat, her favourite Chowlakhi Kothi, which was purchased by the King for ₹4 lakh, was sold to one Nawab Wazir Mirza for ₹40,000. The epoch of nawabi Lucknow was whimpering, leading to its inevitable demise. On 8 July 1859, the British government in India officially declared that war had ended and peace was restored everywhere in the country.

Three years after her settlement in Kathmandu, one day, the Begum came to know from a piece of news published in *Calcutta Times* on 4 April 1863 that Her Majesty, the Queen of Britain had exonerated the names of Hazrat Mahal and her son from the list of offenders in Lucknow. All charges against the Begum had been withdrawn unconditionally, allowing her to return to India and live peacefully.

---

[14]Rizvi, S.N.R., and S.Z.H. Jafri, *The Great Uprising of 1857: Commentaries, Studies and Documents*, Anamika Publishers, 2009, p. 104.

The Begum was growing older. When she left Lucknow, she was only 38. Much water had flowed down the river since she came to Kathmandu nearly 17 years earlier. She had crossed her prime and now her hair was streaked with silver, with wisdom radiating from her gracious face. Her serpentine eyes had lost much of their earlier gleam. Yet, at her age, she continued to be progressive at heart and did not hide behind a veil. It is likely that Hazrat Mahal could well understand that her relentless struggle to make her motherland free from the coils of British oppression was a lost dream. She was practically a hostage in Rana's land. Destiny had meddled with her life, yet the desire of going back to Lucknow or Faizabad, her birthplace, apparently never stirred her emotions. Often she thought of renouncing the material world and going to Mecca. Nonetheless, her last ray of hope was her son.

Birjis had grown up to be an exuberant youth of 32 and she had painstakingly groomed him. Her son was far away from the enticements of the flamboyant court life and Hazrat Mahal was not keen to send him to his father. There was no dearth of endeavour from the Begum to impart the best education to his son in her penury. Birjis had married Mahtab Ara Begum in 1869 when he was 24 and the bride was 10 years older. She was the granddaughter of Bahadur Shah Zafar from his daughter's side. The family came to Lucknow to take part in the struggle and later took refuge in Nepal as followers of the Begum. It was Hazrat Mahal who had given her the name Mahtab Ara.

Birjis Qadar, as the Begum firmly believed, would pick up the baton from her hands one day to complete her unfinished duties. Seemingly, her last ardent desire in the twilight of her life was to meet Jan-e-Alam in Calcutta.

Kamal-ud-din Haider chronicled an incident when a British painter, who visited the Begum for a sitting, urged her to return to her place. She was told that the government would be honoured to accommodate her with a decent pension for her livelihood. However, she would not be allowed to have too many servants. The queen replied with sarcasm that if she was not permitted to spend on her servants, then what would she use her pension for.[15]

On 2 June 1877, after spending 17 years in Kathmandu, Birjis Qadr appealed to F. Henvey, the officiating British Resident of Nepal, through the Nepal Prime Minister Ranaudip Singh Kunwar, who had succeeded the throne following Jung Bahadur Rana's untimely death, urging to allow him to go to British India to arrange the marriages for his children. The appeal was forwarded to Thomas Henry Thornton, officiating secretary to the Government of India Foreign Department but was rejected outright. In an official communiqué, the British India government clearly instructed the Resident of Nepal that the Begum and his son would not be allowed to cross the boundary of India, even for matrimonial purpose. The secretary was of the opinion that since Birjis Qadr was not entitled to get an allowance for his support, he would live in penury at Lucknow and try to rouse the sentiment of the people. In such political uncertainty, the government was not prepared to take the risk. The British could not exorcise the ghost of 1857 from their minds.[16]

Underneath the garb of a glamorous warrior queen, Hazrat Mahal had a romantic heart that harboured poetry amidst ruthless tribulations of life. Her desolation and austerity had brought back all the fond memories of Muhammadi Khanum—the identity that she had long abandoned. Her poems bore the tradition and genre of the shayaris of Lucknow. The Begum had unending leisure to nurture her passion in exile.

---

[15]Santha, K.S., *Begums of Awadh*, Bharati Prakashan, Varanasi, 1980, p. 250.

[16]'1877, Political-A, October', Government of India, No. 359–362, http://tinyurl.com/38cn4swm. Accessed on 16 January 2024.

When Hazrat Mahal chose to pick up the mightier pen, leaving aside her sword, the British sighed with relief that the ghost of mutiny had perhaps been exorcised forever. The Begum was spending her days in self-inflicted desolation. She had refused the offer of amnesty and opted to live in penury in exile. Jung Bahadur Rana was kind enough to grant her a pension of only ₹400 a month, which was spent on her attendants and mostly for the upbringing of her only son. Renunciation was, however, no liberation from responsibility. Jung Bahadur died two years before the Begum, but the pension continued till her last day. Bahadur's successor Ranaudip Singh Kunwar was kind enough to pass it on to Birjis Qadr after the death of the Queen Mother. The Begum also had the remnants of *shahikhajana* (royal treasure) with her, which helped her make ends meet. Whether out of conviction or for reasons of strategy, Hazrat Mahal confined herself within the bounds of her mansion in Barf Bagh, concentrating on writing poetry.

Mellifluous eloquence began to pour forth from her pen and she could not contain her excitement and exuberance in her hermitage. She was extraordinarily graceful, often seen sitting in a remote corner with a manuscript on her lap. The transformation of a warrior to a poetess took place in a remote corner of Nepal. Her writings were personal and exclusive, merely restricted within the walls of her mansion. She had no intention to leave her indelible footprint on the culture of a foreign country.

When Hazrat Mahal was engrossed in writing poetry for her peace of mind, the eloquent flow of Urdu and Persian poetry in the alleyways of Metiyaburj was a truthful testimony of the archetypical Lucknowi culture being imbibed into the intellectual milieu of Calcutta. The beauty of masnavis, soz, ghazals, quasidas, rubais, salaams and marsiyas were springing forth from the pens of lyricists and poets. Credit goes to Wajid Ali Shah who brought with him from Lucknow a bevy of talented poets and composers. He himself was a prodigy of Persian and Urdu literature—a poet, a lyricist and a literary genius. He was a proficient composer in Urdu and Persian under the nom de plume of 'akhtar', meaning star. He was a prolific writer and had an incredible aptitude to dictate more than one poem simultaneously to different transcribers. The tradition of poetic hegemony continued in Metiyaburj.

eighteen

A Legacy Was Born

A queen who would rather have been a poet, an adored bride of a once-wealthy dynasty and a perfect match for a king who was revered down the ages for his literary talents, faded into oblivion. After spending the desolate life of a commoner for 19 long years and following a week-long fever and diarrhoea, Begum Hazrat Mahal breathed her last in a remote corner of Nepal on 7 April 1879 at a premature age of 59. Unlike her husband, the Begum lived in exile, refusing to compromise with the British. She was stubborn enough not to accept the royal pension and spent her life on a meagre allowance conferred by Jung Bahadur, which remained unchanged throughout her life. Nevertheless, till her last breath, Begum Hazrat Mahal strived to keep the torch of liberty burning.

The warrior queen of Awadh, who once fought the mighty British with an unprecedented army of one lakh combatants under her sole command, was buried in an ordinary coffin in a wretched corner of an unknown private graveyard, not worthy of the glory that the Nishapur dynasty of Awadh possessed. Charles Girdleson noted in his official communiqué, 'The Begum has been buried in a separate ground which the Prime Minister gave for the purpose after learning that the Mussalmans of Nepal, who are Sunnis, would not allow her body to rest in the graveyard, as she was

Shia.'[1] The funeral was attended by her son, her daughter-in-law, her attendants and a few representatives from the royal court of Nepal.

The Queen Mother Aliya Begum's resting place was in Paris and so was her son Sikandar Hasmat's. Begum Hazrat Mahal also was fated to lie in the earth of foreign soil. There was no funeral procession for her. The Begum of Awadh received an unceremonious departure. Yet, the Nepal prime minister was generous to allow Birjis Qadr and his family to continue staying at Barf Bagh mansion where his mother had lived for 19 years, with the same amount of pension. 'The Begum's allowance of ₹400 a month has, I hear, been continued to Birjis Kudr by the Durbar,' reported the British Resident in his communiqué.[2] Birjis Qadr decided to remain in Kathmandu with his family.

Monsoon looked spectacular to Wajid Ali from the banks of Hooghly at Metiyaburj. Nature remained bountiful in this part of the country and the lush green exuberance of Botanical Garden on the opposite bank added a fine touch to the surroundings. He loved to watch the downpour on the Hooghly from the windows of Sultan Khana while mellifluous lines of Persian verses poured forth from his pen.

Eight monsoons had passed in his life in Metiyaburj since the news of the Begum's demise in exile reached him. He came to know that at the end of her life, Begum Hazrat Mahal desired to meet him in Calcutta but the British government had rejected her last wish.[3]

---

[1]Foreign Department Political Consultations, No. 264, 1879. See Jain, Simmi, *Encyclopaedia of Indian Women through the Ages: Period of Freedom Struggle,* Kalpaz Publications, 2003, p. 22.

[2]Ibid. 21.

[3]Foreign Department Political Consultations, No. 360, October 1877. See Jain, Simmi, *Encyclopaedia of Indian Women through the Ages: Period of Freedom Struggle,* Kalpaz Publications, 2003, pp. 21–2.

The Oudh Mission in London had taken its toll on the lives of his mother and brother. Since then, ill luck continued to hound him. His son Muhammad Hamid Ali, the third son of Khas Mahal and his heir apparent, returned to him on 29 September 1859—little more than two months after the King came out from his incarceration. Most untimely, Hamid Ali died in 1874 when he was only 34. He was then buried in Sibtainabad Imambara. Following Hamid Ali's death, the King refrained from choosing his heir apparent, although it was not unknown to him that Birjis Qadr, his eldest living son, would have a legal hurdle to claim his throne after him.

As time passed, Wajid Ali Shah could perceive that his Chota Laknau was crumbling down bit by bit. The King was facing financial woes which upset him. A substantial sum from the King's monthly pension was deducted without his consent and distributed amongst his family members whom, previously, he used to pay on his own. The British made full use of their diabolical policy of divide and rule. The government constituted a commission to decide upon the distribution of a portion of the King's pension. The commission allotted ₹3,000 per month to his eldest son, ₹3,000 per month to his second son and ₹150 per month to his other sons in Metiyaburj who were over the age of 12. Some amount of money was also granted to his daughters and the begums living in Metiyaburj. After meeting all obligations, the balance of ₹70,000 was handed over to Wajid Ali per month. By the end of his life, there were perceptible signs of financial inconstancy. The jewels in his treasury, which he had been able to bring from Awadh at the time of his departure, were gradually being depleted. He would often be seen stealthily moving out of the palace in his carriage, without his attendants, only to halt in front of an edifice of a reputed jewel merchant in central Calcutta to exchange a fistful of jewels tied in a silk handkerchief for a bunch of paper notes![4]

Wajid Ali Shah's health was wearing out with time. He was suffering badly from arthritis and piles—his two old companions. He had had a massive heart attack when he was just 27 years of age and remained incapacitated for a long period. A progressive decline in his health had been perceptible to his immediate attendants for a couple of years. He had no faith in European doctors and relied only on indigenous medicines. He was apprehensive of being poisoned by the British agents and stooges. The threat of being poisoned was looming large as he could not get rid of the idea of an assassinator roaming about in his palace. He was apparently in constant dread of being poisoned by his chief wife, or his cohorts and relatives, or by the courtesans, or even by Ali Naqi Khan. His wazir, Munsarim-ud-Daulla, who was a stooge of the British agent Lt Col W.F. Prideaux, placed in Metiyaburj, was also a suspect.

The first blush of the dawn of 22 September 1887 on the eastern bank of Hooghly was ordinary. It was late monsoon and rains were moving past Wajid Ali's estate. The emerging sun on the bank of Hooghly added a red tinge to everything around. Yet, there was something eerie about the dawn, something dissonantly quiet. The *naubat* did not sound the time.[5] A ghost-like silence prevailed over the mimic kingdom of Metiyaburj. Only a bemoaning sound of the ladies fell upon the ears of the passersby. The wailing was reverberating from the Sultan Khana, where the banished King of Awadh was lying in his eternal sleep. The last crown of Burhan-ul-

[4]Mukherjee, Dilip Kumar, *Bangaleer Rag Sangeet Charcha*, Firma KLM Private Limited, 1976, p. 192.

[5]A musical arrangement situated at the entrance of the palace area, used for playing music five times a day at propitious hours

Mulk Saadat Ali Khan's dynasty had breathed his last in the fringes of Calcutta the night before. There was nothing in his wretched death that could even remotely illustrate the past grandeur of the King.

It was Colonel Prideaux who first received the news of Wajid Ali's death. Prideaux managed to reach Sultan Khana within an hour and telegraphed the news to Viceroy Lord Dufferin who was in Simla. Prideaux did not waste his time in posting sentinels, as he apprehended lawlessness, which could arise out of conflicts over succession.

It took 10 hours for the news to reach Khas Mahal who lived in her palace at Suroor Baugh, a stone's throw away from the former King's palace! It was only at the break of day when she was informed about her husband's demise. She was upset, yet she came out of her palace, along with Mirza Jahan Qadr, the King's nephew, to pay her last tribute.[6]

As the day progressed, the muta wives, the princes, the princesses and a crowd of bewailing people started to gather inside Sultan Khana. The British sentinels moved aside to make room for the King's relatives to pay their last homage one by one. The royal family decided that the former king would be interred at Sibtainabad Imambara according to his last wish. At around ten at night, the bier was taken out from Sultan Khana and the funeral procession began.[7] It was preceded by martial music and two platoons of soldiers. The government also gave an impressive Guard of Honour.

Unlike the wretched funeral of Hazrat Mahal, Wajid Ali's bier was followed by a host of notables from Metiyaburj and Calcutta and hundreds of bemoaning followers. The dead body was interred

---

[6]The son of Sikandar Hashmat

[7]Azhar, Mirza Ali, *King Wajid Ali Shah of Awadh*, Volume 2, Royal Book Company, Karachi, 1982, pp. 190–1.

in Sibtainabad Imambara at 11.30 at night, with proper military regalia under government aegis.[8]

Following Wajid Ali's death, the colonial rulers sought to assimilate the estate of Metiyaburj and annihilate the name of the Awadh royalty from the pages of history. A commission was constituted under Colonel Predaux to initiate the process of taking over without delay. The drama that was enacted three decades ago was being repeated once again in 1887, only the place and the artists had changed.

The unfinished job of assimilating the former King's palace in Lucknow was taken up again in Metiyaburj only two days after his death. A new Act was passed on 23 September 1887 whereby British Governor General in council was empowered to administer the estate of Metiyaburj. By strength of the new Act, the government affirmed to dispose of the estate of Metiyaburj and distribute a portion of it to the family members and dependents at their sole discretion.

Again, after a week, on 1 November 1887, Colonel Prideaux issued a notification announcing the forceful retirement of the king's employees and servants against exiguous compensations. In the successive rule of Awadh, the descendants of the king's son or brother who had died during the king's lifetime were barred from inheritance or from seeking any title. They were called *Mahjoob-ol-irs.*[9] Taking this opportunity, the government disqualified the descendants of Mirza Hamid Ali and Mirza Sikandar Hasmat from the inheritance of any property. Instead, the government gave recognition to Prince Qamar Qadr as the

---

[8]Ibid. See also Qudar, Prince Anjum, 'Was Wajid Ali Shah Assassinated? Yes!', *The House of Oudh*, https://oudh.tripod.com/academic/wassasin.htm. Accessed on 16 February 2024.

[9]Sleeman, Sir William, *A Journey through the Kingdom of Oude in 1849–1850*, Volume 1, Richard Bentley, 1858, p. 301.

true representative of the Awadh family in January 1888, leaving behind a throng of avaricious descendants to fight amongst themselves. The last thorn was removed from their pathway.

Prince Qamar Qadr was the ninth son of the King and was the eldest living son in Calcutta. Qamar was born to Begum Fakhr-i-Mahal in Lucknow, most likely before 1850, but his exact year of birth is not known. All other sons born before Qamar Qadr, other than Birjis Qadr, had died during the King's lifetime. The strife continued amongst the descendants and the government was waiting to reap the benefits. The authority immediately formed a syndicate to assimilate all movable and immovable properties in Metiyaburj and put them up for sale.[10] The fund was distributed amongst all eligible heirs, although the process was not free of controversy.

It had taken several years for the King to convert a piece of desolated river bank into a paradise on earth and it took the British only a couple of years to raze it into oblivion. Only the Sibtainabad Imambara, Quasrul Buka and a few other religious places and the graveyard of the King's family remain as evidence of the King's lost glory. Thus laments Sharar,

> The inevitable result was that Matiya Burj was destroyed to the last brick. Property which was worth thousands of rupees were sold for cowries and that place which in a short time had become an earthly paradise was now a veritable hell.[11]

---

[10]Cotton, Evan, *Calcutta, Old and New: A Historical & Descriptive Handbook to the City,* W. Newman, 1907, p. 278.

[11]Sharar, Maulana Abdul Halim, *Lucknow: The Last Phase of an Oriental Culture,* Oxford University Press, 1994, p. 76. 'Cowrie' was the shell currency in ancient days. By 1887, cowries were abolished. Here, Sharar used the term 'cowries' to indicate a meagre amount of money.

The news of his father's death reached Birjis Qadr at his Barf Bagh mansion in Nepal through the British Resident. Birjis, then a family man, aged 42, was striving hard for his living in Nepal with three daughters and a son and a bevy of courtiers and attendants. Of his four children, 23-year-old Amjadi Begum was the eldest, followed by 12-year-old daughter Jamal Ara, his 11-year-old daughter Husain Ara and his youngest child and only son Khurshid Qadr, who was nine. Like his father, Birjis was himself a poet. In his alienation, Birjis Qadr held small but intimate mehfils with the poets in Nepal where he recited his gazals and shayaris written by him in Urdu and Persian. Yet, he had to make his ends meet with his allowance of ₹400. The casketful of jewellery that the Begum had carried with her from Lucknow was dwindling disproportionately.

Shortly, Birjis chanced upon an opportunity, which came suddenly with the year-long Golden Jubilee celebration of Queen Victoria's accession to the throne, which started on 20 June 1887. Her Majesty, the Empress of India, on the occasion of her fiftieth anniversary of reign in 1888, granted clemency to Birjis Qadr. In a communiqué, the last Nawab of Awadh was allowed to return home. Birjis had kept a close watch on the happenings of his father's estate and the English debauchery. The British allowed pension to the King's son Prince Qamar Qadr at the rate of ₹3,000 per mensem, which was much higher than the amount the Nepal court paid him. Colonel Prideaux prepared a detailed report on the methodology and distribution of life pension among the family members and employees of the deceased King and forwarded it to his authority. However, in his report, the name of Birjis Qadr was missing.

Neither the King's heirs nor the British agent were prepared for Birjis Qadr to come all the way from Nepal to Metiyaburj in 1892. The King's eldest living son suddenly landed up in Calcutta and occupied the Atabagh palace in Metiyaburj to claim his rights. Some historians believe that on his arrival, the British government arranged a guest house on Strand Road, but later he moved to Atabagh palace in Metiyaburj.[12] He was accompanied by his wife Mahtab Ara Begum and three children—Jamal Ara, Husain Ara and his youngest child and only son Khurshid Qadr. His eldest daughter Amjadi Begum had died in Nepal three years earlier. What prompted Birjis to come and stake his claim five years after his father's death remained a mystery to all. However, it was not difficult to understand that Birjis had come fully prepared not to lose his battle this time.

Birjis Qadr declared himself as the legal heir to succeed his deceased father and put forth his legitimate claim as the eldest surviving son of Wajid Ali Shah and the titular king of Awadh. Nonetheless, he was the legitimate claimant to his father's pension as his eldest living son. The King's eldest son Nausherwan Qadr was deaf and mute and had died during the former's lifetime. His second son Falakh Qadr had died of smallpox in 1849. The Nawab's third son Mirza Hamid Ali Bahadur was the heir apparent and had passed away in 1874. Mirza Birjis was his fourth son while Qamar Qadr, who was projected by the British agent as a legal heir of the late King, was the King's ninth son. Birjis Qadr's substantive polemics were irrefutable.

Birjis referred to Article V of the proposed Treaty of 1856 and claimed his father's allowance of ₹12 lakh per annum. The referred article reads, 'To each of His Majesty's successors it is agreed that the said Company shall pay twelve lakhs of Company's rupees per annum.'[13] However, as per the treaty, which was signed by the King

---

[12]Naheed, Nusrat, *Jane Alam aur Mehak Pari*, Lucknow Library Helpage Society, 2005, p. 94.

[13]Azhar, Mirza Ali, *King Wajid Ali Shah of Awadh*, Volume 1, Royal Book Company, Karachi, 1982, p. 536.

in October 1859, after his release from Fort William, the successor of the King was not to be accorded any right to retain his title and consequently upon his demise the pecuniary allowances would not continue on their present scale.

Birjis claimed himself as legitimate successor amongst the sons of his father who was capable of looking after the members of the royal family as well as their 20,000 protégés.[14] His claim was not ephemeral and if declined by the government, Birjis would proceed to England with his case and seek justice from Her Majesty. Birjis's unexpected intrusion in the battle of succession brought Prince Qamar Qadr and Colonel Prideaux closer to each other.

While Birjis was preparing to pursue his case and arranging to leave for England if need be, he was invited with his family by one of his relatives for dinner. On returning to his Atabagh Palace, he fell ill from food poisoning and died. On that single night of 14 August 1893, his elder son Prince Khurshid Qadr and his daughter Jamal Ara Begum, along with three companions, succumbed to treachery. His wife Begum Mahtab Ara, who was five months pregnant, remained in her palace and was spared. Birjis' younger daughter Husain Ara Begum, who was with her mother in the palace, was also spared. Birjis Qadr was buried in Sibtainabad Imambara while his children were buried in the royal burial ground in Metiyaburj.

The death of Birjis removed the last impediment in Prince Qamar Qadr's path. Incidentally, his pension was increased from ₹3,000 to ₹4,000 by the government. The tattletales whispered around the alleyways of Metiyaburj—about the invisible hand and role of Qamar Qadr behind the tragedy. On 24 December the same year, Mahtab Ara Begum gave birth to a posthumous child. Prince

---

[14]'Wajid Ali Shah Comes to Town', *United India Periodical*, Vol. 4, No. 26–51, 1962, p. 15.

Maher Qadr, as he was named, was debarred from his grandfather's properties after his father's death by the application of Muslim law Mahjoob-ol-irs. Later, the prince relinquished his claims after the country's independence and breathed his last on 12 March 1961 in independent India. The King's property was fragmented and sold in bits by his descendants down the line to bear the cost of ongoing litigations and to maintain their extravagant lifestyle. Not a single structure of the King's labour of love exists today, except a few religious edifices.

Nonetheless, the picturesque skyline of the King's earthly paradise morphed into gigantic factory sheds, massive pieces of machinery, soot-filled chimneys, dockyards and wharves, jostling with each other for space. The Atabagh Palace does not exist today and has been fragmented to godowns and warehouses. Only a few dilapidated pillars mark the reminiscence of the regal days.

History was never kind to either the King or the Queen. Wajid Ali Shah remained arguably the most controversial man in history, while the queen faded into obscurity. It is difficult to explicate the real man from all that has been written about the King in the pages of history. The ethos of his dynasty urged him to stay away from encounters with the British. His archetypical Lucknowi prudence was taken as his weakness by the enemies. The British conspiracy and debauchment coerced him to turn his face away from the stately affairs; rather, it was never his passion. Wajid Ali was a proponent of oriental culture and was never an astute ruler to govern his kingdom. It would be prudent to judge the King's success story through the prism of his inimitable cultural reformations than to chide him as the fated protector who relinquished his kingdom to the foreign aggressors, uncontested. He was often wrongly accused as an anglophile like his forefathers.

Yet, the King, at times, looked narcissistic in adversity and often compromised dearly to overcome challenges. Nonetheless, he cannot be held culpable for his inability to juxtapose politics and culture proportionately in his life. The British knew that it would be excruciating for the King to spend his days in austerity in prison and that would bring him down to sign the treaty. The result was as expected. The King disavowed all his claims, repudiated the Oudh Mission in London, disowned his spirited wife and finally retreated into romance and art. The Raj was happy with him as long the King remained absorbed with his passion.

Begum Hazrat Mahal remained one of the very few to whom the British showed complacency. No wonder the wave of terror she had inflicted on the British was unprecedented in the annals of Indian history. British soldiers often referred to the Begum as 'the soul of the rebellion'. Indeed, with one lakh combatants by her side, the valiant queen was almost on the verge of expelling the white interlopers from her country in a raging battle where she staged herself as the vanguard on an elephant. Such a remarkable display of valour was epoch-making in the dynasty.

Nitpickers would talk about the queen's murky past, but the controversy deserves to be shelved. She was never a practitioner of stately politics, nor was she a religious leader like Moulvi Ahmadullah Shah, yet she dared to wage a fiery uprising against the British. Having seen a meteoric rise after her husband's departure, the Begum was the be-all and end-all to her countrymen. The queen's patriotic fervour managed to rouse the passion of millions of countrymen afflicted by the pangs of exploitations and sunk in the deepest morass of subjugation. Her clarion call to the people to join her in the struggle of removing the foreign yoke worked like magic. She showed the courage to declare war against the invincible East India Company.

Nevertheless, she was only a regent of a minor king and

at the end of the day, she was alone in her struggle; rather, a stiffer personal challenge was awaiting her. Her compeers neither supported her in the King's jenana nor did she have the support of the King himself. The King had hardly any sympathy for the great uprising of 1857 and had written to the Governor General offering his help to quell it. Time and again, the King reiterated to the British his loyalty, vowing to help the government in any way he could. And although the rebellion was quelled, the fall of Lucknow also marked the eclipse of the mighty East India Company.

By the end of their life, both the King and Queen did not wish to return to Lucknow and were fated to rest in the earth of foreign lands. Birjis Qadr, their only son, and grandsons Khurshid Qadr and Maher Qadr followed their grandparent's trail. Yet, notwithstanding the British conspiracy to obliterate all traces of Awadh royalty and annihilate the last chance of insurrection against the colonial power, the King and Queen left their indelible mark on the sands of time.

Today, the long chronicles of pathos and romance that could be heard from their mausoleums can fill endless volumes. Wajid Ali Shah, the greatest embodiment of the Awadhi gharana, and the Begum Hazrat Mahal, the trailblazer of India's people's movement for freedom, lived in oblivion as the most misunderstood royal couple in the pages of Indian history.

Important Dates

30 July 1822: Wajid Ali was born.

7 July 1837: Muhammad Ali Shah was proclaimed as the eighth ruler of Awadh after the death of Nasir-ud-din Haider.

14 November 1837: Wajid Ali Shah was married to Alam Ara Begum who became Khas Mahal.

7 May 1842: Amjad Ali Shah, father of Wajid Ali Shah, ascended the throne after the death of Muhammad Ali Shah.

20 August 1845: Birjis Qadr was born.

13 February 1847: Wajid Ali Shah became the king after the death of his father Amjad Ali.

5 August 1847: Ali Naqi Khan was appointed as the chief minister.

22 November 1847: Lord Hardinge came to Lucknow and met Wajid Ali Shah at Chatter Manzil.

12 January 1848: Lord Dalhousie came to Calcutta and took the office of Governor General from Lord Hardinge.

6 January 1849: Colonel Sleeman came to Lucknow as the British Resident.

11 January 1849: Colonel Sleeman went to meet the King, who was still indisposed.

1 December 1849: Sleeman went for his famous tour in Awadh

and returned to Lucknow on 28 February 1850.

4 June 1851: Wajid Ali Shah married Akhtar Mahal, daughter of Ali Naqi Khan.

18 July 1853: First jogi mela was held in Kaiserbag.

5 October 1854: Sleeman left Lucknow owing to ill-health.

5 December 1854: Outram set his foot in Lucknow and took his office as Resident of Lucknow.

15 March 1855: Outram despatched his report to Dalhousie with a covering letter.

18 June 1855: Dalhousie signed his infamous minutes and sent it to the Board of Governors.

2 January 1856: Dalhousie received the despatch from England at midnight favouring annexation of Oudh.

30 January 1856: Outram reached Lucknow with a letter from Lord Dalhousie, addressed to the King, and also a draft of the new treaty that the King would be offered to sign.

1 February 1856: Outram met the Queen Mother at Zard Kothi at 4.00 p.m. but could not convince her.

4 February 1856: Outram met the King at Zard Kothi Palace with the proposed new treaty. The King handed over his turban as a symbol of submission.

13 March 1856: Wajid Ali Shah left Lucknow for Calcutta.

25 April 1856: Wajid Ali Shah boarded the steamer *General Mcleod* from Banaras.

13 May 1856: The King reached Calcutta and stayed at Maharaja Burdwan's Kothi.

19 June 1856: The King's Mission boarded the ship *S.S. Bengal* from Garden Reach on their way to London.

29 March 1857: Mangal Pandey fired on Lieutenant Baugh at Barrackpore Cantonment.

8 April 1857: Mangal Pandey was hanged to death.

10 May 1857: The native troops at Meerut revolted.

7 June 1857: Nana Sahib attacked Kanpur treasury.

14 June 1857: 'Panic Sunday' unfolded.

15 June 1857: The King was arrested in Metiyaburj and detained in Fort William.

27 June 1857: Satichaura Ghat massacre took place.

1 July 1857: Historic siege of Lucknow began.

4 July 1857: Queen Mother of Awadh met Queen Victoria in Buckingham Palace.

5 July 1857: Birjis Qadr was crowned as the ruler of Awadh by the sepoy army under Bahadur Shah Zafar with a 21-gun salute.

15 July 1857: Bibighar massacre took place.

25 September 1857: Forces led by Outram and Havelock entered the Residency.

24 January 1858: Queen Mother Aliya Begum died in Paris.

25 February 1858: Sikandar Hasmat, brother of Wajid Ali Shah, died in London.

16 March 1858: The British captured Kaiserbag.

1 November 1858: Proclamation of Queen Victoria was issued.

7 January 1859: Begum Hazrat Mahal entered Nepal.

9 July 1859: Wajid Ali Shah was released from Fort William.

8 February 1860: Jung Bahadur allowed the Begum to enter and stay in Kathmandu.

7 April 1879: Begum Hazrat Mahal died.

21 September 1887: Wajid Ali Shah died in Metiyaburj.

www.ingramcontent.com/pod-product-compliance
Lightning Source LLC
LaVergne TN
LVHW100524110826
845146LV00002B/765